MANAGING THE PRESS

MANAGING THE PRESS

ORIGINS OF THE MEDIA
PRESIDENCY, 1897–1933

Stephen Ponder

St. Martin's Press
New York

MANAGING THE PRESS

Copyright © Stephen Ponder, 1998. All rights reserved. Printed in the United States of America. No part of this book may be used or reproduced in any manner whatsoever without written permission except in the case of brief quotations embodied in critical articles or reviews. For information, address St. Martin's Press, 175 Fifth Avenue, New York, N.Y. 10010.

ISBN 0-312-21384-0

Library of Congress Cataloging-in-Publication Data

Ponder, Stephen, 1942–
    Managing the press : origins of the media presidency, 1897–1933 / Stephen Ponder.
        p. cm.
    Includes bibliographical references and index.
    ISBN 0-312-21384-0
    1. Presidents—United States—History—20th century.
2. Government and the press—United States—History—20th century.
3. Press and politics—United States—History—20th century.
4. Mass media—Political aspects—United States—History—20th century. 5. United States—Politics and government—1897–1901.
6. United States—Politics and government—1901–1953. I. Title.
E176.1.P816 1999
352.23'02748'0973—dc21   98–33865
                                                                            CIP

Design by Letra Libre

First edition: February 1999
10 9 8 7 6 5 4 3 2 1

CONTENTS

ACKNOWLEDGMENTS

Since the beginnings of this project, I have benefited enormously from the advice and support of many advisors, colleagues, students, and friends. I regret that only a few can be mentioned in the space available, and I apologize in advance for the omissions.

Parts of the early chapters originated in graduate work at the University of Washington, where I was fortunate to receive guidance from my dissertation advisor, Gerald J. Baldasty, and the late Robert E. Burke, among others. Portions of the manuscript were published as articles in journals in communications, history, and political science. I am especially grateful for the comments of reviewers and editors for these journals, especially *American Journalism,* published by the American Journalism Historians Association, and *Journalism History,* published by the History Division of the Association for Education in Journalism and Mass Communications.

During the long process of adapting the articles and additional research into book form, I received thoughtful comments and criticism from several reviewers at various points. I appreciated particularly the insights and suggestions of James D. Startt, Donald A. Ritchie, Maurine H. Beasley, and my colleague John Russial, who generously contributed a preliminary editing of the manuscript. None is responsible for my interpretation of any suggestions or the final form of the manuscript.

Completion of the manuscript would not have been possible without the support of the University of Oregon, the Knight Library, and, especially, my colleagues at the School of Journalism and Communication, where I have been a faculty member since 1985. I am grateful for the administrative and personal support of the deans who encouraged me to proceed: Arnold H. Ismach, Duncan L. McDonald, and Tim W. Gleason. I also am grateful for the support of my colleagues, especially those with their own interests in communications history: Tim Gleason, Lauren J. Kessler, and Al Stavitsky. I feel honored to be part of such a supportive department.

I want to acknowledge particularly the help of those colleagues and friends who have shared the rivers as well as the classrooms, including

Charlie Frazer, Deb Merskin, Ken Metzler, John Russial, Bill Ryan, Al Stavitsky, Tom Wheeler, and Jim Upshaw. The importance of their personal support and that of their families and friends cannot be overemphasized.

I am also grateful for the companionship and support of Gaye Vandermyn.

INTRODUCTION

Volumes could be written about the variations of the situation, the mutual helpfulness of the politician and reporter, the way each uses the other and the way the public is played between them.

—Frank R. Kent, 1924

I was fortunate to have an aisle seat when President John F. Kennedy spoke at the University of Washington in Seattle in 1961. As an undistinguished undergraduate, I was far from the stage in Hec Edmundson Pavilion. Nor do I remember much about what the president said. But I do recall that he walked by me on his way out of the hall. He was the first president whom I had seen closely in person.

Yet, because of television, I already had viewed President Kennedy many times. During the previous year, I watched him debate Richard M. Nixon in the first televised presidential debates. I was a regular viewer of his live press conferences, and he was often featured on the 15-minute nightly network news. When I saw the President in person, I was for the first time able to compare the physical presence with the images on the screen, as well as with the photographs and stories that I had seen in newspapers and magazines.

What I recall mostly is that the President in front of me was quite different from the one on the tube. He was, of course, larger than 17 inches across, and in full color, rather than in fuzzy black and white. He also looked heavier and a bit tired. Most importantly, his appearance started me thinking about how dependent I was on the news media for what I knew about the presidency and the political system. I realized for the first time the extent to which my views of national politics and politicians were shaped not by direct observation but by what I viewed, heard, or read at second or third hand. It was one of the experiences that led to my first career, as a journalist.

Since 1961, along with most other Americans, I have become accustomed to receiving most of what I know about the daily interplay of presidents and public policy from the news media, especially network television. Images and stories about President William J. Clinton appear in my living room frequently, filtered and shaped by the correspondents, interviewers, photographers, editors, producers, and others who collectively constitute the national news media, based primarily in Washington, D.C. I am more or less comfortable with this, perhaps because I can recall no other system of presidential communications. This is how presidents have appeared to the public during my lifetime.

However, I am no longer as comfortable with it as I once was. In my years as a journalist, I became familiar with many of the distortions in the prism of mass communications between the Oval Office and my living room. More recently, as a researcher and citizen, it seems to me that these distortions are occurring more frequently and are more troublesome.

The process by which the president speaks to the citizenry through the news media has become more complex and problematic than it was long ago in 1961. At that time, presidential television still was a novelty. The White House relationship with the press corps was mutually respectful, more or less. Over the last 35 years, however, the public's faith in the presidency, the legitimacy of executive governance, and the credibility of the news media all have been shaken by recurring images of failures, crises, and scandals. The relationship between the president and the press, which has been central to the communications process through which American citizens have viewed their national leaders for most of the twentieth century, is in disarray.

Since the national turmoil caused by the Vietnam War and the Watergate crisis, the news media have become more assertive in raising questions about presidents, their policies, and, most recently, their personal lives.[1] Conversely, from the perspective of the White House, the generally deferential journalists faced by Kennedy and his predecessors have been replaced by an adversarial press corps interested more in negativism and scandal than in helping a president to communicate with the citizenry.[2] In the 1970s, the underlying relationship between the president and the White House press corps still could be characterized as largely one of institutionalized continuity and cooperation.[3] By 1995, however, "virtually all Washington politicians say that the mainstream media are too eager to expose the character flaws of the nation's leaders and the failures of public policy rather to inform the country about the positive side of government and the people who run it," observed Kenneth T. Walsh, White House correspondent for *U.S. News and World Report*.[4] The political scientist Thomas E. Patterson described news coverage of the first Clinton administration (1993–97) as strongly negative, which he attributed largely to a cynical view of politics held by journalists.[5] But even before the Clinton administration, critics complained that the post-Watergate news media were only too eager to transmit accusations of scandal and corruption against national leaders.[6] In a series of recurring incidents characterized as "feeding frenzies," individual public officials were barraged by sensationalized stories about official and personal misconduct, sometimes verified and sometimes not.[7]

Not surprisingly, recent presidents have devoted significant amounts of their time and staff resources to try to minimize or to circumvent the filtering of their messages by what they regard as an increasingly irresponsible and disruptive national news media. The White House Office of Communications has developed public relations strategies and tactics intended to allow a president to communicate with the public through other means, including regional, rather than national, news events and conferences; presidential appearances on talk and entertainment shows; and, most recently, use of e-mail and a White House web page aimed at citizen computer owners.[8] All of the above and other presidential publicity tactics have been criticized by journalists in phrases such as "managing the news" or "spin control." From the correspondents' viewpoint, the White House has become increasingly duplicitous and manipulative. A 1997 report by the watchdog group Reporters Committee for Freedom of the Press concluded that "secrecy and control are becoming the watchwords of the Clinton administration."[9] The White House in the first Clinton administration also alarmed journalists by suggesting that new formats and technologies of mass communications made it possible for the President to bypass the obstructive "old media" of news by reaching the public through a more cooperative "new media" of broadcast talk and entertainment shows.[10] A review of 47 news and opinion articles written by journalists about use of "new media" in the 1992 presidential campaign found that more than half warned about the occupational ramifications.[11]

Complaints from the traditional correspondents forced the Clinton administration to become more responsive to their needs early in the President's second term.[12] But sensationalized coverage of Monica Lewinsky, Paula Jones, and other allegations of sexual misconduct against the President in 1998 encouraged the White House to continue its efforts to bypass the Washington press corps, such as by overseas travel or regional travel within the United States.[13]

Despite this dissonance, the news media, especially television, remain important sources of information in shaping citizens' opinions about the presidency. A study of news coverage in the 1996 presidential campaign found a strong relationship between the news and public's preferences for the candidates.[14] Nevertheless, complaints from both the White House and journalists about their deteriorating relationship at the end of the millennium suggest that institutional and technological changes soon may change fundamentally how presidents and other political leaders communicate with the citizenry. The communications presidency of the twenty-first century may be quite different from the one based on leadership of public opinion through the news media that has characterized executive governance in the United States for most of the last 100 years.

If such a paradigm shift in presidential leadership is under way, this seems to be an appropriate moment to re-examine the last comparable transformation, which began in the late nineteenth century. Increased attention to the presidency by the "new media" of that era, commercialized daily newspapers and popular magazines, led to new conventions of journalism that contributed to making the president the leader of the political system.[15] The general outlines of this shift are well known to scholars, although they have been obscured somewhat by the durability of the subsequent relationship between the president, the press, and public opinion. Douglass Cater described that relationship aptly at mid-century as "government by publicity." Of government, Cater observed that "publicity is as essential to its orderly functioning as the power to levy taxes and pass laws."[16]

To some extent, all presidents since George Washington have relied on the press to inform the country about the workings of public policy. "The public papers will be expeditious messengers of intelligence to the most remote inhabitants of the Union," Alexander Hamilton wrote confidently in *Federalist* 84.[17] The Bill of Rights added to the Constitution of 1787 included a prohibition against government abridgment of freedom of expression, specifying the press. But the presidency, the press, and the relationship between the two institutions changed profoundly during in the nation's first 100 years.[18]

Despite broad pledges of freedom, the earliest presidents regarded the press as too important to the survival of the new republic to be left unguided. During the nation's first system of political communication, from 1789 until about the time of the Civil War, publications that concerned themselves with public affairs were sponsored financially by political factions, parties, or individual leaders through a system of loyalties, contracts, and partisan patronage.[19] At the peak of the "party press" era, which one historian labeled as the "dark ages of American journalism," backers of Andrew Jackson organized a network of partisan newspapers to advocate his candidacies and his policies.[20] Census data from 1850 suggest that only 83 out of 2,526 newspapers in the United States at the time were listed as politically "independent" or "neutral." Indeed, political sponsorship in one form or another constituted the dominant economic and ideological base of American newspapers through much of the nineteenth century.[21]

Yet, while most of the antebellum press was institutionally dependent on political sponsors, other forms of published communication had begun to appear.[22] This transition—from small party- or government-sponsored newsletters of the early 1800s to the mass-circulation, advertising-supported daily newspapers and popular magazines of the 1890s—has been the subject of considerable discussion among historians.[23] Some scholars trace the beginnings of this shift to the 1830s and 1840s, when entrepreneurs launched cheap "penny" newspapers, independent of political sponsorship, which relied instead on the readership appeal of entertaining stories about urban life.[24] The financial advantages of political sponsorship were further diminished after the Civil War by the greater possibilities of advertising revenue in a developing retail economy. Improvements in printing technology made possible a potential buying audience of thousands, sometimes millions, of daily readers.[25]

The impact of the decline of political sponsorship on the nineteenth-century press is widely debated among scholars. It is disputed exactly when and how the press became more or less partisan, interpretive, or objective; interested more in sensationalism than politics; or independent of political allegiances entirely. Generally, scholars agree that a major transformation took place. The rise of a mass media less dependent on political sponsorship for economic survival had important implications for the press, the polity, and the information reaching the citizenry.[26]

The outcome late in the nineteenth century was the emergence of a "new media" of advertising-supported newspapers and magazines, which tended to be less connected to the polity than the "old media" of partisan journals. Joseph Pulitzer, the influential publisher of the *St. Louis Post-Dispatch* and the *New York World,* praised advertising revenue for liberating newspapers from the stranglehold of party controls.[27] The decline of official partisanship was accompanied by a decline in the blind loyalty of editors to their political patrons.[28] The political parties themselves had been weakened after the Civil War by a succession of liberal reform movements aimed at ending machine politics and pervasive corruption.[29] As a result of these changes, some newspapers become uninterested in political topics unless they could be sensationalized in story form to draw more readers to attract advertising.[30] But others found that political allegiances could be useful in differentiating themselves in a marketplace with several competing newspapers.[31] Many newspaper owners and editors declared themselves independent of party ties but remained active politically as community opinion leaders or as candidates for elective office.[32]

This emergence of a press institutionally independent of the polity offered the possibility of a marketplace of ideas less influenced by political sponsorship. But from the perspective of presidents and other political leaders, these changes also left the press less reliable in conveying appropriate political information to the public. In 1806, for example, President Thomas Jefferson could send Samuel Harrison Smith, editor of the semiofficial *National Intelligencer,* a letter announcing the success of the recently returned Lewis and Clark Expedition and expect to see it reproduced faithfully in the next issue, then copied again by allied newspapers in other cities. A half century later, President Abraham Lincoln, although a Republican himself, received little support from some of the leading New York City Republican editors for his Civil War policies. Lincoln spent much of his time trying to persuade Horace Greeley and other independent editors of his own party to support him, as well as trying to prevent or to minimize rumors and distortions among the correspondents at the battlefields and in Washington, D.C.[33]

These inconsistencies increased after the Civil War, as the once-predictable, sponsored press placed less emphasis on political advocacy and more on the popular format of news, sometimes sensationally so. In the presidency, Lincoln's successors made fewer attempts to appeal to public opinion, through the press or otherwise. The presidency was diminished after the Civil War by the impeachment of Andrew Johnson and the scandals of the Ulysses S. Grant administration. In the 1870s and 1880s, presidents were regarded as newsworthy when they died, were married, made important speeches, or traveled around the country. They responded regularly to inquiries.[34] But they rarely sought publicity overtly, and few senior members of the Washington press corps called at the Executive Mansion to receive news on a routine basis. According to Washington legend, probably apocryphal but nevertheless indicative, no post–Civil War correspondent covered the White House on a daily basis until 1895, when William W. Price of the *Washington Evening Star* stationed himself by the fence to ask questions of visitors with President Grover Cleveland.[35]

In the last years of the nineteenth century, however, President William G. McKinley began to attract journalists to the Executive Mansion and to encourage them to write more regularly about his activities.[36] Numerous historians and political scientists have commented on the expansion of relations with the press among the presidents who followed McKinley, especially Theodore Roosevelt and Woodrow Wilson, and on subsequent government initiatives in propaganda and censorship during World War I.[37] Although wartime attempts to manipulate public opinion ended in 1919, presidential contacts with the press continued to expand in the 1920s. J. Frederick Essary, a correspondent for the *Baltimore Sun,* complained in 1927 that "Washington has become the great generator of propaganda in this country."[38] Since the presidency of Franklin D. Roosevelt, which began in 1933, White House management of the news media to influence public opinion has been regarded as central to modern executive governance.[39]

This book surveys this transformation in presidential leadership from 1897 to 1933, from the experiments of the McKinley administration to the routine use of publicists, press offices, and the appointment of the first official press secretary in the Hoover White House. It includes the presidencies of the 1920s, which have received somewhat less scholarly attention but represent an essential continuity from the propaganda of World War I to the publicity initiatives of the New Deal. The purpose of the inquiry is to suggest a greater context and an explanatory framework for the late-twentieth-century debate over presidential leadership of public opinion through the news media.

The political scientist Jeffrey Tulis argues that development in the early twentieth century of a presidency based on appeals for popular support constituted a doctrinal shift in American democracy. During development of what Tulis and others characterize as the "rhetorical presidency," activist presidents, especially Theodore Roosevelt and Wilson, sought supportive public opinion to expand their governing authority, rather than relying on the limited powers specified in the written Constitution. Tulis notes that the success of the rhetorical presidency was made possible, in part, by the availability of the rapidly growing audiences for new, popular mass media, especially daily newspapers and national magazines.[40]

When presidents seeking popular support tried to reach those audiences, however, they found that access to the pages of the commercialized press was not necessarily available on demand. Lacking the leverage of sponsorship, presidents of the early twentieth century found that a new form of leadership was necessary to persuade independent publishers, editors, correspondents, and other gatekeepers to grant space and time in these new media for White House messages. Without their cooperation, presidents of the era were limited largely to speaking to citizens within the sound of their unamplified voices.[41]

In attempting to reach the audiences of newspapers, popular magazines, and, after World War I, radio, presidents between 1897 and 1933 experimented with a variety of tactics to persuade media gatekeepers to convey their messages. That process of persuasion is described here as managing the press. The phrase has negative connotations for contemporary journalists, who are confronted daily with manipulation by publicists and official sources. But, in the context of the Progressive period, it describes usefully the experiments by which presidents and executive publicists tried to impose some order and predictability on a system of political communications that seemed increasingly to be in disarray in the late nineteenth century.[42]

To seek increased news coverage, presidents from McKinley forward altered their own activities and the responsibilities of their assistants; encouraged the hiring and use of publicists in the White House and in executive agencies, and tried to adapt their messages to the technological and organizational changes taking place in the media of mass communications. The result of these experiments was to alter the presidency institutionally, to a form characterized in this book as the media presidency—a form of presidential leadership in which popular authority is derived from a president's ability to appeal to public opinion through a mass media no longer dependent on the sponsorship of institutions in the polity.

This book explores the development of the media presidency from experiments by McKinley, who established a foundation for the expansion of press relations under the first Roosevelt, to Herbert Hoover, whose failings as president have been blamed, in part, on difficulties with an enlarged and increasingly assertive White House press corps. It suggests that the successes and failures of attempts to manage the press among the seven presidents from McKinley to Hoover established the outlines of presidential leadership of public opinion through the news media for the rest of the century. It also suggests that the media presidency did not emerge in an institutional vacuum. Presidential experiments with publicity also encouraged the spread of similar practices in the agencies of the executive branch. The president's ability to dominate the news contributed to the decline of Congress as the supreme branch of government. The emergence of the president as the First Source for the news media also encouraged the professionalization of political journalism.

No attempt was made to examine comprehensively all aspects of presidential administrations between 1897 and 1933, which have been extensively studied in other works. However, the book includes original research into those aspects of the presidency involved in managing the Washington press corps, as well as into selected developments in the Congress, the Cabinet, and executive agencies.[43] Evidence cited includes documentation of presidential use of publicity practices, including the introduction and routine use of news releases, press conferences, the creation of newsworthy events, interviews with reporters, and publication of informational statements, pamphlets and reports in summary form for correspondents. I also looked for the creation of organizational structures to support managing the press, including press offices, press rooms, and the hiring of publicity specialists. Evidence of efforts by the executive to influence the press in this period was abundant in presidential manuscript collections, agency records, transcripts of congressional hearings and debates, and the writings of Washington correspondents. Earlier articles from this project have appeared in *American Journalism, Congress and the Presidency, Journalism History, Journalism and Mass Communications Quarterly,* and *Presidential Studies Quarterly.*

Generally, the evidence indicates that during the first third of the century, attempts to manage the press took place under successful presidencies as well as less successful ones. McKinley, Theodore Roosevelt, and Wilson were particularly influential in shaping the president's relationship with the press. So, in their ways, were Warren G. Harding, Calvin Coolidge, and Herbert Hoover, although historians rate them as among the least successful presidents.[44] Of the seven presidencies examined, only William Howard Taft, president from 1909 to 1913, tried to reject entirely the notion of trying to manage the press. Yet important changes took place during his administration as well. Other institutions in the polity also were affected by these experiments, and they reacted in ways that shaped the media presidency.

Chapter one analyzes how McKinley moved in 1898 to attract correspondents to the Executive Mansion to seek popular support for the Spanish-American War. These results were sufficiently satisfactory that George Cortelyou, McKinley's chief of staff, acted after the war to begin to place presidential relations with the press on an organized basis.

Chapters two and three analyze the presidency of Theodore Roosevelt, which long has been recognized for its impact on White House relations with the press. Roosevelt's use of the press to appeal to the public established a benchmark to which subsequent presidents of the early twentieth century were compared. His publicity successes were watched closely by other executive officials and agency administrators, as well as by his critics in Congress.

Chapter three also introduces the influential work of one of those administrators, Gifford Pinchot, who created the first officially designated "press bureau" in the U.S. Forest Service in 1905. Roosevelt encouraged Pinchot's campaign for resource conservation and brought the forester's promotional talents into the White House. Their joint publicity activities prompted the first debates in Congress about executive "press agents" and, eventually, an attempt to ban their hiring.

Chapters four and five address the administration of William Howard Taft, who was unable or unwilling to apply himself to managing the press in the Roosevelt fashion. Chapter four examines Taft's conservative approach to presidential press relations and the reactions in the press corps that Roosevelt had attracted to the White House. Chapter five is a case study of the consequences of Taft's unwillingness to manage the press in his critical first year, when his presidency was undermined by leaks to the news media from rebellious agency publicists, led by Pinchot.

Chapters six and seven examine the influential presidency of Woodrow Wilson. Wilson in his first term became the first president to experiment extensively with regularly scheduled press conferences, although he found the experience ultimately to be unsatisfactory. Frustrated by leaks, Wilson considered creating a "publicity bureau" to try to centralize in the White House the flow of government information from the executive to the press.

Chapter seven examines Wilson's attempts to stimulate public support for American involvement in World War I through propaganda and, on occasion, censorship. The chapter focuses particularly on the persuasive campaigns by two of the wartime information agencies that Wilson created, the Committee on Public Information and the U.S. Food Administration, which have received less scholarly attention but were influential in the expansion of persuasive communications in the 1920s, both within the government and in the growing industries of public relations and advertising.

Chapter eight examines the presidencies of Harding and Coolidge. Harding reinvigorated the presidential press conferences, which Wilson had allowed to lapse. Harding's initiatives, which were continued by his successor, Coolidge, made routine many of practices of managing the press: regular press conferences, frequent photo opportunities, presidential attendance at media social and professional conferences, and use of broadcasting. The regularity of these practices encouraged a parallel professionalization among Washington journalists.

Chapter nine examines the extension of presidential publicity practices into the executive branch in the 1920s. Unlike Wilson, Harding encouraged his Cabinet members to seek publicity independently, which had the effect of giving the President's blessing to greatly expanded agency publicity activity. Hoover, as secretary of commerce, took the opportunity to create a departmental publicity program that became a model for the New Deal agencies of the 1930s.

Chapter ten discusses the paradox of the Hoover's unhappy relationship with the press at the White House. The chapter focuses primarily on the increasing professionalization of the press corps, including the creation of a "literature of complaint" by the correspondents that is often cited as evidence of Hoover's failure as president. It was also an indicator of the tensions within the relationship that had been established between the White House and the press to place the presidency at the forefront of the American political system.

MANAGING THE PRESS

CHAPTER ONE

MCKINLEY AND THE FIRST WHITE HOUSE PRESS CORPS

When President William McKinley led the United States into war against Spain in 1898, it was an extraordinary experience for the presidency as well as for the nation. The major fighting in Cuba and the Philippines was brief, between April and September, and the outcome was never in doubt. But the war marked the beginnings of an "imperial presidency," as Arthur Schlesinger later described it, as well as the foundations of a recognizably modern relationship between the President and the Washington press corps.[1]

These developments were not unrelated. As Robert C. Hilderbrand has pointed out, McKinley needed public support to conduct a war and saw in the press a tool that he could use to shape public opinion.[2] This led to an expansion of the visibility and the authority of the presidency based, in part, on persuading the Washington correspondents for press associations, daily newspapers, and magazines to write about the President's views and actions.

At McKinley's inauguration in March 1897, no organized relationship existed between presidents and the correspondents for these publications, who concentrated primarily on covering Congress. McKinley and the war drew them on a daily basis to the Executive Mansion, where they had called only occasionally in the past. McKinley's assistants, especially George Cortelyou, began to establish routine procedures to answer press inquiries, to arrange access to interviews and events, and to make available presidential statements on which news stories could be based.[3] The correspondents were provided with new working space inside the Executive Mansion and encouraged to accompany the President on his speaking tours. By the time of McKinley's assassination in 1901, the nucleus of a press corps had been attracted to the Executive Mansion, and the presidency had become a more frequent source of news. These developments formed an important foundation for more ambitious attempts by McKinley's successor, Theodore Roosevelt, to shape public opinion through the press.

McKinley's actions seem unremarkable by the standards of 100 years later. But they departed significantly from the defensiveness that characterized the press relations of his immediate predecessors, Grover Cleveland and Benjamin Harrison, the presidents from 1885 to 1897. In 1888, when Richard V. Oulahan, later bureau chief of the *New York Times,* began his reporting career in Washington, correspondents called only occasionally at the Executive Mansion or at the administrative departments.[4] After the urgency of the Civil War, and following Lincoln's assassination, presidential relations with the press had assumed a lower priority. The presidency itself had been diminished by the impeachment proceedings against Lincoln's successor, Andrew Johnson, and by the corruption scandals of Ulysses S. Grant's administrations. Late in the century, Congress was the dominant branch of government, and presidential authority was regarded as limited by the Constitution. The government's budget and administrative appointments were overseen by Congress and its committees, in cooperation with the political party organizations. During the Republican era, when one party dominated both Capitol Hill and the presidency, party leaders in Congress, rather than the president, spoke to the press on behalf of the administration. Publicity in presidential election campaigns was overseen by national party committees composed of leading Republican or Democratic newspaper editors.[5]

To the extent that presidents concerned themselves personally with the press in this period, it was typically by staying on good terms with leading party editors. President Benjamin Harrison, for example, was so generous in his patronage appointments of Republican editors, such as Whitelaw Reid of the *New York Tribune,* that he was accused of maintaining a "subsidized press."[6]

Not surprisingly, Washington correspondents of the late nineteenth century concentrated their newsgathering efforts on Congress, where federal policy was made and where congressional leaders, unlike the president, were willing to speak for publication. The newspapers to which the correspondents reported also tended to be partisan and frequently were allied with regional members of Congress or other political leaders. Covering Congress was a part-time job, and during the congressional recesses, the correspondents sought paying positions on committee payrolls or on election campaigns. Formal admission to the press corps was controlled by the Standing Committee of the Congressional Press Gallery. All this worked to make Capitol Hill, not the executive, the center of national political journalism.[7]

Nevertheless, the relationship between the press, the political parties, and the national government was changing. The number of daily newspapers in the United States quadrupled between 1870 and 1900, and most of those publications were financed by advertising, not political sponsorship. Combined newspaper circulation in 1900 totaled more than 15 million copies a day, nearly 20 percent of the national population.[8] A similar trend was under way in popular magazines. The number of magazines published grew from 700 in 1865 to 3,300 in 1885, and to 4,400 by 1890. The combined circulation of monthly periodicals soared from 18 million to 64 million copies an issue between 1890 and 1905.[9] These advertising- and subscriber-supported publications often were more interested in attracting readers with stories of news or sensations than in publishing the texts of speeches or editorial polemics.[10] The young political scientist Woodrow Wilson complained in 1885 that newspapers no longer reprinted political speeches in their entirety. "Most readers would be disgusted at finding their favorite columns so filled up," he wrote.[11]

Awareness of how to respond to these changes in the press was slow to spread among national leaders. One early adapter, James A. Garfield, was nominated and elected president in 1880 partly because of his skills in managing the post–Civil War "press gang" in Washington.[12] This "Bohemian Brigade" of colorful entrepreneurs had begun to coalesce into a press corps that was at various times professional, partisan, venal, favor seeking, sensational, and, occasionally, respectable.[13] However, Garfield was assassinated after only six months in office. James G. Blaine, another skillful manager of the press while in Congress, failed to become president when he was defeated by Grover Cleveland in the tumultuous election of 1884.[14]

Cleveland's relationship with the press was an unhappy one. He was a Democrat at a time when the press, as well as the Congress, was strongly Republican. In addition, he repeatedly suffered sensational newspaper coverage of his personal life, including Republican-inspired stories about his illegitimate son during the 1884 presidential campaign.[15] When, as president, Cleveland chose to marry his 21-year-old ward, Frances Folsom, in 1886, he discovered that his private life was more newsworthy than were his official activities. Reporters, barred from the Executive Mansion wedding ceremony, camped out in the bushes near the honeymoon cottage. The Republican *New York Times* filled its front pages with stories about the President and his young bride. Cleveland complained about the "colossal impertinence" of "those ghouls of the press," and some journalists sympathized with him.[16] Folsom, however, was made into a national celebrity by the press, and she brought in a social secretary to help her answer the deluge of fan mail.[17]

Not surprisingly, Cleveland remained defensive toward the press throughout his presidencies. Richard V. Oulahan wrote that Cleveland "appreciated the useful function of the press, of course, but seemed to be possessed of the notion that most of those connected with it were personally irresponsible and unfair, and more devoted to sensationalism than to a proper and judicious record of facts."[18] Oulahan noted that Cleveland's dislike of newspapermen was so well known that a Cabinet member pleaded with reporters not to walk near him when he entered the grounds of the Executive Mansion.[19] The publicist George F. Parker, who tried to convince Cleveland to be more responsive to the press, said the President had a strong aversion to newspaper people as a class.[20] Nevertheless, because Cleveland lacked supportive party leaders in the Republican Congress to intercede with the correspondents on his behalf, he was forced to respond to press inquiries. He delegated to his secretaries—Daniel S. Lamont and, in his second term, Henry T. Thurber—the chore of meeting with the correspondents and responding to their questions.[21] In 1895, when William W. Price, of the *Washington Evening Star,* persisted in asking questions of presidential callers for his daily column, "At the White House," Cleveland grudgingly authorized Thurber to supply Price with the names of his visitors. "Few who wished to stand well with Mr. Cleveland were prolific sources of news," Price noted wryly.[22] David S. Barry, a correspondent for the Republican *New York Sun,* complained that news of the Cleveland presidency "was obtained much after the fashion in which highwaymen rob a stage-coach."[23]

Harrison, who served one term as president between Cleveland's two terms, was no fonder of the press. However, Harrison allowed a small number of correspondents to travel with him on an 1891 trip to California. He also hired Elijah Halford, a former Washington correspondent, to be his secretary.[24] Nevertheless, correspondents who tried to interview Harrison on his last day in the Executive Mansion received a tirade against the press "persecution" that he and the First Lady, Caroline Harrison, had suffered.[25]

Before McKinley took office in 1897, then, correspondents called only occasionally at the Executive Mansion, and spoke primarily with the president's secretary. Personal audiences with a president were infrequent. He was unlikely to be talkative or even particularly friendly. Interviews in which presidents spoke for publication were rare. The president was not ignored by the press, but news coverage was focused on major events in his official or personal life, not routine actions. The priority of the correspondents was illustrated by coverage of the president's annual State of the

Union Message to Congress. Many newspapers reproduced the text of the message, but the news stories from Washington correspondents concentrated on describing the congressional reaction.[26]

McKinley, like Cleveland and Harrison, was a private, dignified man who did not seek personal publicity.[27] But McKinley the politician was accustomed to dealing with newspapers, both in Ohio, where he had been governor, and in Washington, where he served for ten years in Congress.[28] He frequently hired former newspapermen as his assistants and continued that pattern as president. His first secretary, or chief of staff, was John Addison Porter, a politically ambitious newspaper proprietor from Hartford, Connecticut. Although McKinley, like Cleveland and Harrison, granted few personal audiences to correspondents and did not encourage familiarity, he took several actions in his first year to make them feel more welcome at the Executive Mansion.

Within days of his inauguration in March 1897, McKinley attended a reception by the Gridiron Club, a group of leading correspondents, who in 1885 had begun to invite prominent political leaders to their sometime raucous dinners. McKinley's decision to accept the invitation was welcomed warmly by the correspondents. Cleveland had refused to attend the gatherings, and Harrison did so only occasionally.[29] McKinley, however, attended Gridiron dinners as a congressman, and he understood the symbolism of attending them as president. He carried his social recognition of the correspondents a step further by formally inviting them to one of the inaugural receptions in the East Room.[30]

McKinley also expanded the working area for reporters inside the Executive Mansion. Although cramped and at first lacking telephone service, it provided an indoor base from which reporters could question the president's secretary and visitors.[31] Because of his daily column, William Price was given a small desk on which to write, a courtesy later extended to other correspondents. Twice a day, at noon and at 4 P.M., Secretary Porter sat with the correspondents and briefed them on the day's activities. Porter was also available for informal chats, although it was understood that the President himself could not be addressed unless he initiated the conversation.[32]

However, McKinley met personally with the correspondents who accompanied him on his first presidential speaking trip. En route to Nashville, Tennessee, in June 1897, he visited their Pullman car to chat with them informally. "Taking a seat in the midst of the party, he threw the hat aside and chatted without reserve for over an hour," according to an article in the *Washington Post*.[33] A few days later, in North Carolina, McKinley refused to enter George Vanderbilt's Biltmore mansion until a caretaker also admitted the correspondents, a gesture that was praised editorially by newspapers around the nation. "Every newspaper man in the country is prouder of President McKinley than ever before," commented the *Toledo Blade*.[34] David Barry, of *the New York Sun*, wrote approvingly that "there are . . . signs that the era of friendliness between public men and newspaper reporters will be restored. . . ."[35]

Late in his first year, McKinley formally invited the correspondents and their wives to one of his official holiday receptions. To be on the President's social list, along with members of Congress and the judiciary, was regarded by the correspondents as a flattering indicator of acceptance.[36] Those correspondents who attended social events in the McKinley administration wrote flattering accounts of the receptions and referred only generally to the health of Ida McKinley, who was subject to epileptic seizures.[37]

That President McKinley was concerned with more than good fellowship is clear from the scrapbooks of newspaper clippings that he had his clerks maintain. Each day, under the general heading of "Current Comment," McKinley was presented with articles clipped from newspapers from around the country and arranged on scrapbook pages for his reading convenience. Clerks scanned newspapers daily for items of interest, especially editorials from the leading Republican journals. The *New York Mail and Express* called the system "quite as extensive as any of the newspaper clipping bureaus in the country."[38] McKinley himself looked at several newspapers daily, particularly his hometown *Canton Repository*. Besides giving the President a means to monitor editorial commentary, which was then regarded as a reliable barometer of public opinion, the scrapbooks helped to familiarize him with what the correspondents were writing.[39]

The scrapbooks were a project of George Cortelyou, who in 1897 became McKinley's assistant secretary. Cortelyou had been a clerk for Cleveland, where he had gained experience in working with correspondents under the guidance of Secretary Thurber and Dan Lamont, then secretary of war.[40] However, Cortelyou disapproved of Thurber's practice of throwing away newspaper clippings, especially the ones critical of the president. Cortelyou, who served three presidents as a staff member or Cabinet secretary, later wrote a memorandum to Theodore Roosevelt that recommended that the president's staff maintain an organized monitoring of the newspapers, among other duties.[41]

Although McKinley went far in his first year to expand the relationship between his presidency and the Washington correspondents, his personal contact with the press was limited. A *New York Times* correspondent complained later that to see McKinley personally, a correspondent first had to persuade his secretary that he had a good reason to do so, then wait a day or two before learning whether the President had approved of the appointment.[42]

In early 1898, however, as the nation moved closer to war with Spain over Cuba, public opinion became too important to the President for such a detached approach to the press and public opinion. McKinley used his State of the Union Message to Congress in December 1897 to publicize his policy toward Cuba, which was to hope for peace while threatening Spain with military intervention. The message was widely praised in the press, although it did not satisfy pro-war members of Congress or the competing New York daily newspapers owned by Joseph Pulitzer and William Randolph Hearst.[43]

The explosion of the battleship *Maine* in Havana harbor in February 1898 spurred newspaper demands for military intervention in Cuba. Even the pro-administration *Washington Post,* not a sensational newspaper, began to run front-page editorials demanding that McKinley reject Spanish appeals to negotiate.[44] The crisis awakened press interest in the presidency on a scale unprecedented since the Civil War. Dozens of correspondents began to appear at the Executive Mansion daily to ask for more information about the explosion and the President's response to the crisis. Porter and Cortelyou found themselves spending most of their time trying to respond to press inquiries. But McKinley wanted to do more than to fend off the correspondents' questions: to keep from being forced prematurely into war with Spain, he wanted to moderate press and public war fever.[45]

Although it was not then customary for the press to quote a president directly, McKinley was the likely source of a series of published official statements calling for restraint. Porter and Cortelyou met with McKinley and prepared typewritten statements to be handed to the correspondents, some of which were printed verbatim. In the press, the statements were attributed variously to visitors with McKinley, to Secretary of the Navy John D. Long or other Cabinet members, and, by implication, to the President.[46] For example, on 10 April 1898, the *Washington Post* carried a story denying rumors that McKinley was changing his plans about asking Congress for a declaration of war: "The *Post* has the highest authority—there could be none higher, in fact—for asserting that these rumors affecting the President's stability of purpose and patriotic desire have no foundation in fact."[47]

In addition, Porter and Cortelyou made themselves available at all times to speak with correspondents, rather than only at scheduled briefings. To Cortelyou, who had seen reporters only sporadically at the Executive Mansion under Cleveland, the contrast was exhilarating. He wrote in his diary about the "suppressed excitement" when 30 to 40 reporters waited daily on the porch, in the front lobby, on the landings, even on the stairs, hoping for official statements. He and Porter were mobbed when official statements became available, and Porter got into "heated discussions" with several correspondents, including Price, of the *Star,* over who would receive the first copies.[48]

In late March 1898, the focus of the press was on the pending report of the military court of inquiry into the sinking of the battleship *Maine.*[49] McKinley was particularly concerned about public reaction to the report's inflammatory conclusion, which was that the battleship likely was sunk in Havana harbor by an external explosion, such as a Spanish mine. By preparing a carefully timed and cautiously worded announcement, to be issued by a Cabinet member rather than by the President, McKinley hoped to moderate the press response and to avoid additional sensationalizing. Cortelyou placed the announcement and a limited number of copies of the report in his office safe over the weekend. But when Cortelyou picked up the *Washington Post* on Monday, 28 March 1898, he found that the Associated Press had already transmitted a "remarkably accurate forecast of findings."[50] After complaints from Secretary Porter, among others, Charles A. Boynton, superintendent of the AP's Washington bureau, signed a statement that the information in the story had not been obtained from anyone in the Executive Mansion.[51]

To avoid future leaks, Cortelyou tried to make McKinley's statements available to reporters as quickly as possible after their preparation. That way there would be less time in which statements could be circulated improperly. On 25 April 1898, for instance, when McKinley sent his message to the Senate asking for a declaration of war, Cortelyou bragged in his diary that the document was in the hands of reporters within minutes after it left the President's office.[52]

McKinley tried to shape press coverage by the timing and wording of announcements throughout the wartime spring and summer of 1898. The President's Cabinet meetings were followed by press briefings by his secretaries.[53] When the Cabinet members and staff left the mansion, sometimes late at night, "they would be escorted home by a group of newspapermen who had to make quick work of it" to meet deadlines, according to David Barry of the *New York Sun.*[54] What the reporters were able to file from these hasty advisories was limited usually to what McKinley and Cortelyou had agreed was appropriate for public consumption.[55]

McKinley was particularly solicitous of the press associations, such as the Associated Press, the *New York Sun* service, and the Scripps-McRae syndicate, which were a more efficient means of getting his views into hundreds of newspapers across the country. He was able to monitor dispatches through new telegraph lines that had been installed in the Executive Mansion. Cortelyou noted in his diary that McKinley more than once took AP dispatches into Cabinet meetings and gave special treatment, including a rare interview, to the AP's Boynton.[56]

To aid McKinley's monitoring of press sentiment toward the war, Cortelyou occasionally wrote the President an analytical summary of the increasing numbers of newspaper clippings that arrived daily. He found himself displeased with much of what he read. "The sensational papers publish daily accounts of conferences that never take place, of influences that are never felt, or purposes that are nothing but the products of degenerate minds that spread them before a too-easily-led public," Cortelyou wrote. He was particularly offended at suggestions that McKinley saw only the favorable stories and letters: "The President sees everything, whether in the shape of mail, telegrams or newspapers, that can indicate the drift of public opinion."[57]

Once war was officially declared, McKinley acted to centralize the flow of information to the press in the Executive Mansion. A "War Room," with maps and 20 telegraph lines, was installed adjacent to the President's office. Relocated and expanded press facilities made it more convenient for reporters to talk with the President or his secretaries than to interview visitors, who might offer dissenting views. Despite press complaints, military censorship was imposed at fleet headquarters in Key West, Florida, and in the New York offices of the press associations. Direct censorship was not imposed in Washington but the reporters found that little information was available except through the Executive Mansion.[58] During peace negotiations in July 1898, for example, nearly 50 correspondents waited all day at the Executive Mansion, only to be handed a one-sentence statement from Cortelyou that a U.S. reply to Spain would not be made public.[59]

These wartime changes in the President's relationship with the press were significant. McKinley shaped the information made available to the press on a regular basis, and the frequent availability of official statements contributed to making the presidency a routine source of news. Increasingly, correspondents included the Executive Mansion, as well as Capitol Hill, in their regular rounds of newsgathering. In wartime, as the magazine writer Ida Tarbell observed, "The President, as a matter of fact, has the newspaper man always with him."[60]

While McKinley recognized the usefulness of dealing with the press on a daily basis during the war, this familiarity had its limits. He was cordial but distant as reporters swarmed about the Executive Mansion. He refused to allow reporters or photographers to attend the formal signing of the peace protocol on 12 August 1898, on the ground that the press might mar the dignity of the occasion.[61]

The correspondents' demands for war information also prompted some experimentation with publicity techniques in the administrative agencies. Prior to the Spanish-American War, these agencies, like the President, had only occasional contact with the daily press. However, once the war broke out, correspondents sought information at the State Department and at the War Department, as well as at the Executive Mansion. In the field, correspondents sought out military commanders for information. McKinley preferred to centralize the flow of information in the Executive Mansion, but he also found it advantageous to use Cabinet members and departmental subordinates as spokesmen. For example, to try to minimize the public reaction after the *Maine* explosion, he authorized Secretary of the Navy John D. Long to announce that there was no cause for alarm. When John Hay became secretary of state in September 1898, he invited a few reporters to meet with him weekly to explain to them the administration's war policies.[62]

The August 1898 armistice officially ended the war in Cuba, but the recriminations lingered on into the fall, as did the fighting in the Philippines. Press attention turned from celebrations of victory in Cuba to complaints about health problems in army camps, spoiled food, military confusion, and censorship in Manila. Although the War Department was the focus of these complaints, McKinley, as president, was held to be ultimately responsible.[63]

These controversies kept in motion the self-fulfilling process that was making the presidency a regular source of news. Correspondents called at the Executive Mansion to seek presidential responses to critical reports, which in turn formed the basis for additional stories. Partly by the President's design and partly by request, the presidency was becoming a "beat"—a process that could be relied upon to produce news predictably. This contributed to the President's growing visibility in the newspapers and presented McKinley with the opportunity to keep on appealing to public opinion through the press in peacetime as well as during the war.

To take full advantage of growing presidential access to the news pages, however, a more organized approach was needed. Dealing with reporters who dropped by several times a day, sometimes in groups, to ask questions or to seek official statements required a more systematic approach than that used for occasional callers. Preparing daily statements for the press demanded more time of the President and his Secretary than the leisurely schedule of, say, annual Messages to Congress.

In the months following the armistice, Cortelyou, who by then had been promoted to the position of McKinley's secretary, moved to make permanent some of the new routines of managing the press that had been developed under wartime pressures. These included having presidential statements duplicated and readied to present to reporters in advance or on demand, rather than by appointment or in delayed responses to inquiries; allowing reporters more opportunities to speak with the President personally, even if off the record; treating the correspondents more or less equally, regardless of partisan affiliation; releasing statements first to the press associations and then to the newspapers; and establishing a standardized system to supply the press with the texts of important statements, such as the Message to Congress, well in advance of delivery.[64]

Cortelyou's organizing of McKinley's relations with the press was praised widely by the correspondents, although it was only one aspect of his job as chief of staff. Albert Halstead, in a magazine profile of McKinley, referred flatteringly to Cortelyou as "the most popular Secretary who has served a President in a quarter of a century."[65] Edward Lowry, another magazine writer, called Cortelyou "very nearly the ideal Secretary to the President."[66]

Among the most successful of these new routines was Cortelyou's initiative to better publicize McKinley's speaking tours. In late 1898, McKinley was concerned both with critical press reports about the conduct of the war and the threat of Democratic congressional candidates in the November midterm elections. The President decided to travel to the Midwest in October 1898 to defend his foreign and domestic policies, which gave Cortelyou the opportunity to try out new procedures for dealing with the traveling newspaper and magazine correspondents.[67]

Previous presidents who had taken the "swing around the circle" had tended to favor local party leaders and editors in issuing invitations to board the train. Cortelyou, who organized McKinley's ten-day October 1898 trip, was more interested in seeing the President's remarks treated as national news than as local commentary. Priority was given to correspondents from the press associations, national magazines, and the most prominent daily newspapers. On this trip, that included the Associated Press, the *New York Sun* Press Association, the Scripps-McRae Press Association, *Leslie's Weekly,* and *Harper's Weekly,* as well as representatives of the largest newspapers in cities to be visited. On subsequent trips, Cortelyou allocated so much of the limited space on the train to this "national" press that he sometimes had to turn down requests from local Republican editors, for which he was unapologetic.[68]

The crowds who greeted McKinley on the October 1898 trip were enthusiastic, and so were the newspaper stories.[69] In between whistlestops, Cortelyou spent considerable time chatting with the correspondents to seek ways to make it more convenient for them to report on the President's public appearances.[70] In one of the most popular innovations,

Cortelyou assigned a stenographer to record McKinley's brief remarks at each stop. Within minutes after the train started up again, he was able to give the traveling correspondents a typed, authoritative transcript, including colorful human-interest notes, which formed the basis for the brief reports they could file at the next telegraph office.

The correspondents welcomed Cortelyou's innovation. David Barry, of the *New York Sun,* called the stenographer's handouts a "great convenience to reporters and it is very important to the president. It puts before the country systematically and completely a correct report of all he says and all that is said to him."[71] A review of Associated Press reports from the October 1898 trip published in the *Washington Post* revealed nearly identical brief accounts of McKinley's remarks at each whistlestop, each one containing a flattering crowd description and anecdote. From Ixon, Illinois, for example, the AP reported that a young man jumped to the railing of McKinley's car and said, "Here, McKinley, give us a shake, please." In another AP report, from Arcola, Illinois, McKinley reportedly led three cheers for the American flag, and an older man near the speaking platform shouted: "[Admiral] Dewey made them honor it."[72]

McKinley was so pleased with the public and press response to his October trip that in December 1898 he set off again, this time to the South, to promote Senate ratification of the final Treaty of Paris, which ended the war with Spain.[73] Between 1897 and 1901, McKinley took at least 40 trips outside Washington, D.C.[74]

Another aspect of presidential-press relations that Cortelyou tried to standardize was the perennial problem of newspapers violating the release times on advance copies of the annual Message to Congress and other formal speeches. These advance texts usually were sent out long in advance by mail, because the messages often were several thousand words long and required many hours of manual typesetting by newspapers. The telegraph was much faster, but the laborious process of transmitting text by Morse code limited the time and space available on AP wires.[75]

The daily newspapers, with the text of the president's message in hand well before its delivery, found it hard to resist using advance excerpts in special editions to "scoop" their competitors. Cleveland had resisted sending out advance copies of his messages for fear of premature publication, despite George Parker's argument that the President's words would receive greater display if the editors received the texts of his remarks earlier by mail.[76]

The problem grew more acute under McKinley because of his increased number of public statements and greater press interest in what the President had to say. After McKinley's Message to Congress in December

1898, the AP complained that Dow Jones had published a 2,000-word abstract 50 minutes early.[77] In August 1899, some New York newspapers broke the embargo on a McKinley speech in Pittsburgh, which angered the others. Cortelyou asked Melville Stone of the AP to investigate the incident and to report back to him.[78]

Concerned that the rancor would reflect on McKinley, Cortelyou created an elaborate process that required representatives of the news services and individual newspapers to sign personally for advance copies of presidential addresses and to assume legal responsibility for keeping them confidential. To receive an advance copy of McKinley's December 1899 Message to Congress, for example, representatives of the news services were required to sign a form that made them responsible not only for themselves but also for the newspapers that subscribed to their services. The most elaborate contract was the one signed by the AP's Stone, which stated that "any violation of this agreement will be a most serious matter, punishable by a refusal to grant similar courtesies in the future."[79]

As McKinley and Cortelyou grew more experienced in dealing with reporters, both became sophisticated in the subtleties of dealing with the questions and with the questioners. Isaac F. Marcosson, who interviewed McKinley, found him to be an "amiable, approachable, kindly man who talked much and said little. I doubt if any American President was quite so cautious and committed himself less on all controversial questions. Yet he was always wise enough to see reporters and communicate something to them."[80]

Cortelyou became, in effect, McKinley's press secretary, although no such official position existed until the Hoover administration. In addition to his regular duties as chief of staff, Cortelyou was McKinley's surrogate source for the correspondents, both in person and over the new device of the telephone. Because he worked long hours and was known to have the President's confidence, Cortelyou was regarded by the correspondents as a valuable and convenient source. David Barry, of the *New York Sun,* observed from a reporter's standpoint that Cortelyou "never slaps them on the back or calls them 'old man' but he always treats them fairly and squarely."[81] Cortelyou also understood the uses of confidentiality. What Cortelyou could say for publication, he would, and he could be candid to reporters who honored his confidences. Albert Halstead wrote approvingly that Cortelyou "must tell the newspaper correspondents what they should know without seeming to suppress information."[82]

Cortelyou had observed that favoring some correspondents over others, especially for partisan reasons, created unnecessary discord and reduced the President's opportunities to get his views into independent and

Democratic papers, as well as the Republican ones. Most of the larger newspapers were Republican in orientation, and few Democratic correspondents expected a welcome at the executive mansion under McKinley. O. O. Stealey, of the Democratic *Louisville (Kentucky) Courier-Journal,* was surprised to find Cortelyou both approachable and willing to leak advance word of a regional presidential appointment. Cortelyou would not respond to Stealey's questioning directly, but he was willing to say that he had heard "a name mentioned in connection with the office." The information gave Stealey a three-day scoop on the official announcement and made him more attentive to news from the Executive Mansion under McKinley.[83]

While McKinley was more forthcoming in addressing the press at the Executive Mansion, he retained the tradition of avoiding correspondents on his summer vacation. In 1900, an election year, McKinley's speaking tours ended in March, and he accepted the Republican nomination for re-election by issuing a statement from his front porch in Canton, Ohio.[84] Arthur Wallace Dunn, the AP correspondent, noted in his memoirs that McKinley was the last president to go on a summer retreat "without a squad of White House reporters in attendance."[85]

By the beginning of McKinley's second term, in March 1901, the President and Cortelyou were recognized widely for their adeptness in managing the press corps to transmit the President's message. Frances Leupp, a veteran correspondent, wrote that McKinley "recognized the value of newspapers as the medium for reaching the people at large and, while apparently not courting publicity, contributed to put out, by various shrewd processes of indirection, whatever news would best serve the ends of the administration."[86]

McKinley's popularity in the nation in the spring of 1901 was such that his most extended speaking tour, a six-week swing through the South and West, resembled a triumphal procession. In addition to nine correspondents, two telegraph operators, and three stenographers, the press car included a photographer under contract for several newspapers and magazines who converted a sleeping compartment into a darkroom. When the trip was cut short in California because of Ida McKinley's health problems, Cortelyou and a clerk, B. F. Barnes, issued frequent reports to the correspondents about the First Lady's condition.[87]

By June 1901, three months before McKinley was assassinated, the relationship between the President and the press had become so established that McKinley could instruct Cortelyou to distribute a statement "through the usual channels." Prior to McKinley, no such "usual channels" existed through which presidents routinely channeled information to the public through the press. According to Cortelyou's diary, that directive followed a sophisticated discussion of the most productive way to release to the press McKinley's statement that he would not seek a third presidential term.[88]

What had been a sporadic, somewhat defensive relationship between the President and the correspondents was becoming a mutually rewarding collection of routines. McKinley had tried to attract the attention of the correspondents and to make writing news stories about the President both easier and more frequent. The correspondents now called regularly at the Executive Mansion to collect such newsworthy information as the President or his Secretary chose to give them. They could expect to be greeted cordially, to receive prompt responses to their questions, and to be given statements and announcements that could be made into news stories. Not only were they welcomed by the staff and, occasionally, by the President, they had expanded their presence in the building. Through these and other now-routine procedures, the presidency was becoming a recognized "beat" for an emerging White House press corps.[89]

By adapting the presidency to conform to the occupational needs of the correspondents, McKinley assured that his views would be transmitted to the nation through the daily newspapers and popular magazines. He was able both to expand and to shape the news about his activities more successfully than his predecessors. On this foundation, Theodore Roosevelt was able to construct a relationship through which presidents could manage the press to influence public opinion later in the century.

CHAPTER TWO

THEODORE ROOSEVELT: PUBLICITY! PUBLICITY! PUBLICITY!

Theodore Roosevelt, who succeeded William McKinley in 1901, accelerated the transformation of presidential leadership that McKinley had begun. Roosevelt's masterful management of the press to generate news coverage of himself and his policies long has been recognized.[1] One study suggests that Roosevelt received the longest press "honeymoon" and the most favorable periodical coverage of any twentieth-century president.[2] From the earliest days of Roosevelt's political career, much of his public and private life seemed to take place in the pages of newspapers and magazines. "He was his own press agent, and he had a splendid comprehension of news and its value," wrote Archie Butt, an aide to Roosevelt and to his successor, William Howard Taft.[3] The journalist and admirer William Allen White agreed: "The spotlight of publicity followed Roosevelt all his life with curious devotion—by no means without Roosevelt's encouragement."[4] To Roosevelt critics such as Willis J. Abbot, editor of Joseph Pulitzer's *New York World,* it seemed that "Publicity! publicity! publicity! was his slogan."[5]

But it was purposeful publicity. Richard V. Oulahan, in 1907 a correspondent for the *New York Sun,* wrote that Roosevelt "was one of the pioneers in the modern method of doing things through the power of publicity."[6] As president, Roosevelt used the news to extend his appearance of personal authority and to shape debates about his policies. A typical Roosevelt policy initiative, wrote the columnist Mark Sullivan, began with a barrage of newspaper headlines intended to stir up public sentiment and to discredit his adversaries, then continued through a series of news releases and public actions that were intended to maintain the flow of news coverage. The process went on until the President either won or started another crusade.[7]

Aided by McKinley's chief of staff, George Cortelyou, who stayed on as secretary until he was succeeded by William F. Loeb in 1903, Roosevelt made managing the press one of his highest priorities. Roosevelt was well aware of the editorial policies and production schedules of newspapers, magazines, and press associations, as well as the occupational demands placed on reporters and writers. He created news about the presidency not only on formal occasions, such as in the traditional Messages to Congress, but on a daily, sometimes hourly, basis. Roosevelt's statements and news releases were made available to correspondents when no other news was likely to be found to fill the news pages, such as on Sundays.

Furthermore, Roosevelt approached the correspondents personally, rather than dealing with them at a distance or through a screen of secretaries. For those whose stories pleased Roosevelt, covering the President became easier and more prestigious. As long as they kept his confidence, they were invited to meet with him daily for a barrage of presidential advice, leaks, story ideas, gossip, instructions on how to write their stories, complaints about coverage, and whatever else Roosevelt thought might influence the news. This constant availability of news both expanded the public visibility of the presidency and encouraged the development of a regularly assigned White House press corps, correspondents whose employment was based on producing regular stories about the President.

Roosevelt had been a magnet for publicity from his first days in elective office as a New York state assemblyman. Early in 1882, when the 23-year-old Roosevelt took his assembly seat, his dandified appearance and bombastic outspokenness brought him instant press attention, not all of it complimentary.[8] Confronted at the beginning of his public career with the realization that he was, in the idiom of the time, a "natural" for publicity, Roosevelt quickly learned how to use it to help accomplish his political goals. Among his first allies in Albany was George Spinney, legislative correspondent for the *New York Times.* In late March 1882, when Roosevelt launched a seemingly quixotic campaign to recall a New York State Supreme Court justice, he was helped by letters and supportive news stories in the *Times.*[9]

By 1889, when President Harrison appointed Roosevelt to his first federal position, on the U.S. Civil Service Commission, Roosevelt was already a critical observer of the press and its ways. In an 1894 letter to Lucius Burrie Swift, he offered his insights into the Washington newspapers: "The

Washington Post is apt to have tolerably full news, but its editor is a particularly blackguard spoilsman. The *Washington Evening Star* is a civil service reform paper, but, like many other evening papers, often does not get the full news. It is a real misfortune that we no longer have any daily paper which will tell the thing in full. I am disgusted with the action of many of our newspapers."[10]

Throughout his public career, Roosevelt was a discerning, and often severe, observer of newspapers and magazines. He was an omnivorous reader and a thin-skinned one. But his early exposure to the workings of the press also showed him how to exploit the process by which news was produced. He learned to create news by stimulating controversy, by conforming to the technological and occupational changes under way in the news media, and by befriending those who gathered and wrote the news: the reporters and writers. Roosevelt honed these insights during his two-year career as a New York City police commissioner, beginning in 1895.

Joseph Bucklin Bishop, then of the *New York Evening Post,* described how Roosevelt approached the job of police commissioner:"He began the fight at once, using in it the weapons he had employed in its predecessors: full publicity, strict enforcement of law, and utter disregard of partisan political considerations."[11] To seek evidence of police corruption with maximum publicity, Roosevelt invited reporters to join him on nighttime prowls of New York streets. He held public trials of police officers who were accused of wrongdoing. Roosevelt understood that controversy made news, and that news furthered his appearance of authority. In his autobiography, Roosevelt acknowledged that as police commissioner "we accomplished some things by assuming the appearance of a power which we did not really possess."[12] It was neither the first nor the last time that the combative Roosevelt would realize the publicity advantages of elevating routine disagreements into a public fight. The furor frequently attracted press attention that he could use to promote his own interests.[13]

Roosevelt regarded journalists as useful sources of information as well as potential publicizers of his exploits. Lincoln Steffens recounted how, on Roosevelt's first day as police commissioner, he asked Steffens and Jacob Riis what he should do.[14] Roosevelt was not merely angling for favorable newspaper coverage. Steffens and Riis knew a good deal about New York City's problems. Steffens was beginning the analysis of urban ills that would lead to his muckraking magazine series "The Shame of the Cities."[15] Riis had published a revealing book on urban poverty, *How the Other Half Lives,* which Roosevelt had read and admired.[16] Roosevelt drew on their knowledge and, in turn, tried to persuade the editor of *Atlantic* magazine to publish an article by Steffens and Riis about police corruption in New York.

The proposed article, not coincidentally, would have supported the reforms that Roosevelt was trying to accomplish.[17]

Roosevelt was less pleased to learn that Steffens and Riis had concocted a New York City "crime wave" to drive up newspaper sales, especially when the sensationalized stories resulted in new public demands on the police commissioner.[18] Nor was the news coverage that Roosevelt generated necessarily as favorable as it was extensive. At one point, he complained to his friend Henry Cabot Lodge that "I have not one New York city newspaper or one New York city politician on my side."[19]

Nevertheless, when he was appointed assistant secretary of the navy by McKinley in 1897, Roosevelt characteristically turned to publicity to overcome what he regarded as the navy's primary problem: "A body of public opinion so important during the decades immediately succeeding the Civil War as to put a stop to any serious effort to keep the nation in a condition of reasonable military preparedness."[20] To stimulate appropriate news stories, he sent a letter to the editor of the *New York Sun* suggesting that the newspaper send a reporter to watch navy maneuvers off Newport News, named the reporter he preferred, and implied that if the *Sun* did not send a reporter, its news service would be left at a competitive disadvantage to the rival Associated Press. The preferred reporter, who was sent, was Richard V. Oulahan, already a Roosevelt favorite.[21]

Long an advocate of military action against Spain, Roosevelt put aside his naval duties to fight personally in the Spanish-American War as leader of the "Rough Riders," an exploit that drew extraordinary news coverage, even by Rooseveltian standards. In his unpublished memoir, Oulahan claimed credit for publicizing Roosevelt's term, "Rough Riders," through the *New York Sun* news service.[22] Given Roosevelt's known propensity for publicity, it is not surprising that the career officers in the expeditionary force selected Roosevelt to write, to sign, and to leak a "round robin" letter to the Associated Press that revealed widespread problems with disease and sanitation.[23]

As governor of New York, his last public office before becoming vice president to McKinley, Roosevelt again identified his major challenge as generating public support to back needed reforms. "When I became governor, the conscience of the people was in no way or shape aroused, as it has since become aroused," he wrote in his autobiography. Opposed by the state Republican Party machine, he "adopted the plan of going over the heads of the men holding public office and of the men in control of the organization, and appealing directly to the people behind them," that is, to the public.[24]

To reach this public, he approached the press corps in Albany in ways that prefigured his management of the presidential correspondents in Washington, using a combination of the carrot and the stick. Governor Roosevelt held briefings for reporters twice a day, once for morning and once for afternoon newspapers. He showered the Capitol press corps with information about his reform proposals.[25] When the carrot of easily available news failed to inspire the reporters to produce the stories he wanted, Roosevelt let their editors know that he was unhappy. In April 1900, for instance, he complained to the *New York Times* that its Albany correspondent was a Tammany Hall man, a tool of the party bosses, and that "he has been persistently, consistently, throughout the winter, perverting the news to discredit me."[26] He also advised Joseph Bucklin Bishop, then editor of the *New York Commercial Advertiser,* not to hire a correspondent from the *New York Tribune* whom Roosevelt regarded as "a tricky and unsafe man."[27]

The intensity with which Roosevelt managed the press in these prepresidential years indicated more than a desire for self-promotion or political advantage. He was a highly intelligent man, and he was developing a rationale for using the press to shape public opinion that drew both from his notion of expanding executive power as a "steward of the people" and from the Progressive view that properly informing the public was necessary to create support for reform.[28]

Widespread among reformers at the turn of the century was the belief that publicizing the "facts" of corporate and government corruption in the American system would prompt responsible citizens to demand change.[29] Revealing the financial manipulations of monopolistic trusts, for example, would create a climate of public opinion that would form a "social control" on the offenders, wrote the influential political economist Henry C. Adams.[30]

However, to Roosevelt and other reformers, the largest mass medium of the day, the advertising-supported daily newspaper, seemed to be part of the problem rather than part of the solution. Instead of providing needed moral uplift, the daily press often seemed to focus on what was vulgar, sensational, partisan, or crass. The utopian novelist Edward Bellamy characterized the late-nineteenth-century press as controlled and managed by private capital "primarily as a money-making business and secondarily only as a mouthpiece for the people."[31]

Without proper guidance, in other words, the press would keep the kind of information that would provoke citizens to support reform from reaching the public. From this perspective, using the techniques of publicity to manage the news was morally, as well as politically, correct. This view meshed well with Roosevelt's belief that the central government, especially the executive, should intervene in the economy on the public's behalf to curb the excesses of laissez-faire. As Robert C. Hilderbrand has pointed out, Roosevelt saw a parallel between the evils of unregulated financial monopolies and the chronic irresponsibility of the press. Both needed proper guidance, by government if necessary, to better serve the public interest.[32]

Roosevelt especially admired the thinking of the sociologist Edward A. Ross, who believed that social control of public opinion could only result from its proper regulation by the newspapers. In an approving letter that became the preface to Ross's 1907 book, *Sin and Society,* Roosevelt wrote that "public opinion, if only sufficiently enlightened and aroused, is equal to the necessary regenerative tasks and can yet dominate the future."[33]

This sort of reasoning provided both moral and pragmatic support for managing the press to support Roosevelt's presidency and his policies. As president, Roosevelt did not, except in a few angry moments, attempt direct government action against newspapers that opposed him. But Roosevelt's overpowering personality, plus his years of experience in using the techniques of publicity to accomplish his goals, were sufficient to exert a commanding influence on the Washington correspondents. McKinley had begun to gain the attention of these correspondents, but it was Roosevelt who persuaded a group of them to specialize in writing about the presidency.

Within hours of returning from the funeral of the assassinated McKinley, Roosevelt summoned the most influential of the correspondents, those from the major news services. No White House correspondents' association existed in 1901, but the Associated Press, Scripps-McRae, and the *New York Sun* press associations collectively telegraphed stories to the news pages of every significant daily newspaper in the nation. The Associated Press, by far the largest of the press associations, tried to avoid offending its diverse newspaper membership by transmitting brief descriptive stories and the texts of speeches.[34] The *New York Sun* was unabashedly Republican, and its bureau chief, David S. Barry, was a lifelong party activist and admirer of Roosevelt.[35] E. W. Scripps, the mercurial left-wing owner of Scripps-McRae, later United Press, was also a Roosevelt admirer.[36]

Significantly, however, the press associations summoned by Roosevelt were represented by correspondents, not editors or owners. As Barry noted, Roosevelt knew that "editorial articles do not mold public opinion now as they did in the days of Horace Greeley. . . . he was greatly impressed with the power exerted upon the minds of the people by the news articles published in the newspapers and he was always keenly alive to what the news columns were carrying." Roosevelt's commands to the three correspondents—Barry; Charles Boynton of AP; and Edward Keen of

Scripps-McRae—left no doubt who would dominate the relationship. The President would be open and accessible to those reporters who had his confidence, while those who published stories that Roosevelt didn't like would be banished.[37]

The correspondents in 1901 lacked the professional stature to object to Roosevelt's heavy-handed approach, even if they were inclined to do so. Newspaper reporting, even political reporting, was regarded as a somewhat marginal occupation at the turn of the century. Although the Washington correspondents tended to take themselves more seriously than did their raffish colleagues in newspaper city rooms around the country, they had limited autonomy from their editors or from their political patrons and sources, many of whom were members of Congress.[38] Will Irwin, in a 1911 muckraking article on newspaper journalism in *Collier's* magazine, said that to make the right acquaintances and to get the best sources, the correspondents needed to surrender "to the Washington point of view. . . . So Washington correspondence, viewed in bulk, tends always toward the side of the powerful."[39] Writing about political affairs was often a way station to elective office, a political appointment, or a full-time job as a government or corporate publicity agent.[40]

Moreover, the newspaper and press association correspondents, unlike publishers and editors, lacked the education or social standing to challenge a president. Few had attended college, and some had been promoted to Washington after years of service on lesser newsroom beats or for faithful editorial work. McKinley had encouraged these correspondents to make covering the presidency a regular "beat," but he kept his distance from them professionally and socially, leaving them to talk to his secretaries or to party spokesmen in the Cabinet or Congress. However, Roosevelt, unlike McKinley, could not rely on his conservative party colleagues in Congress to speak to correspondents on his behalf. In any case, Roosevelt throughout his career had found journalists interesting as well as useful. He preferred to deal with them himself.[41]

The result was that correspondents accustomed to polite but distant treatment at the Executive Mansion found themselves confronted directly with an outspoken, often bellicose, President in an unavoidably personal relationship. Those whom Roosevelt favored, especially the Republican correspondents who knew him before he became president, received frequent personal audiences and were allowed to overhear the President's disarmingly candid remarks during his informal "shaving hour" press conferences. Louis Brownlow described these events as "more fun than a circus." Brownlow wrote: "'Teddy' in an ordinary armchair would be lathered, and, as the razor would descend toward his face, someone would ask a question. The President would wave both arms, jump up, speak excitedly, and then drop again into the chair and grin at the barber, who would begin all over."[42] Oulahan wrote that one correspondent whom Roosevelt favored frequently with trial balloons, presumably himself, was so shaken at the barber's near misses with the razor that he often failed to overhear what the President was trying to tell him.[43]

For a working-class correspondent to be a confidant of an aristocratic President, especially one with a powerful personality like Roosevelt's, was a heady experience. Walter E. Clark, of the *New York Sun,* boasted to an editor in Seattle that "I had a bully long confab with Teddy yesterday; he was having a haircut and a shave. I wish I had time to tell you all the funny things he said; he talked a blue streak even while the barber was shaving him." Although Clark later became disillusioned at being "used" by Roosevelt, he was entranced at first. "We went up to Teddy Saturday morning and had the finest time," he wrote. "(Attorney General Philander C.) Knox was there, and Teddy told stories and performed war dances around his office. He laughed so long that he disturbed the neighborhood."[44]

For the most favored correspondents, called by critics the "fair-haired boys," personal exposure to Roosevelt's charm and endless crusading led to hero worship.[45] Oulahan, an admirer of Roosevelt's since his days as assistant secretary of the navy, was invited to all the "seances," as the exclusive conferences were called, and enjoyed unlimited access to the President.[46] A less fortunate correspondent complained that favored members of the press corps had become Roosevelt's "cuckoos" and "assistant press agents." The cuckoo was described as "a journalistic bird that is permitted to make its principal roost close to the executive chambers and report for the delectation of his editor, for the enlightenment of the public, and the accommodation of the President such outgivings of internal operations of the presidential mind as may suit the purpose and the whim of the nation's chief magistrate."[47] Walter Clark, who fell out of favor with Roosevelt after quarreling with Loeb over a promised patronage appointment, complained that "we have constantly been pulling his chestnuts out of the fire, and have been constantly used to grind his axes."[48]

Whether or not the correspondents liked Roosevelt personally, maintaining the President's confidence was critical to gathering the information necessary to produce authoritative news stories. As Clark observed, "There is no limit to his fund of ready comment on the inside of the administration, and on men and affairs nearly or remotely touching the administration."[49] Roosevelt's remarks could not be quoted, but his wide-ranging talks frequently set the stage for future stories. Oscar King Davis, a correspondent for the *New York Times,* said: "You might have an hour with the

President, and talk all around the horizon, politics, diplomatic affairs, military, naval or congressional situation, money trust, labor, undesirable citizens, and what not, and yet not get out of it all a word that you could write today. Then, within a week, something might happen that would be trivial and unimportant to one who had not had such a talk with the President, but which furnished a good story to one who had."[50] Oulahan agreed: "Ten minutes of conversation with President Roosevelt usually gave me more material for my press dispatches than longer interviews with each of a half a dozen principal officers of government."[51]

In contrast to his exuberant private remarks, the President's public statements were guarded. "Roosevelt seldom spoke without seeing a picture of how the sentence would look in type, and how it would affect the mind of the readers," noted Henry L. Stoddard, a correspondent for the *Philadelphia Press*.[52] Isaac F. Marcosson wrote that while Roosevelt at times granted interviews, they were one-way conversations limited to what the President intended to say.[53] Charles Willis Thompson, bureau chief of the *New York Times* during Roosevelt's presidency, doubted that any reporter ever provoked Roosevelt to make an unplanned public comment. Thompson said Roosevelt "never said one word more than he had already decided to say. . . . although no man ever talked more freely to reporters—not for publication."[54]

When Roosevelt did decide to comment publicly, he would repeat his message until he felt it had received the proper amount of news coverage. Oulahan noted that "if opportunities were not presented frequently enough to reiterate his statement of policy in a message to Congress or a public speech, he would repeat his words to Washington correspondents, day after day, as long as the hostile clamor lasted. His ingenuity would enable him to dress his ideas in some new garment each time he felt that repetition was necessary. In that way he gave the correspondents the means and the excuse for keeping fresh and alive the Roosevelt viewpoint. He made no excuse for resorting to this method. The Colonel's theory was that if you wished the people to understand your attitude, you must constantly, insistently, remind them of it."[55]

His torrent of words, colorful temperament, and endearing candor notwithstanding, Roosevelt could be ruthless to correspondents who violated his confidences. "It was all or nothing with him," Davis wrote. "He either talked, with entire frankness and freedom, about everything, or he didn't talk at all."[56] Violators were sentenced to his "Ananias Club" and could be banished from the President's presence, a loss of access that could end the correspondent's usefulness to his newspaper and, consequently, his job.[57] As bureau chief of the *New York Sun,* Oulahan was ordered to withdraw from the White House a correspondent whose only offense had been to obtain an advance copy of a congressional committee report, which angered a competing correspondent, who complained to the President. Roosevelt was dissuaded only after Attorney General Knox, a friend of the correspondent, interceded on his behalf. In another incident, Roosevelt wrote a personal note to Frank B. Munsey, then owner of the *Washington Times,* demanding that the newspaper recall correspondent John Stauffer, who had written that Senator Nathan B. Scott of West Virginia left the Executive Mansion in a huff because the President kept him waiting. Munsey complied.[58] While professing to welcome criticism, Roosevelt was notoriously thin-skinned, and the correspondents knew that angering Roosevelt or his Secretary would bring at least a scathing letter to their editors.[59]

Roosevelt knew that one way to counter unwanted newspaper stories was to upstage his critics by creating new sensations. This technique, which Oulahan called "Roosevelt's back-fires," worked to crowd unwanted stories off the front pages or to overshadow the display of a story that the President did not want to be read. In one incident cited by Oulahan, Roosevelt, who had been reading Upton Sinclair's shocking novel *The Jungle,* abruptly ordered a federal investigation of meatpacking houses to preempt a forthcoming "first page feature which was not to his liking."[60]

Dictatorial or not, Roosevelt's management of the press raised the professional stature of the correspondents at the same time that they were elevating the public visibility of his presidency with their news stories. To "cover" the presidency, previously a secondary, somewhat intermittent activity by the correspondents, was becoming a full-time job under Roosevelt. Practices that began as novelties under McKinley were becoming routine expectations: the frequent briefings,[61] the convenient advance distribution of formal speeches and presidential messages,[62] and, in the person of secretary Loeb, the availability of a key staff member to serve the press.[63] In his autobiography, Roosevelt praised the leading Washington correspondents as "on the whole, a singularly able, trustworthy and public-spirited body of men, and the most useful of all agents in the fight for efficient and decent government."[64]

Roosevelt's interest in appealing to the public through the press extended well beyond the newspapers and press associations with representatives in Washington. The President was also interested in the publicity possibilities of a relatively new medium, the mass-circulation national magazine. Magazines prior to the late nineteenth century tended to be literary in outlook, limited in circulation, and directed at specialized audiences, especially women. In the 1880s and 1890s, however, entrepreneurs such as J. Walter Thompson and Cyrus Curtis discovered that magazines were an attractive medium for national marketing through advertising. Fueled by advertising revenues, technological advances in printing, and lowered postal rates, magazines proliferated in numbers and in circulation during the first decade of the century. As noted earlier, the combined circulation of monthly periodicals rose from 18 million to 64 million per issue between 1890 and 1905. The circulation of Curtis's *Ladies Home Journal* reached 1 million per issue in 1913, and kept growing.[65]

Not only did the *Ladies Home Journal* and other leading magazines such as *McClure's, Munsey's, Saturday Evening Post, Good Housekeeping, Woman's Home Companion, McCall's, Collier's, Cosmopolitan,* and the *Outlook,* reach increasingly into the nation's homes during Roosevelt's presidency, they frequently focused their editorial content on public affairs, especially on the need for political reform.[66] Before becoming president, Roosevelt had met many of the more prominent magazine editors and writers and found them predisposed to the reform cause.[67]

As president, however, Roosevelt found that persuading the magazine writers to champion his policies required a somewhat different approach than the forceful techniques that he used on the Washington correspondents. For one thing, he had to seek out the gatekeepers of this new medium, rather than to wait for them to come calling at the Executive Mansion. Once the Washington correspondents had been persuaded to cover the President routinely, getting into print could be accomplished simply by being available to them on a daily basis. Getting the President's message into the national magazines, which were published mostly in New York City and did not send correspondents daily to the Executive Mansion, required more presidential planning and time.

Here, Roosevelt benefited from his background in New York politics and his social and professional acquaintanceships with the editors and writers who were sympathetic to the reform movement. Roosevelt's challenge was not only to place himself and his views on prominent display in these magazines. He wanted the articles written to support his policies as well. But the most prominent magazines demanding reform, such as *McClure's* and the *American,* tended to favor stronger remedies to cure the ills of American government and society than Roosevelt found acceptable politically. Also, the blunt methods of managing the press that he used to manipulate the Washington correspondents were less likely to succeed with the better-educated, politically independent magazine writers and editors.[68]

Roosevelt tried persistently, both in person and by letter, to befriend and influence the leading magazine writers, particularly William Allen

White, Lincoln Steffens, and Ray Stannard Baker. To court these writers, or at least to try to limit the political fallout from their stories, Roosevelt conducted an extensive campaign of personal persuasion. The President consulted with them on story ideas, suggested sources, argued his views to try to shape their articles, arranged for access to government offices and records, and sometimes fed the writers damaging information about his political rivals.

For example, Roosevelt's leaks to White led to a critical profile of New York Republican boss Sen. Thomas Platt, a long-time conservative foe of Roosevelt, in the December 1901, issue of *McClure's*. Platt, suspecting correctly that Roosevelt was behind the article, demanded that White be barred from the White House. Platt's angry reaction made news, and White sent an alarmed and apologetic note to the President. Roosevelt sent back a cheerful letter reassuring White that "the only damage that could happen to me through such articles would be if you refused to continue to champion me. Now, old man, don't talk nonsense. If Senator Platt comes in again, I shall show him your note and tell him that of course I never inspired any attacks on him, but that equally of course I must continue to have as my friends whomever I wish."[69] In his autobiography, White confirmed that Roosevelt had been behind the story: "This was true, though I was cautious enough never to print any story that Roosevelt gave me without getting the story from another source. Generally, he told me where to find the other source, for he loved intrigue."[70] White was a willing ally. His unctuous praise in the advance proof of another article for *McClure's,* "Roosevelt: A Force for Righteousness," was too much even for the President, who questioned the favorable comparisons with George Washington, Abraham Lincoln, and Benjamin Franklin.[71]

Roosevelt was less successful with some of the other reform writers, including Steffens, who was one of the most prolific. When Roosevelt was a New York City police commissioner, he and Steffens worked together closely. As president, however, Roosevelt was disturbed by the dark portraits of greedy businessmen, corrupt political bosses, crooked or ineffective city officials, and ubiquitous graft that Steffens drew in his "Shame of the Cities" articles, which had begun to appear in *McClure's*. Roosevelt called in Steffens and his editor, S. S. McClure, to urge, without noticeable success, that Steffens "put more sky in his landscape."[72] In 1907, when Steffens, bearing a presidential letter of support, starting asking Roosevelt's subordinates pointed questions about the behavior of key congressmen, the President tried to rein him in. In 1908, Roosevelt tried to distance himself from a Steffens article in *Everybody's* magazine about the upcoming presidential election.[73]

Like Steffens, Ray Stannard Baker, another prominent reform writer, initially was drawn to Roosevelt but later became suspicious of his political motives. The President at first took Baker into his confidence and gave him information and access to his administration, then withdrew when Baker's stories proved to be embarrassing politically. Baker wrote numerous articles in *McClure's* and, later, the *American,* about problems in labor unions, race relations, and, especially, monopolistic practices by railroads, all issues which concerned Roosevelt. The Hepburn Act of 1906, intended to reform railroad rates, was a centerpiece of Roosevelt's "Square Deal" legislative proposals, and he wrote to Baker repeatedly as the writer prepared and published a series of articles critical of the railroads. Roosevelt reviewed early drafts of some of the articles and tried to restrain Baker's attacks on railroad officials.[74]

Roosevelt's tenuous relationship with the reform writers grew more complicated after his critical remarks about "muckraking" in 1906. Roosevelt's characterization of these journalists, who henceforth became known as "muckrakers," was delivered first in a private talk to the Gridiron Club and then publicly in a speech on 14 April 1906. Roosevelt was aiming at those whose criticism had gone too far, in the President's view, or who had caused him political embarrassment, such as David Graham Phillips, author of "The Treason of the Senate," which recently had appeared in *Cosmopolitan* magazine. He compared them to John Bunyan's "Man with the Muckrake, who could look no way but downward with the muckrake in his hand."[75] After his remarks, Roosevelt tried to placate the offended writers, particularly Baker and Steffens. "I want to 'let in light and air,' but I do not want to let in sewer gas," Roosevelt wrote to Baker, who was alienated by the President's criticism. "If a room is fetid and the windows are bolted I am perfectly content to knock out the windows; but I would not knock a hole into the drain pipe."[76]

Roosevelt's attempts to manage the magazine writers were not limited to muckrakers. Mark Sullivan, a sympathetic columnist for *Collier's,* magazine, received an 11-page letter from Roosevelt, with considerable underlining, after he made a mildly critical editorial allusion to the President's judicial appointments.[77]

Roosevelt's constant appeals for public support through all available means of mass communications contributed to the personalization of the presidency. To seek governing authority by appealing through the press to the public, the President had to reach through the filters of the newspapers and magazines to establish some sort of personal relationship with the citizenry, however distant. In doing so, the President increased the curiosity of both journalists and the public about the person behind the office, about the President's personality as well as his policies. To some extent, this personalization was an inevitable consequence of the emergence of the president as the public symbol of government. But Roosevelt's self-exposure to the press as policymaker, his flamboyant personal style, and his rambunctious family life all contributed to making him the twentieth century's first celebrity president.

Roosevelt's promotion of himself and his policies as president was constant and calculated. He was less pleased at press and public fascination with the "First Family," its vigorous sporting activities, and the social adventures of "Princess Alice," the President's rebellious teenage daughter from his first marriage. It is doubtful that Roosevelt and his colorful family could have escaped frequent news coverage under any circumstances. But Roosevelt himself contributed to the intrusion of the press into his private life when he invited correspondents to cover his activities at his summer retreat at Oyster Bay, Long Island.

Prior to Roosevelt, the press had paid only occasional attention to the First Family or to the president's summer vacations. Marriages, deaths, births, and formal social events were reported dutifully in the news and social pages of newspapers. But neither Caroline Harrison nor Ida McKinley had sought or received the volume of press coverage received by Frances Folsom Cleveland. When the McKinleys left Washington in the summer to spend weeks in Canton, Ohio, it was generally regarded as a vacation. The machinery of government did not follow the President and his family, and neither did most correspondents.[78]

But the Roosevelts were not just another family. The President and his second wife, Edith Kermit Carow Roosevelt, had four rambunctious sons in addition to Alice. In addition, there was Roosevelt himself, whom Edith Roosevelt regarded as her fifth boy, the one who led the younger ones on adventures that resulted in headlines while he was governor of New York. On one occasion, as reported in national magazines, the Roosevelt children broke up an official party at the governor's mansion by opening the windows to let in the barnyard smells from their menagerie.[79] In another incident, described by Gifford Pinchot, the forester arrived at the mansion to deliver an official report and found the Governor lowering the children on bedsheet ropes from a second-floor window. Roosevelt then insisted that Pinchot put on boxing gloves and spar with him before accepting the report.[80]

In 1902, President Roosevelt unintentionally increased the press spotlight on his family by declaring that official business would be conducted from his summer home on Long Island while the Executive Mansion in Washington was being renovated.[81] The President's formal statement stated that while access to the family home, Sagamore Hill, would be restricted, "the regular business of the administration will be carried on the same in Oyster Bay as if the President were in Washington."[82] As a result, the press associations and a half dozen of the leading newspapers sent correspondents to Long Island to cover Roosevelt's activities.[83]

Once in residence, the correspondents felt daily pressure to come up with stories that would justify their employers' expenses.[84] When Roosevelt was less diligent about furnishing them with news than he had been in Washington, the correspondents used their ingenuity to create stories about the family's vigorous recreation activities, especially the President's horseback riding and sailing. Clark, of the *New York Sun,* was bemused at Roosevelt's "funny stunts," including climbing into the rigging of a sailboat.[85] Roosevelt, however, was upset. He complained to the editor of the *New York Sun,* Paul Dana, that "your man" was making up stories and invading his privacy. He was particularly incensed about a humorous reference to his daughter, Alice, as "Alice in Wonderland." Roosevelt wrote: "The plain truth of course is that I am living here with my wife and children just exactly as you are at your home; and there is no more material for a story in one case than in the other!" He demanded and got the *Sun* to withdraw reporter Frank O'Brien, which angered the newspaper's other correspondents.[86]

Much of the press fascination about the Roosevelt family centered on the President's adventurous daughter, Alice. If Roosevelt was the first president to be made into a celebrity by the modern mass media, Alice was the first celebrity presidential family member.[87] She was an outspoken debutante and party-goer, who turned 18 in February 1902. In that same month, she publicly christened the family yacht of the German Prince Henry, brother of Kaiser Wilhelm, and was dubbed "Princess Alice" in the newspapers. Subsequent stories traced her active and controversial social life, and photographers waited outside the White House to record any appearance. Her stepmother, Edith Roosevelt, tried to control the press frenzy by commissioning official photographs of the First Family, including Alice, which were then widely distributed. But Alice continued to speak directly, and frankly, to reporters, against her stepmother's wishes. The volume of news coverage surrounding the First Daughter occasionally rivaled the media exposure of her father.[88] Press fascination with "Princess Alice" did not begin to subside until early 1906, when she married Nicholas Longworth, a congressman from Cincinnati. Edith Roosevelt refused to admit the press to the White House for the ceremony.[89]

Roosevelt's other children were caught occasionally in the press spotlight as well. Roosevelt tried to protect his troubled son, Ted, from press inquiries into his academic and disciplinary problems at Harvard University, with limited success. At one point, the President advised his son to "not make a fuss about the newspapermen, camera creatures, and idiots generally."[90] In 1907, Secretary Loeb tried to protect the family by banning reporters from congregating on the White House grounds at night and peering into the windows.[91]

Edith Roosevelt disliked the press intensely and tried to devise defensive publicity tactics to protect the children. She became a public figure at times to draw attention to herself and away from her children. In doing so, however, she unwittingly contributed to the establishment of the first lady as a public, semiofficial entity as well.[92]

The President tried to keep the correspondents occupied with news that was more useful to his official purposes. But he was unable to stop the press fascination with his family or with his own demanding outdoor activities, which included skiing, fishing, boxing, and bear hunting.[93] Press coverage of the President's annual summer retreat became one of the expanding routines of news coverage that underlay the personalization of the media presidency.[94] Ike Hoover, chief usher in the White House for 42 years, observed in 1934 that no President's family received as much press attention as the Roosevelts. "News was always abundant, and it was a poor reporter indeed who did not pick up a column or two a day in these strenuous times," Hoover wrote.[95]

Despite Roosevelt's underlying disdain for the press and his willingness to manipulate the news media by persuasive means, he usually resisted the temptation to use the authority of government to retaliate directly against his newspaper critics, at least until late in his second term. Then, his anger against the New York press, specifically Joseph Pulitzer's *New York World,* led the President to order his attorney general to try to indict Pulitzer for criminal libel, something rarely attempted since the earliest days of the nation. Although Roosevelt ultimately failed to intimidate or to punish Pulitzer or to censor the *World,* the President's action was a reminder that the emerging relationship between the media presidency and the news media raised fundamental issues about the limits of executive authority and of freedom of the press.

Pulitzer's *World,* which was nominally Democratic, long had been a frequent and partisan critic of Roosevelt. During the presidential campaign of 1908, the *World* published a story that suggested that well-placed Republican financial speculators had profited excessively from a $40 million government payment to French investors in the firm that built the Panama Canal. Named in the story were William Cromwell, a friend and advisor to William Howard Taft, the Republican presidential candidate; Charles P.

Taft, the candidate's half brother; and Douglas Robinson, brother-in-law to Roosevelt. All denied the allegations. Roosevelt, who was supporting Taft's candidacy, ignored the charges publicly, even when they were repeated on the day before the election by the *Indianapolis News,* owned by a Republican rival of Roosevelt.[96]

Taft won the election, despite the controversy. Nevertheless, on 8 December 1908, the *World* ran an inflammatory editorial that accused Roosevelt and others named in the earlier stories of lying. A week later, Roosevelt sent an angry special message to Congress stating that the government was suffering from "a string of infamous libels" and that he had instructed the attorney general to seek legal action against Pulitzer.[97] Roosevelt then began preparations to leave for Africa on safari once Taft was inaugurated. However, the Justice Department followed up the President's order and obtained grand jury indictments against Pulitzer and the *World,* first in Washington in February and then in New York on 3 March 1909. The government's legal authority to obtain the indictments was shaky at best, based on an obscure statute dating back to the Alien and Sedition Acts of 1798. The *World* fought back, demanding a congressional investigation of the $40 million payment. The subsequent investigation cleared Taft, Robinson, and Roosevelt of any involvement. Nevertheless, the government's case against the *World* continued until it was dismissed on technical grounds and the dismissal was upheld on appeal, in 1911. By then, Roosevelt had left office and Pulitzer was near death. The legal outcome failed to establish presidential authority to sue the press for criminal libel. Nevertheless, the incident was a reminder of the official fist within the glove in the President's attempts to persuade the press to promote his policies.

The result of Roosevelt's incessant management of the newspapers and magazines was to place him and his presidency in the forefront of the public discourse during his years in the White House. The newspaper trade journal *Editor and Publisher* described Roosevelt in 1908 as "the man who best understands the press agent game."[98] According to observer Mark Sullivan, "Roosevelt's fighting was so much a part of the life of the period, was so tied up to the newspapers, so geared into popular literature, and even to the pulpit (which already had begun to turn from formal religion toward civic affairs), as to constitute, for the average man, not merely the high spectacle of the presidency in the ordinary sense, but almost the whole of the passing show, the public's principal interest."[99]

McKinley found that publicizing his views by managing the press could be a useful adjunct to policymaking, especially in wartime. To Roosevelt, managing the press to produce supportive news coverage was central to presidential leadership. He tried daily to appeal to the public through whatever media were available, and he succeeded in keeping the presidency on the front pages during his terms in office. To the Washington correspondents, the Roosevelt administration seemed to be an uninterrupted series of presidential announcements, statements, interviews, controversies, stunts, and trips. To "cover" the President's activities became, in the Roosevelt years, a full-time job.

The ability of Roosevelt to dominate national reporting of public affairs affected more than the presidency and the press. Reading about Roosevelt's views every day frustrated members of Congress, who were more accustomed to presidents who deferred to congressional authority. Under McKinley, the Republican congressional leadership had been allied with the President and frequently spoke to the press on his behalf. But Roosevelt was often at odds with the party leadership, and he used the press to circumvent congressional objections to his policies. In addition, Roosevelt's success at gaining public support by appealing more or less directly to the citizenry through the press was closely watched by leaders in the executive branch, Cabinet members, and agency administrators, who soon launched their own experiments in managing the press.

CHAPTER THREE

THE WHITE HOUSE AND
THE FIRST "PRESS BUREAUS"

Theodore Roosevelt's attempts to lead the nation by appealing to the public through the press changed the polity as well as the presidency. Roosevelt made news constantly, and his ability to dominate the headlines made a strong impression on his supporters and critics throughout the government, as well as among the citizens.

The ability of the President to bypass the congressional party leadership by appealing for popular support through the press was watched closely by administrators in the executive branch, whose agency promotional and publishing activities were overseen closely by congressional committees. Cabinet members and agency administrators took note of Roosevelt's success at generating "free" publicity in the newspapers, rather than through the congressionally supervised pamphlets of the Government Printing Office. Newspaper and magazine coverage could reach out to larger audiences than could official publications, while also avoiding the stifling oversight of Senate and House committees.

Prior to Roosevelt's presidency, few executive agencies attempted to communicate to the press or to the public without particular approval of Congress and its committees. Those that did, such as the Agriculture Department, acted with explicit congressional authorization to disseminate information to specific constituencies, such as farmers. Instead of seeking out newspapers and magazines to publicize their work as news, these agencies tended to rely on the official pamphlets and reports published by the Government Printing Office (GPO) and distributed by members of Congress under their individual mailing privileges.

However, Roosevelt's publicity successes suggested other possibilities. Particularly inspired was the forester Gifford Pinchot, who already had begun to try to promote press coverage of his agency. Pinchot had been appointed by McKinley in 1898 as chief of what was then called the Division of Forestry, a tiny arm of the Agriculture Department. The division, which at that time had no supervisory authority over public lands or natural resources, existed primarily to exchange technical information among scientists and to promote more efficient industrial uses of trees. Pinchot's predecessor, Bernhard Fernow, described the office's role as one of "propaganda and primary education." Besides serving as a nexus for information, Fernow lectured extensively and encouraged the development of university courses in forestry.[1]

Collection and distribution of technical information to specialized constituencies was consistent with the traditional mission of the parent Agriculture Department, which was the largest source of Government Printing Office publications in the late nineteenth century.[2] Departmental books, reports, pamphlets, and other publications in this period were published by the GPO under the close oversight of the congressional committees that controlled the budget and hiring. For instance, the General Printing Act of 1895 detailed how much money each agency could spend on individual publications and authorized a specified number of printed pages.[3] The Agriculture Department's most popular publication, the annual *Agriculture Yearbook,* was not distributed directly to the public by the agency, but by members of Congress under their congressional franking privileges. In 1889, for example, 375,000 of the 400,000 copies of the *Yearbook* went directly to members of Congress for mailing to their constituents.[4]

Despite firm congressional control over agency publications, administrators long had been curious about the possibilities of reaching the larger audiences of commercial newspapers and magazines. In 1889, Jeremiah Rusk, the first Cabinet secretary of agriculture, experimented with sending summaries of department reports to the newspapers and press associations, where they were widely used.[5] Some bureaus, such as the Weather Service, discreetly made their research information available for publication by newspapers and magazines. Pinchot, however, was the first Agriculture Department administrator to appreciate fully the potential of using publicity to seek public support for agency activities.[6]

Pinchot, like Roosevelt, was an aristocratic reformer who was enthusiastic about using publicity to create public support for his goals. In 1893, while working as a private forester, Pinchot prepared an exhibit for the Columbian Exposition in Chicago on his work at the Biltmore estate in

North Carolina and sent a pamphlet describing the exhibit to thousands of newspaper editors.[7]

Pinchot's appreciation of the possibilities of publicity was sharpened by his experiences as a member of a forestry commission created in 1896 by the National Academy of Sciences to study environmental abuse and wasteful resource practices on public lands in the West. Commission members, including Pinchot and John Muir, traveled throughout the West in the summer of 1896, largely without news coverage or public notice. This absence of publicity, in Pinchot's view, worsened the angry response in the West when, in early 1897, Cleveland followed the commission's advice to set aside vast forest reserves by presidential order. Pinchot was sent back to the West later that year as a special forest agent to survey the new reserves. He spent much of his time trying to persuade hostile regional newspaper editors to accept the government's decision. In his autobiography, Pinchot credited the experience with giving him "some inkling into how public opinion is credited or directed."[8]

In Seattle, for example, the two daily newspapers vehemently had opposed creation of the forest reserves in the spring of 1897 and competed over who could argue the most strongly against them. When Pinchot visited the region several months later, he was able to persuade a prominent local developer, Judge Thomas Burke, to intercede with the editor of the Seattle *Post Intelligencer* to grant Pinchot an interview. The subsequent front-page story was the first wholly favorable report on the issue to appear in the Seattle press in eight months. Earlier, in Spokane, Washington, Pinchot had called upon a Yale classmate, William Hutchinson Cowles, to get his story into Cowles's *Spokesman-Review*.[9]

Encouraged by these early attempts to use the press to mold public opinion about government policy, Pinchot substantially expanded the publicity work of the Division of Forestry when he became its chief in 1898. He increased the agency mailing list from 1,200 to 6,000 names, which included 2,000 newspapers. He set the tiny staff, supplemented by students and scientific "collaborators," to work producing new booklets and pamphlets for publication by the Government Printing Office.[10]

Pinchot's view of the primacy of publicity was revealed in a 1903 letter, in which he wrote: "Nothing permanent can be accomplished in this country unless it is backed by sound public sentiment. The greater part of our work, therefore, has consisted in arousing a general interest in practical forestry throughout the country and in gradually changing public sentiment toward a more conservative treatment of forest lands."[11]

Given the division's limited resources, Pinchot's agency publicity campaign was a remarkable achievement. He used his personal fortune to supplement the agency budget to hire technically trained men with literary skills. They produced a stream of pamphlets, bulletins, magazine articles, speeches, lantern slides, and photographs that promoted the agency's activities. Pinchot's publicists were organized into the first formally designated federal "press bureau" in 1905, after Congress greatly expanded the agency into the U.S. Forest Service.[12] In June 1905, *Chatauquan* magazine listed 68 separate publications on forestry that were available to the public from the agency. By fiscal 1908, the agency's annual report listed the publication of nearly 4.4 million copies of 220 publications. During Pinchot's tenure as chief of the agency, between 1898 and 1910, his employees published 10.8 million copies of official advisories, pamphlets, bulletins, and reports, according to the cumulative annual reports of the Agriculture Department's Division of Publications.

These publications were sent to a list of editors, reporters, community leaders, and scientific leaders, which had reached 750,000 names by Pinchot's last annual report in 1909. In November 1909, two months before Pinchot was fired by President Taft, the chief of the Forest Service's press bureau complained that the addressees on the list had been sent only 1.5 million copies of news publications in the last year, an average of only two to each. He urged the division chiefs to come up with more newsworthy material.[13]

One source of the names for the mailing list was an extensive lecture program maintained by Pinchot and his aides. In an era before broadcasting, lecturers crisscrossed the country to speak to community meetings, trade associations, women's clubs, civic organizations, and schools. Pinchot hired special lecturers to promote the work of the Forest Service, and they were expected to gather names from their audiences to add to the agency's mailing list. Notices of the lectures, and sometimes summaries of the talks themselves, were sent to local newspaper editors. Publicity from these tours and the prominence of agency employees at public meetings and conventions prompted congressional critics of Pinchot to demand investigations into agency travel. A 1907 congressional report listed 1,530 occasions in the previous fiscal year when Forest Service representatives had attended or addressed public meetings.[14]

No aspect of agency publicity work was more important to Pinchot than placing news in the commercial newspapers and magazines, which he considered "free" publicity that reached a larger audience than that of government publications. In his 1907 annual report, he wrote: "For certain kinds of information related to forestry, millions of readers can be reached through newspapers and magazines for thousands who could be reached through official publication and distribution of the same matter."[15]

Beginning in 1902, the agency had experimented with the issuance of "press bulletins," an early form of news release. Three bulletins were mailed that year to the 4,000 editors then on the mailing list. In fiscal 1908, the number had grown to 418 releases sent to the press, many accompanied by return envelopes for tear sheets so Pinchot could estimate how many actually were printed. Taking the claimed circulation of the newspapers that printed his releases, Pinchot calculated that the press bulletins were reaching an average monthly audience of 9 million readers.[16]

Pinchot sought space in national magazines as well as newspapers, especially the reform-minded ones. Evidence of his success is illustrated by the indexing in the *Readers Guide to Periodical Literature*. During the period from 1900 to 1904, there were 29 articles concerning forests, or forestry, in 69 periodicals. During the 1905 to 1910 period, this expanded to 204 articles in 99 periodicals. The term "conservation," which Pinchot used to describe his work, was indexed as a subject heading for the first time, and, under Pinchot's name, 19 personal profiles of the forester were listed in national publications.

The extent of Pinchot's agency publicity campaign was unique in government in this period. Nevertheless, when Roosevelt became president in 1901, Pinchot was still the administrator of an obscure, somewhat specialized agency buried deeply in the Agriculture Department.[17] In Roosevelt, however, Pinchot found a president who shared his enthusiasms for reform, conservation, vigorous outdoor activity, and, importantly, for publicity.

For a president to concern himself with the details of executive administration, let alone obscure agencies in the Agriculture Department, was somewhat unusual. Presidents in the late nineteenth century tended to deal with administration only indirectly, through the Cabinet or the Congress. Congressional committees influenced agency activities through budgeting and oversight, and the party leadership often was consulted in hiring employees, despite civil service.[18]

However, Roosevelt's expansive view of executive authority included presidential influence into the administration of government as well as setting policy.[19] Roosevelt was concerned particularly with the emerging issue of conservation, where he shared Pinchot's view that the central government should act to protect and to develop natural resources on public lands. When Pinchot and Frederick H. Newell of the Reclamation Service called upon the new President to seek his support for their agencies' conservation policies, they found him to be an enthusiastic advocate. Roosevelt agreed to support their goals and, by incorporating them into his presidential agenda, to advance both the cause of conservation and his own authority over administrative policy.[20] With the President's backing, Pinchot greatly expanded his agency publicity campaign for conservation and began to coordinate it with the White House. Pinchot became Roosevelt's conservation advisor, a member of the President's "Tennis Cabinet," and an important contributor to the President's other publicity campaigns.[21]

Roosevelt's interest in Pinchot went beyond their shared views on reform, conservation policy, enthusiasm for vigorous outdoor activities, and good fellowship. Pinchot and his publicity staff offered institutional support to the White House at a time when the President had only a handful of professional employees. Roosevelt had little support in conducting his publicity campaigns except from his secretary, Loeb, who had other responsibilities as the President's chief of staff. Pinchot and his agency publicists became important contributors to Roosevelt's media presidency.

Pinchot's publicity work for Roosevelt began with the writing of presidential messages and speeches on natural resource issues. With the assistance of Herbert A. Smith, head of the forestry press bureau, Pinchot became one of Roosevelt's principal speechwriters. An index prepared for Pinchot's autobiography lists more than 30 presidential messages, speeches, letters, and proclamations on conservation that he drafted between 1901 and 1909. These included segments of the annual presidential State of the Union Messages to Congress in 1901, 1903, 1904, 1905, 1907, and 1908. Pinchot claimed to have drafted the entire 1905 message. He also contributed to presidential speeches to various interest groups, such as to the National Irrigation Congresses in 1903, 1904, 1906, and 1907. "I was able to incorporate the bulk of the suggestions you sent," Roosevelt wrote in 1907. "I shall use your speech to the Irrigation Congress to give me material for my message."[22]

Pinchot also supplied Roosevelt with briefing material, including speech drafts and notes for newspaper interviews, for the President's national speaking tours. In May 1903, after a lengthy trip that ended in California, Roosevelt wrote: "I am very much obliged for your notes on forestry. You may have seen that I have used all of the material you have given me."[23]

Pinchot also began to incorporate the President into the Forest Service's own publicity program. Agency pamphlets described Roosevelt as a supporter of forestry, and articles written by the department's staff appeared under Roosevelt's name both in agency bulletins and in articles reprinted in popular magazines.[24] Roosevelt also occasionally released Forest Service bulletins at the White House, which brought him news coverage on the popular issue of conservation while adding to the agency's standing in the press as well.[25]

Despite the President's assistance, the publicity campaign for government conservation in Roosevelt's first term was not sufficient to advance Pinchot's primary bureaucratic goal: congressional transfer of management authority over the forest reserves from the Department of the Interior to his own agency in the Department of Agriculture. Roosevelt was sympathetic to Pinchot's cause, but, as he wrote to Pinchot in 1903, he needed more indications of public and congressional support from the West.[26]

Pinchot's response was to suggest a new sort of presidential initiative that could generate political support and publicity: the presidential commission. The key to the commission concept was that the President would use his executive authority to appoint agency administrators to a new quasi-presidential body, in this case the Public Lands Commission, that would stimulate public discussion of issues stalled in Congress. As the chief instigator of several Roosevelt commissions, Pinchot envisioned a more specific use: generating publicity for conservation through the "educational" process of public hearings and investigations. The President's involvement made deliberations of the commissions more worthy of attention by newspapers and magazines. The resulting news stories also increased the visibility of Roosevelt on an issue popular with many of his reform supporters.[27]

How Pinchot used the Public Lands Commission as a vehicle for generating supportive publicity was revealed during hearings the commission held in Oregon, California, Nevada, Utah, and Wyoming. The visit to Portland, Oregon, in January 1904 was timed to coincide with the conventions of two public lands interest groups, the National Livestock Association and the National Wool Growers Association. Pinchot and Newell, of the Bureau of Reclamation, who was also a commission member, sent telegraphed statements to the local newspapers well in advance of the hearings, called on the local editors when they arrived in the city, and helped to stimulate favorable newspaper coverage of the commission's deliberations. The main headline in the city's largest newspaper, the *Portland Oregonian,* declared: "Make Friends for President; Visit of Pinchot and Newell Wins Over Opponents of Administration Policy."[28]

Once Roosevelt had been elected to a full presidential term with western support in 1904, Roosevelt told Pinchot he was ready to support Pinchot's proposal for an enlarged forestry agency. The final push for congressional approval to transfer the public lands into Pinchot's authority came during the American Forest Congress, held in Washington in January 1905. Four hundred representatives of the forest industries attended, as well as many government officials. Pinchot's agency had organized the conference to generate more publicity and to put additional lobbying pressure on the U.S. Congress. Roosevelt agreed to be the honorary president of the conference and to deliver the major address.[29]

The President's presence drew the correspondents, as did the lengthy news releases that Pinchot sent out in advance. Roosevelt's speech was summarized by the press associations, and the text was transmitted to newspapers across the country. In addition, Roosevelt preceded the conference with a convenient announcement to the press that two of the leading opponents of the legislation, Senator John Mitchell and Congressman Binger Hermann, had been indicted in Oregon on land fraud charges. The announcement, delivered by the President during the dead news time of a holiday Sunday, was widely reported on the eve of the Forest Congress. No direct evidence links presidential release of news of the indictments to Pinchot and the conference, but the timing was certainly fortuitous.[30] Pinchot later described the Forest Congress as "a powerful influence not only toward the transfer, but also in spreading sound knowledge and wise conclusions about forestry throughout the length and breadth of America."[31]

The collaboration of Roosevelt and Pinchot to promote publicity that supported government conservation achieved its greatest successes in the creation of news events to dramatize the work of two other presidential commissions: the Inland Waterways Commission in 1907 and the subsequent White House Conference on Conservation, the first national governors' conference, in May 1908.[32] Both events, as well as other presidential commissions on national conservation and on rural life, reflected important presidential experiments in publicity as well as promoting the administration's policy in the press over congressional opposition.

The first in this sequence was the Inland Waterways Commission, which was intended to promote regional planning among the states in the Mississippi River system. Pinchot, whom Roosevelt appointed to the commission, made a preliminary trip on the Missouri and Mississippi Rivers in the spring of 1907. In a report to Roosevelt, Pinchot referred to the prospect of the commission generating popular support for the conservation cause: "The Waterways Commission has gone far enough to make it practically sure that its work will be successful internally and, I believe externally, in getting action."[33]

At Pinchot's urging, the commission invited the President to take a steamboat tour in fall 1907 on the way to a speech to the Deep Waterways Association in Memphis, Tennessee. The steamboat cruise, a variation on traditional presidential swings around the country, was intended to draw press coverage in both Washington and the region. In his autobiography, Pinchot explained how creating the event brought publicity for the President's conservation policies: "Action is the best advertisement. The most effective way to get your cause before the public is to do something the papers will have to write about. So when the Inland Waterways Commission wanted to impress the need for inland waterway improvement on the whole United States, the commission asked T. R. to sail down the Mississippi River with it and the Mississippi Valley Improvement Association on river steamers provided by the latter."[34]

Roosevelt was delighted with the trip and at the subsequent news coverage, which made it one of his most successful public appearances. In the President's autobiography, he wrote that "this excursion, with the meetings which were held and the wide public attention it attracted, gave the development of our inland waterways a new standing in public estimation."[35] The St. Louis newspapers, the *Globe-Democrat* and the *Post-Dispatch,* filled their front pages with reports on the President's trip for three consecutive days. The *Memphis Commercial Appeal's* front-page headline described the event dramatically as the "greatest gathering in the history of the South." Newspaper coverage outside the Mississippi region was extensive on both the East and West Coasts. Among the national magazines, *Collier's* published a full page of photographs, and the *American Review of Reviews* devoted four pages to the trip. At his speech in Memphis, Roosevelt revealed plans for the White House Conference on Conservation, the first national governor's conference, the following spring. Pinchot was named chairman of the arrangements committee for that conference, and Thomas R. Shipp, a veteran newspaper and publicity man who worked for Pinchot, was appointed conference secretary.[36]

The May 1908 conference on conservation was probably the most successful presidential publicity event created by Roosevelt and Pinchot. All the nation's governors were invited, and 34 attended. All members of Congress were invited and many attended, although critics of Roosevelt and Pinchot in Congress blocked public payment of the conference expenses. (The wealthy Pinchot paid much of the cost himself.) The gathering of officials, which also included the U.S. Supreme Court, the Cabinet, and leading industrialists, left the nation's newspapers searching for new superlatives. William Randolph Hearst's *New York American,* no friend of Roosevelt or Pinchot, displayed what was called "Probably the Most Notable Group of United States Statesmen Ever Photographed" across its front page.[37]

Publicity arrangements for the conference were extraordinary, even by the standards of the Roosevelt administration. Pinchot and Shipp, working with conference organizer W J McGee and the President's secretary, Loeb, deluged newspapers across the country with such volumes of advance material that the publicity campaign itself became the subject of admiring

news stories. "The public interest is being whetted in advance of the con-
claves by volumes of literature," noted a story in the *Chicago Record-Herald*.
The *Grand Rapids (Michigan) Press* reported that "ample provision has been
made for the newspaper and magazine writers, and they are expected to
rise to the occasion in describing the first appearance in conference of so
many notables."[38]

The congressional press galleries were consulted in selecting 40 correspondents from the major newspapers and the press associations, as well as
another 21 magazine correspondents.[39] Not surprisingly, given the presence
of the President and other officials and the advance publicity work, which
included drafting of the major speeches by McGee and Pinchot, the press
coverage was all that the White House had hoped for. In Pinchot's enthusiastic estimation, "The Governor's Conference made front-page news all over
the United States, as was natural, and in many other parts of the world also,
while it was in session. Afterward followed a flood of friendly editorials and
magazine articles, with only here and there a touch of opposition in some
trade paper or from an unusually alert and acrimonious political opponent.
The general tone was of unstinted praise. Conservation became the com-
monplace of the time."[40] In Roosevelt's autobiography, the President praised
Pinchot for coordinating the "educational" campaign for conservation: "It is
doubtful whether there has ever been elsewhere such effective publicity—
publicity purely in the interest of the people—at so low a cost."[41]

Although the conference and the subsequent National Conservation
Commission, led by Pinchot, failed to make Congress more receptive to
Roosevelt's conservation policies, it demonstrated the potential of presi-
dential-agency collaboration in generating supportive press coverage. By
allowing Pinchot to capitalize on the President's cooperation, Roosevelt
gained credit for the Forest Service's policies and shared in the publicity
rewards. The Forest Service also benefited from the President's support,
both administratively and in public prominence. By 1909, it had become
the largest single agency in the Agriculture Department.

The Forest Service's success in reaching beyond Congress to gain additional public support through publicity was closely watched by other administrators, who also began to hire former newspapermen to publicize
their agencies. Here again, Roosevelt set an example. Not only did the
President encourage Pinchot at the Forest Service, Roosevelt himself appointed a former newspaperman, Joseph Bucklin Bishop, to lead and to
publicize the work of the government commission created to oversee the
building of the Panama Canal.[42]

The adoption of publicity practices in the executive branch, as well as
Roosevelt's constant appeals to the public through the press at the White

House, angered leaders of Congress, who perceived correctly a threat to their traditional authority over both the presidency and the agencies. Congressional opponents of Roosevelt and Pinchot tried repeatedly from 1905 onward to block both their policies and their publicity. The attacks, which were led by western critics of restrictive public lands policies, focused on Pinchot rather than attacking the President directly.[43] But Roosevelt's conservative critics were active in the debate, which came to focus on Pinchot's press bureau and on executive branch spending for publicity.

Pinchot was attacked not only for publicizing Forest Service practices opposed by western developers and entrepreneurs but for using his press bureau to generate newspaper attacks on his critics, especially those in Congress. Neither Roosevelt nor Pinchot was hesitant to use publicity as a weapon, as well as to promote their policies.

It was Roosevelt, not Pinchot, who was behind the regional news stories aimed at Senator Weldon B. Heyburn of Idaho, who opposed emphatically the creation of more forest reserves in his state. Heyburn was Republican national committeeman for Idaho, and Roosevelt had needed his support in the election of 1904. After the election, however, Roosevelt refused Heyburn's request for veto power over the creation of new reserves and sent the Senator a sharply worded letter saying so. The President then forwarded a copy of the letter to Pinchot and added. "You can have my letter and Heyburn's response to it made public any way you see fit." Pinchot took the hint. He reprinted the exchange of letters in an agency publication and also leaked the story to sympathetic newspapers in the Pacific Northwest. The resulting news stories, in fall 1905, described Roosevelt as angry with Heyburn. The President, the stories said, had chastised Heyburn during a meeting at the White House.[44]

Heyburn did not attack Roosevelt directly for the unfavorable stories, but he led what became an annual assault on Pinchot's publicity activity during consideration of the Forest Service budget. In January 1906, Heyburn appeared before the Senate Committee on Public Lands to charge that Pinchot maintained a press bureau to attack congressmen and to seek self-glorification.[45] Heyburn led in similar attacks on Pinchot's publicity activities in 1907, 1908, and 1909, during which amendments were proposed to curb Forest Service spending on the press bureau, on official travel, and on participation in the presidential commissions. These were major debates. Floor discussion in spring 1908 spread over a week, including a night session, before the Senate voted to dilute a House-passed amendment that would have forbidden the agency to spend money on the preparation of newspaper and magazine articles. At one point, Senator

Charles Fulton of Oregon warned prophetically that "if the right be accorded this bureau, you must accord every bureau that right; and the first thing you know, every official will have its own special correspondent, whose duty it is to exploit and glorify the particular work."[46]

Congressional attacks on agency publicity continued after Pinchot's firing by Taft in January 1910. Within weeks, one of Roosevelt's conservative critics, Congressman Roger Tawney of Minnesota, tried unsuccessfully to amend the Forest Service budget to forbid the agency from giving information to the press unless specifically requested to do so by newspapers and magazines. Tawney noted that while "this press agent service is comparatively new in the departments here and at the seat of government," it was rapidly spreading. "One reason why many appropriations for a number of bureaus in the various departments of government cannot be kept down is because of the influence which these bureaus exert today in the press of the country in the districts of the several Members of this House."[47]

Interestingly, reaction in the press to the congressional debate over the propriety of agency publicity was minimal. Even during the lengthy debates over the Forest Service budget in 1908, the Washington newspapers noted only briefly that Congress was considering the Agriculture Appropriations bill. Earlier, when the bill was before the House, the *Washington Post* supported editorially the creation of more government press bureaus, because they made available more printable material for the newspapers. "It is probable that the press agent will become a regular and legitimate part of the government equipment," the *Post* commented. But the *Washington Herald* was less enthusiastic: "If this practice were to become general in the executive departments, we fear it would lead to serious abuses. It happens in the case of the Forest Service, the exploitation has been undertaken on behalf of a good cause, and by people who are above the accusation of self-seeking. This fact has undoubtedly saved the Forest Service from the criticism that might have been aroused by the development of a like enterprise in some other branches of the federal service."[48]

In the press corps, the response to the spread of agency publicity also was ambivalent. Roosevelt and Pinchot were both personally popular among the correspondents, who found them charming and helpful, with admirable backgrounds in the reform movement. However, Walter E. Clark, of the *New York Sun,* disliked the Forest Service press bureau: "It is wrong, although it is pointedly Rooseveltian, for a bureau to employ four men for publicity work by falsifying a payroll; and, besides, some of the work of this press bureau is absurd. The whole object of it is to influence public opinion against the Congress—as Roosevelt himself has tried to do and has succeeded in doing ever since his accession."[49]

Other newspapermen found agency press bureaus a welcome convenience, since they provided publishable material, becoming known as "handouts," that the correspondents would not otherwise have gotten. Few correspondents had the time to concern themselves with the activities of the executive departments, since they were fully occupied trying to keep up with Congress, the party leadership, and, increasingly under Roosevelt, the White House. Moreover, agency press bureaus provided another source of income for the poorly paid correspondents, who were accustomed to taking part-time work or congressional patronage positions to supplement their newspaper incomes. Pinchot, for example, considered hiring Gilson Gardner, a correspondent for Chicago newspapers, to write part-time for the forestry press bureau.[50]

Despite congressional opposition, the practice of hiring publicists spread quickly among the administrative agencies. By 1912, a House committee hearing into the hiring of departmental press aides elicited testimony from newspaper correspondents that publicists had been employed by agencies as diverse as the Bureau of Soils, the Bureau of Biological Survey, the State Department, the Census Bureau, the Bureau of National Roads, the Smithsonian Institution, and the Post Office.[51]

Roosevelt's media presidency, then, stimulated the spread of publicity experiments in the executive branch, as well as in the presidency. When Roosevelt left the presidency in 1909, numerous agency experiments in managing the press to seek public support were under way, despite congressional opposition. Administrators found that appealing to the public through the press was a promising way to develop popular support for an agency and its policies, with or without congressional support. Newspaper publicity had helped Pinchot to expand the authority and the budget of the Forest Service, as well as to defend the agency against attacks by western congressmen. Moreover, Pinchot's collaboration with Roosevelt suggested new possibilities in using publicity cooperatively in executive leadership at both the agency and at the White House.

Roosevelt's presidency benefited as well. The President embraced the cause of conservation as his own and used publicity to try to circumvent congressional opposition to his legislative proposals. Moreover, Pinchot and his publicists provided institutional support for Roosevelt in dealing with the press on other issues.

These experiments in government publicity outside the White House provide additional evidence of the institutional breadth of the transformation in executive governance under way at the beginning of the century.

But attempts to manage the press by publicists in other parts of the government represented both an opportunity and a challenge to the media presidency, as well as to the Congress. By encouraging the hiring of publicists by administrative agencies, Roosevelt also increased the likelihood that news stories would appear that promoted agency viewpoints, not necessarily his own. One outcome of increased agency contacts with the press was an increase in the number of leaks, which led to unwanted news stories which Roosevelt, like other presidents, struggled to prevent or at least to minimize.

By bringing Pinchot into the White House inner circle, Roosevelt had been able to establish some control over the Forest Service's publicity apparatus. But Roosevelt was well aware of the possibility of unwanted leaks to the press or competing publicity initiatives from other agencies or from members of Congress. The President read the newspapers carefully, and he responded quickly to what he regarded as undesirable or unauthorized stories. Archie Butt, Roosevelt's military aide, noted that when the President spotted a story he didn't like, "he would at once begin an investigation as to how it got there, and if he could locate the author of the leak he would dismiss him or else have him transferred to some other department."[52] In 1906, for example, Roosevelt strongly reprimanded the Secretary of Interior Ethan Hitchcock for using his department's "bureau of publicity" to criticize a western senator.[53] Roosevelt also tried to prevent negative publicity by advising agency administrators on how to handle inquiries from journalists. After appointing Joseph Bucklin Bishop to be secretary of the Isthmus Commission, he advised him on how to publicize the progress of construction on the Panama Canal.[54]

By keeping a firm hand on press coverage during his presidency, Roosevelt was able to minimize leaking, despite a growing number of media-savvy administrators and publicists. But Roosevelt's handpicked successor, William Howard Taft, had quite different ideas about the importance of managing the press and about the limits of presidential authority. As a result, Taft became the first twentieth-century president to demonstrate the pitfalls, as well as the possibilities, of the media presidency.

CHAPTER FOUR

TAFT: AVOIDING THE PRESS

William Howard Taft long has been regarded as among the twentieth century's least successful presidents, despite an extensive public career that later included nearly ten years as chief justice of the U.S. Supreme Court. Taft was elected president in 1908 with broad electoral support and the enthusiastic backing of his predecessor, Theodore Roosevelt. But when he sought reelection in 1912, he received only eight electoral votes and finished third in the popular vote behind the Democrat Woodrow Wilson and Roosevelt, who ran against his protégé as an independent Progressive candidate.

The collapse of Taft's popularity has been attributed largely to his unwillingness or inability to exercise the presidential authority that had been wielded so vigorously by Roosevelt. Unlike his dynamic predecessor, Taft held what his most recent biographers regard as a conservative, strict constructionist view of the presidency, one more in keeping with the dignified, aloof presidents of the late nineteenth century than with the media presidency practiced by Roosevelt.[1] Roosevelt's penchant for maximum publicity had put the President on the front pages almost daily and raised expectations in the press and public that Taft could not or would not fulfill. A *New York Times* editorial in 1913 described Taft succinctly as "the victim of too much Roosevelt."[2]

The contrasts in presidential leadership between Roosevelt and Taft were substantial. In few areas were they more visible than in Taft's unwillingness to appeal to the public by managing the press. For nearly eight years, Roosevelt had used the news media to proclaim his authority as a national leader and to appeal for public support to override congressional opposition to his policies. His unrelenting publicity campaign had so changed Washington journalism that correspondents now were expected to cover the presidency regularly in addition to their traditional focus on

Congress. Under McKinley and Roosevelt, the nucleus of a White House press corps had gathered to meet with the president or his spokesman daily and to write newspaper stories about not only his public activities but his private life as well. In Elmer Cornwell Jr.'s formative work, *Executive Leadership of Public Opinion,* he credited Roosevelt with creating the twentieth century model of leading public opinion by exploiting the mass media. Taft was described as taking a step backwards.[3]

Taft simply did not agree with Roosevelt's view that seeking public support by cultivating the press was necessary to presidential leadership. He regarded appealing to the correspondents as unnecessary and disagreeable, if not demeaning. Instead, Taft preferred to take a laissez-faire approach to public opinion, based on the notion that his accomplishments would speak for themselves. In a rare magazine interview in 1910, he stated: "What I hope for my administration is the accomplishment of definite results, which will be self-explanatory."[4] Richard A. Ballinger, Taft's secretary of the interior, described Taft's approach as one of "nonpublicity."[5]

Taft's seeming indifference to the press and public opinion contrasted sharply with the assumptions and the expectations that underlay the emerging media presidency. When Taft did not follow the procedures of dealing with the press at the White House that McKinley and Roosevelt had developed, he alienated many of the correspondents that his predecessors had attracted. To meet the daily demands of their editors for news, the correspondents turned to other sources of information, including their traditional sources in Congress. They also turned to Taft's critics, who included a number of holdover Roosevelt reformers in the administration who were becoming increasingly unhappy with Taft's policies.

Prior to his inauguration as president in March 1909, Taft was highly regarded by the correspondents, especially the "fair-haired boys" who had been the closest to Roosevelt. When Taft served as Roosevelt's secretary of war, it was an afternoon custom for favored correspondents to "go Tafting"—to call on Secretary Taft and to hear his candid remarks, which frequently revealed a good deal of news. Furthermore, in 1908, prominent Republican correspondents such as Richard V. Oulahan, of the *New York Sun,* and Oscar King Davis, of the *New York Times,* worked in Taft's presidential campaign, at Roosevelt's request. Oulahan served as chief of the "Literary Bureau" of the Republican National Committee, while Davis wrote supportive magazine articles and part of a campaign biography praising Taft.[6]

After the election, however, the correspondents found Taft oddly aloof. When they called on President Taft at the White House after the inaugural ceremonies in March 1909, they were shocked at the rebuff they received. In his autobiography, Davis described how the reporters were initially refused entrance by Fred W. Carpenter, Taft's secretary, and eventually admitted only after agreeing to offer Taft only their personal respects, rather than to ask questions. On what started out to be a routine newsgathering visit a few days later, Davis ended up waiting for two days in Taft's outer office before he was allowed to ask the President about his views on tariff legislation.[7]

Taft's withdrawal from making news in the first days and weeks of his presidency was both a personal and professional blow to the correspondents. In the 12 years since the inauguration of McKinley, the presidency had become an expected source of news, and the jobs of a growing number of correspondents depended in part on their ability to produce authoritative stories about the White House. The correspondents had become accustomed to ready access to the president or his secretary to ask questions; to daily, if not hourly, presidential announcements; and to frequent and colorful White House events to describe in their stories. When Taft declined to continue these publicity practices, he was accused of withholding news. Within weeks of Taft's inauguration, the correspondents were talking about the "good old days."[8] Edward G. Lowry wrote nostalgically that Roosevelt's activity "was a wonderful stream, and it furnished entertainment and gossip not only to Washington but to the whole country. Washington correspondents counted the day lost if the White House beat provided no 'color story' of some new Roosevelt performance."[9]

Less than three weeks into the Taft's presidency, a spokesman for the distressed correspondents, Alfred Henry Lewis, appealed to Taft's personable military aide, Archie Butt. Although Butt was alarmed privately at Taft's insensitivity to publicity, he loyally told Lewis "that the press, with the rest of the country, would have to readjust itself to the new conditions just as the people would have to do later. It is impossible for Mr. Taft to do as Mr. Roosevelt did and keep the press fed with news every hour of the day." When Butt told Taft of the conversation, the President said bluntly, "the people of the country elected me, I believe, and damn it, I am going to give it to them whether they like or not."[10]

Taft remained cordial to the few correspondents that he saw. But the first media presidency was clearly over. The spring and summer of 1909 brought a continuing series of disappointments with the new administration. "Since Roosevelt, very little news has come out of the White House," an anonymous correspondent complained in *American* magazine.[11] Not only was Taft generally unavailable—his secretary, Carpenter, was less cooperative than McKinley's Cortelyou or Roosevelt's Loeb had been. The correspondents found that in Cabinet meetings and at the Justice Department, "the new lid is gradually being closed on government information," according to the trade journal *Editor and Publisher*. The journal ran an editorial cartoon of dejected correspondents standing outside the White House gate, on which a sign read: "Administration news made public only on rare occasions; newspaper men kindly but firmly requested to keep away."[12]

The flow of presidential statements, advice, and events at the White House had dried up. Even the texts of Taft's formal speeches were no longer distributed in advance, in contrast to Roosevelt's, which were sometimes sent out weeks ahead of delivery. "The President simply is not forehanded about these things, but, on the contrary, is extremely dilatory," a sympathetic Walter E. Clark, of the *New York Sun*, wrote to an editor in Seattle. "It is a condition which does not seem likely to improve."[13] Prior to Taft's first annual State of the Union Message to Congress in late 1909, the President complained to Butt that "the press was urging him to finish the message so that it could be sent all over the country by mail, but he was not going to do it, and the press would have to send it by wire."[14]

Left without briefings, handouts, speech texts, or presidential events to fuel their daily stories, the correspondents turned to writing about rumors, the remarks of Taft's enemies, and the President's primary leisure-time activity, golf. These stories irritated Taft and further convinced him that he should have nothing to do with the press, if possible.[15] When the correspondents complained about the lack of news, Taft said he saw no reason why he should have to go out of his way to entertain them or to do their work for them. In a letter to William Allen White, Taft wrote: "I am not constituted as Mr. Roosevelt is in being able to keep the country advised every few days as to the continuance of the state of mind in reference to reform. It is a difference in temperament. He talked with correspondents a great deal. His heart was generally on his sleeve and he must communicate his feelings. I find myself unable to do so."[16]

Even when the correspondents could get through to Taft with story ideas, he squelched them. In his diary, Butt described a conversation he had with a group of correspondents, including Davis, of the *New York Times*, who were complaining about the lack of news. Davis told Butt that he had gone to Taft with four possible topics: a Cabinet shake-up, Taft's lack of communication with Roosevelt, a diplomatic incident, and an upcoming campaign speech. Instead of commenting, "he killed four good stories," Davis said. Butt asked Davis what he was going to write about Taft, and Davis replied, "Nothing."[17]

In June 1909, when the correspondents first traveled to Taft's summer cottage at Beverly, Massachusetts, they found that another of the routines of newsgathering created under Roosevelt, reporting on the summer White House, also had changed. Roosevelt had invited correspondents to write about the President's official activities at his summer retreat at Oyster Bay, Long Island. The assignment quickly became an expected annual assignment for the correspondents, who also wrote about Roosevelt's family and the President's colorful sporting activities.

Taft, however, like McKinley and other late-nineteenth-century presidents, regarded his summer retreat as a vacation. He took few official actions, made no announcements, and played only golf, an elitist and comparatively dull sport from the viewpoint of a press corps accustomed to a president who boxed with professional fighters, roughhoused with his children, climbed to the top of the mast in sailing ships, and hunted bears. Instead, Taft preferred to ignore the correspondents, who he felt had been sent to bedevil him. When Arthur Wallace Dunn of the Associated Press proposed to break the tedium by writing a series of articles on Taft's first months in the White House, he found himself blocked from talking with Taft by the President's secretary, Carpenter. Dunn was forced to wait out in the rain with other correspondents until a sympathetic Butt invited them to take shelter on the porch of the President's cottage. Before Taft reluctantly appeared, Dunn wrote, the correspondents overheard the President complain around the corner: "Must I see those men again! Didn't I see them just the other day?" Taft was then unresponsive to questions. Dunn noted in his autobiography that that was the last time he saw Taft at his summer retreat. The series of articles was never published.[18] Butt's account of the incident was more sympathetic to Taft, but he noted also that the President objected to a photographer taking his picture "at the sacrifice of dignity."[19]

Taft had worked briefly as a newspaperman in Cincinnati early in his career, between graduation from Yale and admission to the bar to practice law in Ohio. But, as president, he seemed to be unaware of, or uninterested in, the mechanics of how news was produced, and how they dictated the deadlines and work practices of the correspondents.[20] In April 1910, after Taft decided late one day to nominate Charles Evans Hughes as an associate justice of the U.S. Supreme Court, he was elated to find that the reporters in the White House press room had already gone home. Oblivious to the missed opportunity of getting the story in the morning newspapers, he proudly told Butt that "I think I have scooped the boys this time."[21]

Underlying Taft's unwillingness to indulge in publicity was his restricted view of the president as a public person. Roosevelt saw himself as someone whose rhetoric was significant to the citizenry and whose "bully pulpit" could be used to articulate a national purpose. Taft seemed to regard the presidency as an administrative or judicial position. The journalist William Allen White described Taft as "as insensible of public opinion and of currents of public thought as an oriental satrap."[22]

Taft also did not seem to realize that a president's informal or formal comments, when published, could have far-reaching consequences. Edward G. Lowry described Taft as "as lacking in all craft and guile as a child. He was too frank and naive for his own good."[23] When Taft, as secretary of war, spoke unguardedly to the correspondents, they protected him by not publishing his overly candid remarks. Charles Willis Thompson, then bureau chief of the *New York Times,* recounted an incident in which Dunn, of the Associated Press, persuaded Taft to forbid reporters from quoting his impolitic remarks about President Roosevelt. In Thompson's view, Taft had a "childlike frankness" and was unable to comprehend the difference between being a president and a private citizen. As president, Taft was no longer protected from himself by Roosevelt or by solicitous correspondents. Thompson wrote: "Now, for four years, his conversations were to be with the people of the United States, and he was to demonstrate the same quality in public that he often had shown in private; and now the effect was to be calamitous, for he was talking to millions who did not know him and would make no allowances."[24] Butt complained in his diary that "it is the hardest thing to keep the President from talking. He does not seem to realize that every word he utters is repeated and often exaggerated."[25]

Taft's indiscreet remarks more than once were leaked to reporters by those to whom he had carelessly spoken. They quickly became the subject of stories that embarrassed the President. In a somewhat defensive letter to William Dudley Foulke in late 1909, Taft admitted that he was surprised to read about their confidential correspondence in an Indianapolis newspaper. "I see very few newspapermen myself; but I presume that in discussing the situation in Indiana I may have recited to people who are interested some of the correspondence without the slightest intention of having it published. That I understand from my Secretary is the way in which the matter was probably brought to the attention of the public. I can not be responsible for the correspondent of the *Times-Star* in Washington or for the correspondent of any other newspaper."[26] When another Taft indiscretion led to a leak and a story in the Indiana press a few months later, Taft seemed bemused.[27]

Taft's record in weighing the public impact of his formal remarks was not much better than in his informal ones. He considered speechmaking bothersome, performed it only reluctantly, and spent as little time as possible in preparation. As a result, he was a poor public speaker, and he damaged his presidency repeatedly with ill-considered remarks. Before his first extended national speaking tour, in the fall of 1909, Taft procrastinated for weeks over preparing the presidential addresses that he had promised to deliver. Instead of writing speeches, Taft rested for a month at his summer cottage, spending his days playing golf. "I am expected to make a good many speeches, and that frightens me: for I do not know exactly what to say or how to say it," he wrote candidly to his daughter. "I shall stagger through the matter some way, but not in any manner, I fear, to reflect credit on the administration."[28]

Taft ended up hastily dictating his speeches to a stenographer on the train, which meant that they were delivered with little forethought or preparation. Repeatedly, across the country, Taft made statements that dismayed or angered his audiences and that were transmitted to the nation by the traveling press corps. Particularly damaging was Taft's praise of the widely unpopular Payne-Aldrich tariff bill in a speech delivered at Winona, Minnesota, in September 1909. His statement that the tariff was "the best bill that the Republican Party ever passed" made headlines around the nation and brought him severe criticism. That the telegraphed stories of the nine correspondents on the train emphasized this impolitic remark was a direct consequence of Taft's dilatory approach. Because of his delay in preparing the speech, no advance text had been available. Restricted by the limitations of the telegraph to transmitting only one or two sentences, the correspondents focused on the first phrase they heard Taft speak that would make a headline.[29] In an interview later in his presidency, Taft admitted that "if I had prepared it two or three weeks before and revised it deliberately, as I ought to have done, I should have clarified several passages."[30]

Taft also was reluctant to exploit the symbolism of the presidency in public. He declined to acknowledge the crowds that gathered at railway stations to watch his train go by. He did not wave, raise his hat, or make other public gestures, which led Jimmie Sloan, a Secret Service agent, to warn that Roosevelt had educated the public to expect more than that, and that Taft "will be a dead card if he doesn't change."[31] When Butt tried to get Taft to seat himself prominently among the fans at a baseball game for publicity purposes, Taft insisted that all he wanted to do was to watch the game. "You don't care whether I see the game or not," Taft chided Butt. "What you want is for me to be seen, and I will tell you frankly I don't care whether I am or seen or not, but what I really want is to see."[32]

As criticism of his administration increased, Taft seemed to pride himself on defying the "bugaboo" of public opinion. In a letter to William Kent during the Pinchot-Ballinger controversy in September 1909, Taft wrote that "I don't propose to allow it to influence me. When the people comprehend the facts and then condemn, it is one thing; but when they are induced to assume a position without respect to a knowledge of the facts, one has to bear the burden of criticism in order to do right."[33] Dismissing newspaper criticism of the gaffes on his western speaking tour, Taft wrote instead that he was encouraged by how warmly the public received him in person. "I have the confidence of many of the people sufficient to carry me over the dead point in an administration and to secure a waiting judgment until the whole evidence is in and the time comes for the verdict. I have gone through the trial thus far quite successfully."[34]

Taft's hopeful statement masked the resentment that he felt toward press criticism. For all of his outward disdain for publicity and public opinion, the President was just as hypersensitive to news stories as Roosevelt had been. He ordered his first secretary, Carpenter, to stop sending him editorials from the *New York Times* that were critical of the western trip. "I don't think their reading will do any particular good, and would only be provocative of that sort of anger and contemptuous feeling that does not do any body any good."[35] He complained to the First Lady, Helen Herron Taft, that the newspapers "are especially determined to show that this trip has done me and the party no good."[36]

Helen Herron Taft was a key advisor to the President, and she understood better than her husband the importance of being accommodating to the press. She was taken aback at first with the increased public and press expectations about the president's private life at the White House. But she allowed herself to be interviewed and quoted directly, the first incumbent First Lady to do so. However, her ability to work with the press, to write speeches, and to advise her husband was reduced by a stroke she suffered in June 1909.[37]

How much a healthier Helen Herron Taft would have been able to alter the President's view of the press is unclear. When the newspapers criticized Taft, he stopped reading them. Archie Butt described a breakfast conversation between the Tafts in 1911, at which the President refused to accept a copy of the Democratic *New York World* from the First Lady. "I have stopped reading it. It only makes me angry," Taft declared. "But you used to like it very much," she responded. "That was when it agreed with me, but it abuses me now and I don't want it," he replied. "You will never know what the other side is doing if you only read the [New York] *Sun* and the *Tribune*," she pointed out. "I don't care what the other side is thinking," Taft declared, ending the conversation.[38]

Butt also was concerned that Taft seemed to overreact to the newspapers' praise as much as he did to their criticism. "I believe it would be better for [the *Sun*] to abuse the President than to be continually praising him," Butt wrote. "The President is really affected by editorials. He does not like to read disagreeable truths any more than he likes to hear them."[39]

Taft found offensive even the mild skits of the correspondents at Gridiron Club dinners. While riding to one in December 1909, Taft remarked: "I am getting very tired myself of these dinners, and if they are at all rough with me this evening it shall be the last one I attend. It is an undignified thing to do at the best, and yet it is very difficult, as all other Presidents of late years seem to have made it a custom to go."[40]

Yet, despite his hypersensitivity to newspaper stories and comments, Taft could not or would not bring himself to employ the techniques of managing the press that worked so well for Roosevelt. In the summer of 1911, when his administration was under attack in the E. W. Scripps newspapers for supposed corruption involving mineral claims on public lands in Alaska, Taft refused to respond to reporters' questions. Instead of calling in friendly correspondents to hear him denounce the allegations or to issue a sharp statement of rebuttal, as Roosevelt would have done, Taft composed a 10,000-word legal brief in the administration's behalf and then tried to persuade the Associated Press to telegraph the entire text. A dismayed Butt wrote, "He may be right, but I think a sweeping denial would have been just as effective."[41]

Only in private letters to his brother Horace D. Taft and to a few other intimates did Taft vent his frustrations about the press. Taft had offended both newspaper and magazine publishers by opposing the former's efforts to keep down the price of imported newsprint and wood pulp and the latter's attempts to retain generous postal subsidies.[42] Angered when both used their publications to voice their self-interested objections to his policies, Taft declared in January 1910 that "If I live I will have three more years to do what I 'dern' choose, and to follow what I believe to be right and to regard threats of popular ill will as of no moment whatsoever if their expressions are directed against what I know to be right or in favor of what I know to be wrong." He raged at the "groveling hypocrisy" of a conciliatory speech to the magazine publishers by Iowa Senator Jonathan Dolliver.[43]

In late 1909 and early 1910, Taft had tried to ignore months of press attacks on Secretary of the Interior Ballinger over allegations of fraud involving Alaskan coal lands. Finally, Taft wrote that he had given up hope of changing public opinion through the press. "I am going to do what I think is best for the country, within my jurisdiction and power, and then let the rest take care of itself. I am not looking for a second term, and I am not going to subject myself to the worry involved in establishing a publicity bureau, or attempting to set myself right before the people in any different way from that which is involved in the ordinary publication of what is done. The misrepresentations which are made by the muck-raking correspondents I cannot neutralize, and I don't intend to."[44]

Despite Taft's protests, the decline of his popularity was too precipitous for him to ignore. As George Juergens has pointed out, Taft in his first year was well on his way to becoming one of the most vilified presidents of the twentieth century.[45] Press and public criticism of his competence, his remarks on the tariff, the fallout from the Ballinger-Pinchot affair, and unflattering comparisons to Roosevelt all contributed to a critical loss of public support by the spring of 1910. That November, in the midterm elections, the Republicans lost control of Congress to the Democrats for the first time since 1894.

Taft's estrangement from the correspondents had been worsened by the lack of a presidential assistant skilled in dealing with the press, as Cortelyou or Loeb had been. Carpenter, Taft's secretary in his disastrous first year, was scorned by the correspondents. Dunn, whose position with the Associated Press made him familiar with the White House staff, described Carpenter scathingly as "a self-effacing, patient, painstaking little man. . . . He had been with Taft for many years, and had learned that the most pleasing service he could render his chief was to keep people away from him."[46] Carpenter left the White House in May 1910 and was replaced by Charles Dyer Norton, who tried to place Taft's public relations on a more sophisticated basis. Norton proposed to Taft some strikingly modern innovations in presidential publicity.[47]

At Norton's urging, Taft late in 1910 began to hold the first regularly scheduled White House news conferences open to all correspondents, an experiment more fully developed by his successor, Woodrow Wilson. Roosevelt had seen favored correspondents at his daily "shaving hour," but attendance was by invitation only, and the meetings were not formally recognized. Under Taft, however, all accredited correspondents were invited at a fixed time, 4 P.M., once a week. The first conference was held in the Cabinet Room, which caused the meetings to be called Taft's "Newspaper Cabinet."[48] The setting was more formal than Roosevelt's had been; the 15 correspondents who attended the first meeting sat on chairs around a table, rather than standing around the President.[49] Once having gathered the correspondents, however, Taft seemed to have little to say. The President also found it difficult to show up on time. The correspondents sometimes had to wait until 6 p.m. or later for Taft to make an appearance.[50] Because of the lack of news and the wait involved, the conferences were not popular with the correspondents. Taft didn't particularly enjoy them, either. They were soon discontinued. Oulahan, of the

New York Sun, suspected that Taft, like Woodrow Wilson after him, disliked the "town meeting" aspect of the questioning by correspondents.[51]

Norton had other ideas about improving the President's public relations, but neither his plans nor his personal ambitions were welcomed universally in the Taft White House.[52] Ashmun Brown, of the *New York Sun,* wrote that the correspondents found Norton to be an improvement over Carpenter, "but he has an awful case of swelled head and actually thinks he is running the government."[53] Norton's arrogance and some impolitic remarks about Roosevelt eventually prompted Taft to acquiesce in his resignation. Norton was succeeded by Charles D. Hilles, who left in the summer of 1912 to become chairman of the Republican National Committee, and Carmi Thompson, who served in the last few months of the Taft presidency.[54]

None of Carpenter's successors was able to reverse Taft's slide in popular opinion. But they were able occasionally to improve the President's standing with the press.[55] Taft even allowed himself to be interviewed on the record a few times, still a rare presidential action.[56] For many reporters, the most useful source close to the Taft White House was fellow correspondent Gus J. Karger, of the *Cincinnati Times-Star,* which was owned by Taft's brother Charles P. Taft. Karger served as an unofficial liaison with the correspondents when no assistance was forthcoming from the President's staff.[57]

Only in his last year as president did Taft seem to be making headway in a sustained effort to reach the public through the press.[58] After a two-month speaking tour in the fall of 1911, Taft was upbeat about both his press coverage and the upcoming presidential campaign. Along the way, Taft had made 30 speeches and succeeded in getting headlines in regional newspapers. In Detroit, he told local editors about his days as a reporter in Cincinnati, and he spoke later in the trip to the Louisville, Kentucky, press club.[59] In a long letter to a sympathetic southern editor, J. C. Hemphill, Taft rejoiced in getting his speeches into the news pages despite the reluctance of the Hearst newspapers, the Democratic *New York World,* and the United Press news service, which was owned by the left-wing publisher E. W. Scripps. "In this way I got my case before the people, and, since I have returned, I have had a great many evidences that it was an advantage to me."[60]

Greater success in persuading the press to carry his messages had not improved Taft's view of journalism, however. In the same letter to Hemphill, he deplored the insurgent Republican and Democratic newspapers who belittled his presidency. "But, being a member of the newspaper craft, you know what infernal liars your profession can produce, and you will accept their stories accordingly," he wrote. Referring to his own early work as a reporter, Taft added: "I had a slight experience in that craft years ago, but constant effort has rid me of the tendencies that pursued such a profession, and therefore you must accept me as a truthful witness."[61]

Unfortunately for Taft, his belated honeymoon with the press ended several weeks later, after Roosevelt, dismayed at Taft's performance in the White House, decided to run again for president. Many of the Republican correspondents who had come to accept Taft's presidency quickly switched their allegiances to Roosevelt, along with the insurgents who had been supporting the reform candidacy of Robert M. La Follette. Taft's party regulars were able to keep Roosevelt from winning the nomination for president at the Republican National Convention in June 1912. But when Roosevelt bolted the party to lead an independent Progressive campaign for president, he split the Republican vote and ended Taft's chances for re-election.

Had Taft been president 15 years earlier, his hands-off approach toward the press and publicity would have been less damaging to his presidency. Like Cleveland or Harrison, he could have limited his dealings with the correspondents of that era, and they likely would have kept to their main work of writing about Congress and partisan affairs. But the relationship between the press and the president had changed during the days of McKinley and, particularly, under Roosevelt. They had attracted the spotlight of the press to the White House by making available a steady supply of information and guidance that could be used to make news. The correspondents, in turn, had come to regard the president as someone of significance who was accessible to them as a frequent source of authoritative stories.

Under the outline of the media presidency that had emerged between 1897 and 1909, the chief executive was now regarded as regularly newsworthy, and he could usually rely on a White House press corps to transmit his appeals for public support. But the president's new opportunity to seek public support by managing the press was a two-edged sword. To maintain the benefits of the relationship, the president was now expected to produce and to interpret news on a regular basis for the press corps that had formed to receive and to distribute it. When those expectations were not met, the correspondents would turn to whatever other sources were available, including the president's critics, to do their job of writing stories.

The damaging consequences of Taft's policy of nonpublicity were dramatized during his first year in office, which is reviewed in more detail in the next chapter. By declining to try to extend Roosevelt's relationship with the press corps after his inauguration in 1909, Taft forfeited his initial opportunity to use the mass media to influence public opinion favorably toward his administration. He also left himself vulnerable to other government leaders who had learned under Roosevelt how to use publicity to advance their causes. Key agency publicists, especially Gifford Pinchot, were dismayed when Taft, in their view, betrayed Roosevelt's reform legacy.

CHAPTER FIVE

THE CONSEQUENCES OF "NONPUBLICITY"

William Howard Taft's refusal to try to influence public opinion by managing the press, especially in his critical first year as president, had important consequences for the Taft administration and for the media presidency. Inspired by the supportive press coverage generated by the Roosevelt White House, an increasing number of executive branch administrators had hired publicists, usually former newspaper reporters, and created press bureaus to try to appeal to the public through the press themselves. When Taft, unlike Roosevelt, showed no inclination to restrict leaks or to try to coordinate executive branch publicity activity, the practices spread rapidly.

By early 1910, a congressional committee confirmed that the Census Bureau, among other agencies, had hired a press agent.[1] In 1912, newspaper correspondents told another House committee that publicists had been hired by agencies as diverse as the Agriculture Department, the Bureau of Soils, the Bureau of Biological Survey, the State Department, the Bureau of Public Roads, the Smithsonian Institution, the National Museum, and the Post Office.[2]

Widening adoption of publicity practices by administrative agencies constituted a potential challenge to the emerging media presidency, as well as to congressional supremacy. Theodore Roosevelt had been well aware of the possibility of distracting leaks to the press from agency publicists, and he moved aggressively to punish departmental sources of unwanted stories. Taft, however, seemed unconcerned about unauthorized leaks to the press, and he left the details of agency administration to the Cabinet and Congress.[3]

Taft failed to respond in 1909–10 when Gifford Pinchot and other rebellious holdover administrators used leaks and other publicity techniques to dramatize what they regarded as the betrayal of Roosevelt's conservation legacy by Richard A. Ballinger, Taft's secretary of the interior. The Ballinger–Pinchot conflict was one of the most damaging episodes of the Taft presidency. Nothing in Taft's experience and outlook had prepared him for a publicity war, especially one within the executive branch. In the end, Taft was left estranged from Roosevelt's supporters and from Roosevelt himself. The conflict also demonstrated that in the spreading practice of executive leadership by publicity, management of the press by agency press bureaus could be a threat to the media presidency as well as a potential source of support.

Underlying the Ballinger–Pinchot conflict of 1909–10 was a fundamental disagreement between the Taft and Roosevelt administrations over how federal authority should be used to manage natural resources on public lands. Roosevelt, acting in concert with his secretary of the interior, James R. Garfield, and Pinchot, his conservation advisor, had created in the executive branch a federal conservation "movement" that overlapped statutory and bureaucratic boundaries. Relying on his expansive interpretation of presidential authority, Roosevelt issued executive orders that withdrew from commercial development millions of acres of public land on which there were timber, mineral, water power, and other resources. In addition, Pinchot used his position as the President's advisor to intervene in the affairs of agencies concerned with natural resources in both the Department of Agriculture and the Department of the Interior.[4]

President Taft, however, was less enthusiastic than Roosevelt about restricting commercial development on public lands. He also disapproved of the constitutionally questionable authority that Roosevelt had relied upon to order the land withdrawals. Instead of reappointing Garfield as secretary of the interior, Taft replaced him with Ballinger, a westerner and former judge who shared Taft's conservative views on both conservation and the constitutional limitations of presidential authority. In the first weeks of the Taft administration, in early 1909, Ballinger began to challenge and to reverse some of the Roosevelt land withdrawals.[5]

Ballinger's actions angered Pinchot and other holdover executive administrators from the Roosevelt administration, including Frederick H. Newell, chief of the Reclamation Service. When Taft refused their request for a presidential reversal of Ballinger's decisions, Pinchot and Newell turned to the press with their complaints. Increasingly, through the summer and fall of 1909, they used the press bureaus and publicity specialists in their agencies to launch a series of newspaper and magazine articles that were sharply critical of Ballinger's policies, Ballinger himself, and, by extension, Taft's presidency.

Pinchot's success in undermining popular support for Ballinger and the Taft presidency was due in part to the President's reluctance to try to manage the press himself or to restrain executive branch publicity. Taft's refusal to follow Roosevelt's example of keeping the correspondents supplied with news from the White House had created an occupational vacuum for the press corps. Left without presidential announcements, advisories, events, or activities to provide the grist for their daily stories, the correspondents turned to other sources of news, including Taft's critics, such as Pinchot. Pinchot was known to the correspondents as a close friend of Roosevelt's, a leader in the progressive reform faction of the Republican Party, and a prolific source of news during the Roosevelt administration. His leaks to reporters about conflict and possible corruption in conservation policies quickly became news stories that badly damaged the Taft administration's popular support.

Nor was Ballinger, the immediate target of the leaks, any more adept than Taft at understanding the ways of the press and public opinion. One of Ballinger's first acts after becoming secretary of the interior in April 1909 was to cancel the office's contract with a newspaper clipping service, because "I haven't even time to read clippings from newspapers."[6] Neither was Ballinger well known to the Washington correspondents, despite a previous appointment as commissioner of the General Land Office under Roosevelt.

The leaks from Pinchot and his supporters to the press began in the early summer of 1909. By fall, the story of Ballinger's betrayal of Roosevelt's conservation policies and possible corruption had grown into a national front-page scandal in the daily newspapers and was the subject of critical articles in muckraking magazines.

The first stories appeared in publications sympathetic to the Roosevelt reformers, including the *Philadelphia Press* and *Outlook* magazine, where Roosevelt himself was now a columnist. The *Press* carried a story on 9 May 1909 warning that Secretary Ballinger was about to turn over 5 million acres of publicly owned land to the private "water power trust." Ballinger denied to the editor of *Outlook,* E. F. Baldwin, a former college classmate, that he was trying to reverse the Roosevelt conservation program or that he disagreed with Pinchot and Newell. However, additional stories appeared in June and July of 1909 that accused Ballinger not only of betraying the Roosevelt legacy but also of trying to fire Newell.[7]

That these and the later stories were prompted by leaks from Roosevelt holdovers in executive agencies was never in question. Oscar Lawler, the assistant attorney general for the Interior Department, warned Ballinger in mid-July that Newell and Pinchot were organizing a propaganda campaign against him. Lawler was concerned at the lack of a response due to the "aversion to newspaper exploitation throughout the administration."[8] Ballinger was warned again in early August by a sympathetic Republican newspaperman, Walter E. Clark, of the *New York Sun,* who blamed specifically the press bureaus of the Reclamation Service and the Forest Service. Clark named one publicist in the Reclamation Service, who he said was carried on the payroll as a statistician.[9]

Before Ballinger responded to these warnings, however, he found himself the target of a nationally telegraphed United Press story that accused him of turning over to the "power trust" more than 15,000 acres of hydroelectric power sites on public land in Montana. The story was wildly overstated, according to the subsequent congressional investigation. Only 158 acres of land were involved, not 15,000. But the story was widely published by the nation's newspapers, and its timing was particularly damaging to Ballinger.[10] United Press distribution of the story coincided with Ballinger's arrival in Spokane, Washington, to address the National Irrigation Congress, an important industry group. Because of earlier reports of conflict between Pinchot and Ballinger, several of the Washington correspondents had traveled to Spokane to hear both men speak. The timely appearance of the water power story effectively set the news agenda for the conference. The next day's stories focused on the accusations against Ballinger, which were taken up by Pinchot's allies at the conference, and on Ballinger's unwillingness to respond to them.[11]

The content and timing of the United Press story were far from coincidental. Lawler wrote to Ballinger that existence of the story was widely known in Washington, D.C., before it was transmitted. Circumstantial evidence points to Pinchot or his allies. The United Press reporter, Samuel M. Evans, was an acquaintance of Pinchot's. Furthermore, Pinchot also was close to Gilson Gardner, the chief Washington correspondent for the Newspaper Enterprise Association, which, like United Press, was owned by the left-wing newspaper publisher E. W. Scripps. Pinchot had a quite pleasant meeting with Scripps in California three weeks after the first story appeared.[12]

The water power story was followed within days by another, more damaging newspaper story, which charged that Ballinger was about to be accused of personal corruption in the handling of an investigation into improper claims on federal coal lands in Alaska. This story, and the Forest Service's role in promoting it to newspapers and magazines, led eventually to Pinchot's firing by Taft in January 1910, to a congressional investigation, to Ballinger's resignation in 1911, and to a widening rift between Taft and Roosevelt. It also demonstrated how unanswered news stories from agency press bureaus could undermine popular support for a president.

The primary source of the allegations against Ballinger was Louis Glavis, a disgruntled employee of the General Land Office, an agency of Ballinger's Interior Department. Glavis believed that Ballinger was hindering an investigation into questionable mining claims in Alaska that had been filed by, among others, Clarence Cunningham, a former legal client of Ballinger's in Seattle. To Glavis, this was part of an elaborate plan by unscrupulous Wall Street interests to seize public mineral resources in Alaska. Although news coverage of the Glavis charges eventually destroyed Ballinger's career, no convincing evidence of his personal corruption was found during the subsequent Senate investigation. Ballinger had, however, improperly taken Cunningham as a law client shortly after resigning as commissioner of the General Land Office in 1908.[13]

Rebuffed by his supervisors and after an unsuccessful appeal to Ballinger himself in May 1909, Glavis looked outside his own agency for help in publicizing his complaint. In July 1909, Glavis sent a telegram promising sensational revelations against Ballinger to Forest Service headquarters in Washington, D.C. Pinchot was traveling in the West, but Overton W. Price, the associate forester, and Alexander C. Shaw, the agency's legal officer, started an investigation. Shaw went to General Land Office headquarters in Washington, D.C., to search the files on the Cunningham claims. A similar search took place at the General Land Office's regional headquarters in Portland, Oregon. Meanwhile, Glavis, impatient with the pace of the Forest Service response, traveled on his own to Spokane to meet with Pinchot at the forester's hotel during the irrigation conference.[14]

Pinchot had not expected the meeting with Glavis, but, as he wrote afterwards to Garfield, he was "mighty glad" for the information about Ballinger.[15] Pinchot advised Glavis to take his complaint directly to President Taft, who was then at his summer retreat at Beverly, Massachusetts. Pinchot gave Glavis two introductory letters for Taft, one of which advised the President, somewhat disingenuously, that "various parts of Glavis' story are so much known that I believe it will be impossible to prevent it becoming public, in part at least, and before very long. Many persons have knowledge of more or less essential portions."[16] Pinchot also ordered Shaw to meet with Glavis in Chicago and to help him to prepare the presentation to Taft.[17]

Pinchot's assistants quickly leaked word of the forthcoming allegations against Ballinger to friendly correspondents. Stories outlining these charges closely followed the United Press story about water power sites, as well as earlier reports about feuding between Pinchot and Ballinger. The cumulative result ignited a front-page newspaper frenzy in the slow news atmosphere of summertime Washington, D.C. The first stories appeared on 13 August 1909, and, fed by continuing leaks from the Forest Service, stayed on the front pages for nearly a month without rebuttal from either Taft or Ballinger.[18] By late August, the *Washington Post* had received a complete copy of the Glavis charges, as well as leaked copies of General Land Office files. The editor of the *Post,* which supported Taft, advised the President that the newspaper had received the information and requested his response.[19]

Taft inadvertently helped to fan the furor in the press by agreeing to meet personally with Glavis at Beverly. The President's involvement immediately made the controversy more newsworthy. But, after the meeting, Taft refused to issue a statement to the correspondents. The President's only public response was to summon Ballinger from the West to respond to the charges, which seemed to confirm the seriousness of the allegations. The *Washington Post* concluded in its story that the charges were "of a much more serious nature than at first intimated."[20]

Not only did Taft refuse to respond publicly to the charges against Ballinger, neither he nor his staff supplied the correspondents with the kind of behind-the-scenes guidance on how to shape their stories that was always available from the Roosevelt White House. For nearly three weeks after Taft met with Glavis, normally sympathetic Republican newspapers in Washington, D.C., and New York filled their front pages with repetitions of the Glavis charges and rambling speculation about what was going on in the Taft administration. Daily stories traced Ballinger's hurried train trip from Seattle to Washington, D.C., where he was met by a crowd of reporters. Ballinger, following Taft's instructions, refused to speak with the press, other than to remark, somewhat enigmatically, that "incidentally, I plan to kill some snakes."[21] Three days later, more reporters took the train to Beverly with Ballinger to be nearby when the Secretary personally delivered his response to Taft. After weeks of repetition without rebuttal, the Glavis charges had been so widely accepted by the correspondents that even the solidly Republican *Chicago Tribune* referred to Taft's "subpoena" of Ballinger.[22]

At Beverly, Taft met with Ballinger but, again, provided no public statement or private guidance to the press, which prompted another week of newspaper speculation. Taft then left for the West on a speaking tour. Finally, after leaving Ballinger to suffer a month of unanswered allegations in the press, Taft allowed his staff to hand a letter to the correspondents on the train that declared the Glavis charges unfounded.[23] The resulting stories, based on reports telegraphed from the railway station at Albany, New York, were widely displayed. Some of the Washington, D.C., newspapers turned over their entire front pages to Taft's belated response.[24] But Ballinger's reputation had been damaged badly by the weeks of newspaper speculation.

Taft's statement, however belated, helped to take the story off the front pages by mid-October 1909. The newspaper frenzy was over, at least temporarily. Some of the leading correspondents had left Washington to travel west with Taft and to write instead about the President's speaking tour. Moreover, as described in the previous chapter, Taft committed a series of gaffes on the trip that also helped to push the Ballinger story off the front pages. At Winona, Minnesota, delivering a hastily prepared speech, Taft praised the unpopular Payne-Aldrich tariff as "the best bill that the Republican Party ever passed." Lacking an advance text, the nine correspondents traveling with the President seized on the phrase for their brief telegraphed dispatches.[25]

Back at the Forest Service, however, Pinchot's assistants were helping Glavis shape his allegations into an article for the leading muckraking magazine in 1909, *Collier's Weekly.*[26] When the article appeared in the magazine's 13 November issue, its dramatic presentation reignited the controversy. The text of the story was cautiously worded, but the headline on the magazine's front cover asked provocatively, "Are the Guggenheims in Charge of the Department of the Interior?" Inside, the story was headlined, "The Whitewashing of Ballinger." Following the lead of *Collier's Weekly,* other muckraking magazines published similar articles, prompting renewed calls for a congressional investigation.[27]

From the earliest stages of the Glavis controversy, the primary sources of the leaks to the correspondents were well known in Washington and inside the Taft administration. When the allegations of personal corruption involving Ballinger first appeared, in mid-August, the Democratic *New York World* claimed to have conducted the "first authorized interview" and identified Price, of the Forest Service, in its page-one story.[28] Lawler, the Interior Department assistant attorney general, repeatedly warned both Ballinger and George Wickersham, Taft's attorney general, about the Forest Service press bureau.[29] Secretary Ballinger sent a personal letter of complaint to Taft, arguing that newspaper stories originating in the Forest Service press bureau reflected badly on the President as well as himself.[30] In addition, Walter E. Clark, of the *New York Sun,* wrote that he told Taft personally about the source of the leaks and watched while the President took notes.[31]

These sources and Taft's own correspondence indicate that the President was aware of the campaign of leaks against Ballinger, and that he

knew they were coming from agency administrators and their press bureaus. Yet Taft chose deliberately not to reply publicly to the charges, and
he ordered Ballinger to do the same. This policy of nonpublicity was
adopted partly because Taft did not want to force the resignation of Pinchot, who was an important link to Roosevelt and his followers. Instead,
Taft suggested mildly to Pinchot that "you assist me by using your influence to prevent further conflict between the Departments by published
criticism in the newspapers."[32] But it is also apparent from Taft's letters that
he was unable or unwilling to comprehend the impact on popular support
for his administration from the avalanche of unfavorable publicity.

Taft first tried to minimize the conflict as a misunderstanding between
Ballinger and Pinchot. The pro-administration *New York Evening Telegram*
reported that Taft did not want to become involved in the controversy, and
that Ballinger could take care of himself.[33] When the editor of the *Washington Post* appealed to Taft for help in rebutting the Glavis charges, the
President declined to respond publicly on the ground that any statement
would be misunderstood. Privately, however, he deplored the use of "advertising methods and unfounded statements to create an impression of
bitterness that has no reason for existence."[34] As the stories continued, Taft
complained that "there is too much of a disposition to charge people with
bad faith, and too great encouragement to newspaper controversy," but he
declined to reply publicly or to chastise Pinchot.[35]

Taft only reluctantly released to the correspondents the 13 September
letter dismissing the Glavis charges. And when he did so, he again urged
Ballinger to keep silent and to keep Pinchot's name out of the controversy.[36] Taft then tried to appease Pinchot in a letter that referred only
obliquely to the publicity campaign. He wrote that he was somewhat concerned by the controversy, and that he hoped there would be less official
leaking to the press.[37] Privately, Taft described Pinchot as a "fanatic," with
a "publicity machine" in his agency, and someone whose supporters were
willing to make reckless statements against Ballinger.[38]

Taft was warned in advance about the muckraking *Collier's Weekly* article. But he seemed unable to take it seriously or to comprehend its potential impact on public opinion. Taft replied to Attorney General
Wickersham's warning by writing that " . . . I feel as if we may exaggerate
the importance of the paper's attitude." Pinchot, Taft acknowledged, "is at
the bottom of the *Collier's* action, and at the bottom of a good many other
attacks. That will come out eventually; and the injustice of the attacks will
aid in showing the necessity for the action that I fear we must take in time.
I shall be glad to have your analysis whenever it is ready, but there is no
particular hurry."[39] Taft also seemed unconcerned in a letter to his brother

Horace: "I have been advised of some attack on Ballinger in *Collier's*, but I am rather disposed to think that their attitude is hardly judicial, and that they are mistaking for evidence what is more assumption by enthusiasts who in the interest of their cause seize upon shreds of suspicion that would have no weight to a man used to a man to weighing evidence." Making no mention of his order to Ballinger to remain silent, Taft went on to criticize Ballinger for being overly sensitive and for taking "but little means to defend himself."[40]

Privately, again, Taft was seething. He wrote to the First Lady that "Pinchot has spread a virus against Ballinger widely, and used the publicity department of his bureau for the purpose. He would deny it, but I see traces in his talks with many newspapermen on the subject, who assume Ballinger's guilt, and having convicted him treated any evidence that he is a man of strength as utterly to be disregarded."[41]

Ballinger was deeply hurt, personally and politically, by the accusatory stories, but he followed loyally the President's orders not to respond. The Secretary of the Interior was no more capable of comprehending the new prominence of publicity in executive politics than was Taft. Despite Ballinger's Washington, D.C., experience, his primary background as a public official had been as mayor of Seattle, where Republican newspapers supported their party's public officials. Indeed, the two Republican daily newspapers in Seattle, the *Post-Intelligencer* and the *Times,* remained loyal to Ballinger throughout his ordeal. Although Walter E. Clark's primary employer was the *New York Sun,* he also served as the *Post-Intelligencer's* Washington correspondent and the newspaper's agent in national Republican Party affairs. Taft later appointed Clark to be territorial governor of Alaska.[42]

The appearance of critical news articles in nominally Republican newspapers in New York and Washington, D.C., baffled Ballinger. He wrote to Clark that "the whole affair is so contemptible . . . that I hardly know how to deal with it, except by conference with the President, and after obtaining more definite facts."[43] In a letter to E. F. Baldwin, however, Ballinger expressed confidence in the outcome: "Standing securely on my conscious rectitude, the efforts of newspaper correspondents to impugn my motives and the integrity of my acts will ultimately be shown to be absolutely groundless."[44] Writing to an ally, Erastus Brainerd of *the Seattle Post-Intelligencer,* Ballinger said that "as they can find nothing worthy of criticism that will stand the light of investigation, I am not giving any serious concern to these articles, for I believe that the future will make everything plain and show who the instigators are."[45] Ballinger discouraged Brainerd's offer to stage a rally in Seattle at which *Collier's Weekly* would be denounced. He wrote: "This is a state of mind that only time can correct, and it is not to be corrected by public clamor, in my opinion."[46] In December 1909, after months of mostly unanswered charges against him in newspaper and magazine stories, Ballinger wrote to another regional Republican editor that: "I have felt so thoroughly conscious of the justice of my position in all these matters and of the injustice and unfairness of criticisms emanating from certain sources that I have felt assured that the public would ultimately understand the truth without the necessity of my entering upon a campaign of publicity. I have always believed in and adopted the course of nonpublicity in my private as well as my official life, endeavoring to justify my course by the results accomplished."[47]

Ballinger's supporters grew increasingly angry at the lack of public support from Taft. After weeks of reading about the Glavis charges, Ormsby McHarg, a Commerce Department official and friend of Ballinger's, called his own news conference to make intemperate remarks about Pinchot, Roosevelt, and Roosevelt's conservation policies. The outburst, which was widely reported, cost McHarg his job.[48] The McHarg incident also prompted the correspondents themselves to complain publicly about Taft's silence and the lack of presidential guidance. The *Chicago Record-Herald,* a Republican paper, said it was time for Taft to speak up and to defend Ballinger.[49] The *Washington Star* commented that Taft's policy of silence was difficult to understand, since Pinchot's publicity campaign against Ballinger was well known. The *Star's* correspondent wrote, "The administration's end of the controversy appears to be somewhat hampered, either by a sense of official dignity or ethical backwardness at tooting its own horn, markedly at variance with the good Roosevelt methods and days, so nothing is coming out from departmental sources. . . ."[50]

Late in 1909, both Taft and Ballinger took heart from the increasing likelihood that a Senate investigation into the conflict would lead to political vindication by the Republican majority.[51] Taft and Ballinger exchanged hopeful letters over the favorable newspaper response to Ballinger's departmental annual report. "I am glad to say that this is only one of a great many articles of a similar character that the people are becoming sensible and that the newspapers are getting a little light," Taft wrote.[52] The President wrote to his brother Horace that "I think we are settling down to a condition where Ballinger's position will be better understood, and some people will find themselves beating the tom-tom without any listeners."[53] Taft said he looked forward to the forthcoming congressional investigation, which he believed would reveal "the methods adopted by these publications to disseminate the press bureau matter that is worked on by the Forestry Service."[54]

Ballinger was further cheered when Taft fired Pinchot in January 1910. Pinchot forced the President's hand by sending a letter to Senator Jonathan P. Dolliver that admitted the depth of his agency's role in instigating the press attacks on Ballinger. Ironically, Taft's firing of Pinchot overshadowed press coverage of Attorney General Wickersham's formal vindication of Ballinger.[55] But, again, Taft and Ballinger were outmaneuvered by Pinchot in both the subsequent congressional hearings and in the press. Pinchot's supporters hired an astute trial lawyer as Glavis's attorney: Louis Brandeis, later associate justice of the U.S. Supreme Court.[56] Under Brandeis's guidance, Glavis presented testimony that further damaged Ballinger's reputation, as did Pinchot. The chief forester testified that Ballinger was an enemy of conservation and unfit to be secretary of the interior. Pinchot also defended the publicity activities of his assistants, Price and Shaw, as appropriate to an administrative agency. They had, Pinchot said, helped "direct critical public attention to the actions of the Interior." He said also that "if they appealed to public opinion, it must be remembered that they belong to a service which has been, and is now, wholly dependent upon enlightened public approval."[57]

In addition, Pinchot kept up his publicity campaign during the congressional hearings. Besides his official testimony, which he helpfully released to the press in advance of its delivery, Pinchot and his brother, Amos, prepared and sent to the nation's newspaper editors a packet containing a summary of the testimony against Ballinger, excerpts from Pinchot's remarks, and a digest of the lengthy hearings to serve as a handy reference guide for their stories.[58]

As before, Taft was indignant at Pinchot's continuing publicity activities during the congressional investigation, but he seemed to be at a loss over whether or how to respond. In a letter to his brother Horace, he complained: "The investigation goes on, and highly moral people like our friends Pinchot and Garfield are engaged in a publicity bureau by which they circulate fantastic and wild statements made by a witness who will say almost anything founded on hearsay or even less. They have a man here who makes a short statement of the evidence of the unfairest character, and then gives it out to the newspapers. But we are living in an age of supreme hypocrisy, when the man who can yell the loudest against corruption in general has the advantage and the man who has the responsibility of affirmative action is at a disadvantage."[59]

Unfortunately for Ballinger, he had hired as his legal advocate an attorney friend of Taft's, John J. Vertrees, who went out of his way to antagonize the press and to alienate the correspondents further. At the congressional hearings, Vertrees spoke pointedly only to members of Congress, not the press. He also accused the correspondents of "habitually" doing injustice to persons "who may be assaulted and impugned" only to sell newspapers.[60]

Taft remained steadfast in refusing to resort to publicity techniques but, by March 1910, Ballinger had suffered enough. With neither the Senate hearings nor the press coverage helping to restore his reputation, Ballinger reluctantly accepted the advice of his supporters to hire a publicist.[61] Ashmun Brown, a correspondent for the *Seattle Post-Intelligencer* told his editor that Ballinger had approached him. "He didn't call it press agenting, but that is what it is. He wanted someone to stick around the hearings and wise up the newspapermen as to the significance of the testimony." Brown declined the job, but a correspondent for the *New York Tribune* agreed to try to help Ballinger.[62] By the time Ballinger appeared to testify before the investigating committee, in May 1910, however, newspaper editors were bored with the story. Ballinger's testimony in his own defense drew little coverage, except for Associated Press dispatches about his grueling cross-examination by Brandeis.[63]

The Republican majority on the Senate committee eventually cleared Ballinger of wrongdoing, but Pinchot was the uncontested winner of the publicity war.[64] Ballinger's career was destroyed, and Taft's presidency was deeply damaged. Not only had Taft been forced to fire Pinchot and thereby alienate the Roosevelt progressives, the President had shown himself to be ineffective in defending a member of his Cabinet or himself against Pinchot's publicity campaign. In a comment echoed by other correspondents, Samuel G. Blythe, of the *New York World,* remarked that, after one year in the White House, the rotund Taft had become a "stranded whale."[65] In a painful epilogue, Taft blundered one final time in the handling of publicity about the Ballinger-Pinchot affair when he abruptly announced Ballinger's resignation in March 1911. He revealed the resignation to reporters before notifying other members of the Cabinet, who were then left to deny what the President had already announced.[66]

In May 1910, Taft replaced his secretary, Carpenter, and began to experiment with some of the techniques of presidential persuasion of the press used by Roosevelt, such as occasional interviews and formal news conferences. But his underlying reluctance to use the techniques of publicity did not change, and his relationship with the press at the White House never fully recovered from the disastrous first year.[67]

The causes of Taft's ineptness with the press were both philosophical and personal. But they also reflected a lack of understanding of how White House use of publicity techniques to manage the press to influence public opinion had changed the nature of executive leadership. Not only Roosevelt but other political leaders had discovered the possibilities of appealing to the public by managing the press. Agency press bureaus were being created to promote press coverage and public support favorable to that agency's policies and interests, which were not necessarily those of Congress or the president. The newspapers and magazines that Roosevelt enlisted to build up his popular support also could undercut public opinion when manipulated by publicists in agency press bureaus.

Taft's plight demonstrated that by the end of the first decade of the twentieth century, the president's developing relationship with the new mass media had become too established to be overlooked. News coverage was too important to the success or failure of the media presidency to be left unguided, whether at the White House or, increasingly, in the administrative agencies of the executive branch.

CHAPTER SIX

WILSON: CENTRALIZING EXECUTIVE INFORMATION

President Woodrow Wilson, Taft's successor, long has been recognized for his attempts to use the press to appeal for public support. Wilson held the first sustained, regularly scheduled presidential press conferences between 1913 and 1915. In 1917, after U.S. entry into World War I, Wilson created the nation's first ministry of information, the Committee on Public Information, to launch a propaganda campaign to persuade U.S. citizens to support the war effort.[1]

This chapter examines Wilson's first term, from 1913 to 1917, in which he placed a high priority on seeking supportive public opinion as a foundation for expanded presidential authority. As a political scientist, Wilson long had been a student of the presidency, and he recognized the potential usefulness of the news media to shape what the public was thinking about national issues and leaders. As soon as he took office in 1913, Wilson tried to reinvigorate the relationship with the Washington correspondents that McKinley and Roosevelt had encouraged and that Taft had neglected. Wilson also tried to establish White House control, or at least coordination, over the spreading use of publicity practices in agencies across the executive branch. These first-term experiences formed an important context for the stronger measures taken by Wilson in his second term to control government information and to manage the press in wartime.

Wilson's drive to expand presidential authority by managing the press to shape public opinion was based on important philosophical, as well as pragmatic, concerns. During his academic study of the political system,

Wilson had come to believe that properly guided public opinion, rather than the limited authority of the written Constitution, was the appropriate foundation for a strengthened presidency. Only a president backed by supportive national opinion could impose his will on the polity. To create this favorable public opinion, a strong president needed to formulate a consistent message and to transmit it clearly to the citizenry.[2]

But, as Wilson wrote two years before being elected president, neither the institutions of government nor mass communications could, without guidance, be relied upon to create and to transmit the messages necessary to unify public opinion behind the president. In the late nineteenth century, in Wilson's view, constitutional separation of powers and the hegemony of congressional committees had led to a fragmentation of government authority. In mass communications, those media with the largest public audiences—advertising-supported newspapers and magazines—preferred to attract readers with entertaining stories and sensations, rather than to publish what Wilson regarded as appropriate political information. To create and to communicate a message clear enough to shape public support for a strengthened presidency, then, was a two-part process: The president needed to be able to speak for a unified central government, and he would have to find a way to persuade the mass media to communicate that message to the citizenry.[3]

Wilson's analysis of the public roots of presidential power was a significant theoretical contribution to the development of the media presidency. Roosevelt's vigorous campaigns to influence public opinion had been based on a mixture of pragmatism and zeal, an expansive view of executive authority, and the progressive notion of informing the citizenry to support reform. But Wilson placed guided public opinion in the forefront of American democratic thought. To Wilson, shaping the public's views was not just a useful adjunct to executive policymaking; it was the key to restructuring the polity around a more authoritative presidency. Once in the White House, however, Wilson found that managing the press to create popular support for his presidency was much more challenging in practice than in theory.

For one thing, Wilson's exemplar of the president as national opinion leader had been that of the great orator, who speaks to his audience in person. Wilson was, by all accounts, a compelling public speaker. "Mr. Wilson had a sense of the dramatic which enabled him to capitalize some of his actions in a way to make them popular," Richard V. Oulahan noted approvingly.[4] But to reach beyond the sound of his voice, a president had to turn to the newspapers and magazines, which were more inclined to publish summarized stories or commentary than the full texts of political speeches. In a telling observation, the correspondent David Lawrence wrote that the reporters covering Wilson's campaign for president in 1912 were impressed with the candidate's ability to speak extemporaneously. However, few of them telegraphed Wilson's remarks to their editors because the speeches were too long and because a text was not available in advance.[5] As president, Wilson continued to use oratory to seek public support. But to reach the audiences beyond the sound of his voice, he had to make presidential oratory a news event, not just a speech. For example, he made news, in addition to making a speech, when he revived, after 113 years, John Adams's custom of personally delivering the president's annual State of the Union Message to Congress.[6]

To reach mass media audiences, then, the new President had to adapt his activities to accommodate and to manage the complex process involved in making news. Theodore Roosevelt began to learn the techniques of managing the press in his earliest days in elective office as a New York assemblyman. Wilson, however, had only two years of elective experience as governor of New Jersey before he was elected president. He did not have Roosevelt's understanding of how the press worked as an organizational process, and he was often frustrated with how the news media treated his remarks and activities. Ray Stannard Baker observed: "If the President was ever fearful of anything in his life, it was publicity; he was afraid, I think, not so much of the facts themselves, but of the way they were presented. As a highly cultivated scholar he disliked exaggeration, distrusted sensationalism. And yet he recognized the need for publicity and often seemed irritated and offended if the clear stream of news was fouled at its sources or muddied with propaganda."[7]

Wilson's most sustained attempt to appeal to the public by managing the press in his first term was through the still-experimental means of regularly scheduled press conferences open to all correspondents. Beginning in March 1913 and continuing intermittently until July 1915, these press conferences drew crowds of reporters to the White House. Even if Wilson, like earlier presidents, rarely spoke for publication, regular and frequent access to his conferences was a welcome change from Taft's aloofness. Taft had experimented with open press conferences, but the results had been disappointing both to him and to the correspondents. Wilson's press conferences usually provided the correspondents with material for stories on what the President was believed to be thinking.[8]

Wilson's press conferences were arranged to try to accomplish several objectives. Inviting all the correspondents to attend, not just the favored representatives of supportive newspapers, helped the President, a Democrat, to overcome the partisan imbalance among the largest daily newspapers, which were heavily Republican in orientation. Roosevelt, as a Republican, had been able to restrict his comments largely to the "fair-haired boys" from leading party newspapers, such as the *New York Sun,* and still reach most of the newspaper reading audience. Wilson had no comparable base of support in the daily press in a period when partisanship flavored the news pages as well as the editorial pages. Furthermore, the owners of the largest groups of ostensibly Democratic papers, William Randolph Hearst and E. W. Scripps, either had opposed Wilson's candidacy for the party's presidential nomination in 1912 or offered him lukewarm support in the general election.[9]

Meeting with most of the correspondents as a group also allowed the President to limit the time he spent with them individually, encounters that Wilson did not enjoy. Roosevelt had found journalists to be a bully audience. Wilson regarded them as a necessary evil. While governor of New Jersey, he tried to maintain an "open door" policy for journalists and found that his published comments were often garbled, misrepresented, or sensationalized.[10] He viewed the Washington correspondents generally as unimpressive intellects who were primarily concerned with trivia and with invading the President's family life.[11]

Not surprisingly, given Wilson's defensiveness, the President's first press conference, 11 days after his inauguration, went awkwardly. The magazine writer Edward G. Lowry described it as "chill and correct." Lowry wrote: "Mr. Wilson stood behind his desk, his visitors filed in and stood in a thickened crescent before him. There was a pause, a cool silence, and presently some one ventured a tentative question. It was answered crisply, politely, and in the fewest possible words. A pleasant time was not had by all."[12] Wilson tried again a week later, beginning with a conciliatory statement that invited the 200 correspondents in attendance to join him in a partnership for the good of the nation. However, he also left them puzzled when he called upon them not to "tell the country what Washington is thinking, for that does not make any difference. Tell Washington what the country is thinking."[13]

Nevertheless, the President kept trying, in his fashion, and the correspondents appreciated the personal access, which at first was twice a week. At the conferences, Wilson rarely made opening announcements. Instead, he prepared himself diligently to receive questions on the policy issues of the day and to give what he regarded as responsive replies. But transcripts of the conferences indicate that he often was evasive, answered questions as briefly as possible, resisted speculation on issues that had not been decided, and rarely allowed himself to be quoted, directly or indirectly. Asked to allow the quotation of his remarks about a pending tariff bill on 26 May 1913, Wilson at first replied, "I don't know what I just said, because I am on guard in talking to you fellows this way." However, the statement he subsequently dictated, which denounced lobbying on the bill, made headlines across the country.[14]

The correspondents generally welcomed the President's willingness to meet with them regularly and to provide them something to write about. But the conferences themselves sometimes seemed more like lectures at which Wilson, the professor, rebuked the correspondents for inadequate homework on their questions. "Well, now, gentlemen, do I have to go over that ground again and again?" Wilson complained on 30 October 1913 when asked about relations with Mexico. "I have given you all that I know about the subject."[15]

Oulahan, who had left the *New York Sun* to become chief correspondent of the *New York Times* in Washington, admired Wilson but nevertheless noted that the President was quick to detect hostility in any but the most respectful inquiries.[16] Charles Willis Thompson, another *New York Times* correspondent, said Wilson did not apologize after his angry outbursts but would try to make amends later. Thompson was impressed at first with Wilson but later came to regard the President as often misleading and sometimes untruthful.[17] Hugh Baillie, later president of United Press, was impressed with Wilson's oratory but found the President's news conferences "small but very formal. What you saw there was his severe manner, his long Covenanter countenance, his cold and challenging eye. And he could be brutal to anyone he didn't respect."[18]

Wilson often quibbled with or evaded questions to which he did not want to respond directly. "Of course, I bluffed you," Wilson admitted at his 3 January 1914 press conference. "This has been a real 'much ado about nothing,' as a matter of fact, because I think I earned your gratitude by presenting you with a live opportunity to make copy, but as a matter of fact, and speaking seriously, what I gave you at first was literally true."[19] Privately, he told his close advisor, Col. Edward House, that he saw nothing wrong with "grazing the truth" on sensitive issues, especially when foreign policy was involved.[20] Hugh Baillie described Wilson's answers as "so artful that the meaning of what he said didn't dawn on the people in the delegation until they were outside."[21] David Lawrence, once Wilson's student at Princeton University and later a columnist and founder of *U.S. News and World Report,* said the reporters gradually lost faith in Wilson's candor, even if they still attended his press conferences. Wilson could be imperious or evasive, but he was still the president and a source of potentially useful information.[22]

Wilson, in turn, was displeased when the correspondents' stories failed to reflect what he wanted them to say. He frequently used the press conferences to complain about newspaper stories that he did not like, although he tried to maintain a bantering tone. "Who fanned the fiction that I have abolished Cabinet meetings?"Wilson demanded at his 9 October 1913 press conference.[23] On 26 January 1914,Wilson chided the correspondents about "some interesting fiction" he had read about U.S. troops being sent to Mexico.[24]

Wilson's private letters bristle with hostile comments about the press.[25] In letters to his first wife, Ellen Axson Wilson, and to a close friend, Mary Allen Hulbert, in the summer and fall of 1913, he repeatedly criticized the press. "Believe very little that you read in the *Times*," he wrote to Mrs.Wilson on 7 September 1913."Do not believe anything you read in the newspapers. If you read the papers I see, they are utterly untrustworthy," he wrote to Mrs. Hulbert on 21 September 1913.

At least part of Wilson's frustration resulted from renewed press interest in the president's family. Unlike the rambunctious Roosevelts, Taft's children had grown to college age and moved out on their own by the time he became president.The First Lady, Helen Herron Taft, did not often seek publicity after suffering a stroke in 1909 that hampered her ability to speak.Wilson's presidency, however, coincided with the dropping of barriers against women participating in politics. Both the First Ladies in his administration, Ellen Axson Wilson, who died in 1914, and Edith Bolling Galt, whom the President married in 1915, took public positions on political issues.[26]

Especially irksome to Wilson was the press fascination with his three teen-age daughters, which began during the campaign of 1912. "Father was very courteous and patient when he himself was questioned, but he resented almost fiercely the attempts to pry into family affairs and tried to protect us as much as he could," recalled Eleanor Wilson McAdoo. "I have always believed that the first rumors of his 'aloofness' and 'unfriendliness' were the result of his annoyance at this first onslaught upon us."[27]

The President's daughters were independent young women with active political and social lives. Two of the daughters, Jessie and Eleanor, were married in the White House within a six-month period in 1913–14, in the full glare of newspaper and magazine coverage.The press's fascination with his daughters' romances so displeased Wilson that he lost his temper and harangued reporters at length after newspaper stories revealed Eleanor's engagement to William G. McAdoo,Wilson's secretary of the treasury.[28]

Wilson's ostensible reason for discontinuing the presidential press conferences in June 1915 was the sensitivity of the deteriorating international situation. However, the President clearly was frustrated with the conduct of the press conferences, even though, by other measures, they had been reasonably successful. Despite Wilson's complaints and the strained atmosphere, the presidency had received increased prominence in news coverage. Most of the stories about Wilson that appeared in newspapers and magazines were quite favorable.[29]

The correspondents as well as the President had benefited from Wilson's press conferences, despite the conflicts and complaints. The opportunity to meet with the President regularly and to hear his pronouncements not only gave the correspondents something to write about, it raised their stature professionally. The press conferences were at first so popular an attraction that they drew large, mixed crowds to the White House, which nearly proved to be their undoing. Confronted with correspondents and hangers-on who competed with one another for attention and for "scoops" or tips that might influence the stock market, Wilson threatened in July 1913 to discontinue the conferences after "certain evening newspapers" quoted him without permission on his comments about Mexico. The President demanded some sort of self-regulation, which led to the founding of the White House Correspondents Association, patterned after the Standing Committee of Correspondents of the Congressional Press Galleries. Oulahan, then chairman of the Standing Committee, drew up regulations stipulating that the President could not be quoted without his consent, among other rules of conduct. The regulations also restricted access to the press conferences to accredited reporters, a significant step in the establishment of an organized White House press corps. After Wilson ended his regularly scheduled press conferences, the correspondents' association continued to meet as a social group until Warren G. Harding called upon it to screen attendance at his revived presidential press conferences in 1921.[30]

The consensus among the correspondents was that President Wilson had found the press conferences tiresome and unproductive, too much like a "town meeting," from which irrelevant questions led to irresponsible news stories.[31] The opening question at Wilson's 2 February 1914 press conference, for example, sought the President's thoughts on Groundhog Day.[32] After ending the regularly scheduled conferences in June 1915, Wilson held only one more open press conference during his first term, late in the reelection campaign of 1916. Otherwise, he delegated the chore of meeting with the correspondents in his first term to his secretary, Joseph P. Tumulty. Tumulty's background was in New Jersey Democratic politics, not in newspapering, but he understood the importance of lobbying the correspondents to generate favorable publicity for Wilson. Tumulty befriended the correspondents, supplied them with newsworthy information, jollied them on Wilson's behalf, and smoothed over the President's frequent complaints. He held his own informal news briefings, at 10 A.M.

each day, with a calculated candor and good humor that contrasted with Wilson's prickliness. Tumulty also wrote the President daily advisories on trends in news coverage and stage-managed Wilson's most important first-term announcements.[33] In his memoirs, Tumulty described his job as "the connecting link between the President and the outside world." He wrote that "the Secretary is the political barometer of the White House, the creator of White House atmosphere, the 'inexhaustible fount of copy' for the press of the country, as the Washington correspondents like to believe, although the belief is never wholly realized."[34]

However, Tumulty fell out of favor with Wilson after he joined the President's other political advisors in recommending against his marriage to Edith Bolling Galt, at least before the reelection campaign of 1916 was over. Ellen Axson Wilson, the President's first wife, had died of liver disease in August 1914. Wilson's courtship of Mrs. Galt, less than a year later, became the subject of ribald jokes and considerable newspaper speculation. Over the objections of Tumulty and other political advisors, Wilson married his second First Lady in December 1915. She demanded subsequently that Tumulty be fired.[35] After his reelection in 1916, Wilson sought Tumulty's resignation. However, Tumulty's popularity with the press prompted David Lawrence and other correspondents to appeal to the President to retain him as secretary. Wilson agreed eventually to do so, although Tumulty never fully regained the confidence of Wilson or of the new First Lady.[36]

Despite the successes of the press conferences and Tumulty's lobbying of the correspondents on the President's behalf, Wilson remained dissatisfied with the press. In March 1914, Wilson wrote to Senator W. J. Stone that "I am so accustomed to having everything reported erroneously that I have almost come to the point of believing nothing that I see in the newspapers."[37]

Wilson more than once considered creating a presidential "publicity bureau," a peacetime ministry of information, to try to centralize in the White House the growing flow of information from government sources to the press. Wilson was concerned not only with news coverage of his messages but also with distracting leaks, announcements, and other unwelcome stories from publicists in the executive branch, including some hired by his Cabinet members. Taft had tried to ignore these leaks, with disastrous results, during the Ballinger-Pinchot controversy. Despite, or perhaps because of, Taft's seeming indifference to departmental publicity, practices such as hiring publicists and issuing "handouts" to stimulate news coverage had been adopted by numerous executive agencies.[38] Even Gifford Pinchot, who had done as much as anyone to encourage departmental publicity under Roosevelt and Taft, was impressed with how widely such practices had spread. Writing after the election of 1916, Pinchot advised Roosevelt that editors were becoming so inundated with press bureau handouts that their automatic publication could no longer be assured.[39]

The use of these publicity techniques by the President and agency press bureaus had been more or less accepted by the Washington press corps. One reason for this was that the increasing number of publicists and their handouts made it easier to do their jobs. By 1916, the flow of handouts to the press was such that some correspondents were able to make a living simply by rewriting the daily supply.[40] The new government press offices also offered reliable employment to correspondents who were paid previously on space rates and only when Congress was in session. Wilson's victory in 1912 increased the prospects for the hiring of Democrats, as well as Republicans, for these prized government publicity jobs. A 1913 story in *Editor and Publisher* referred to Democratic correspondents who "may have had their eye" on the job of "press representative" in the Wilson administration's Post Office.[41]

From Wilson's perspective, however, these publicists generated a continuing stream of unwanted leaks and news stories that interfered with his goal of projecting a unified administration point of view to the citizenry. Unlike Taft, Wilson did not have an aggressive agency publicist like Pinchot campaigning to undermine his policies. But Wilson struggled from the beginning to persuade his Cabinet appointees and other executive administrators to accept his authority and to present the White House's viewpoint in their dealings with the press.

For Wilson to try to exert substantial influence over Cabinet members was in itself novel in a period when such appointments traditionally went to semiautonomous party elders.[42] Wilson, however, believed that a strong president should also be the party leader and policymaker. Cabinet members should be administrators, rather than policy advocates.[43] Nevertheless, party demands for prominence and patronage had forced Wilson to appoint a Cabinet that included such independently outspoken members as Secretary of State William Jennings Bryan, the three-time Democratic presidential candidate.[44] Bryan, whose powerful oratory for reform had made him a shaping force in the Democratic party and in national public opinion, insisted on being allowed to continue his paid lecture tours. Bryan's oratory may have helped to stimulate public support for the Wilson administration, but his speaking engagements also led to embarrassing news stories about Wilson's secretary of state appearing on stage with jugglers, female impersonators, yodelers, and other entertainers.[45]

Several other Cabinet appointees followed the emerging custom of hiring personal publicists, which further complicated Wilson's goal of having the administration speak to the press and public with a single voice.[46] One week after Wilson appointed Josephus Daniels, a newspaperman, to be secretary of the navy, Daniels met with the admirals to see about increasing publicity about the Navy. "Too little is published, and I planned to see that the public is acquainted with all that happens of interest," he noted in his diary.[47] The new attorney general, James C. McReynolds, hired as his "confidential secretary" John T. Suter, a prominent former newspaper correspondent who had previously been a publicist for the Post Office.[48] Wilson's secretary of the interior, Franklin K. Lane, was a talkative former West Coast newspaperman with many acquaintances in the press.[49]

Not surprisingly, some of the Cabinet members, especially Lane, talked freely with the correspondents after their meetings with Wilson, leading to newspaper stories that irked the President by prompting questions at subsequent White House press conferences. On 11 April 1913, for example, only weeks after his inauguration, Wilson was asked by correspondents about a leaked story that the Cabinet was considering requiring all government employees to start work at 8 A.M.[50] One week later, Wilson faced unwelcome questions on the sensitive issue of alien land ownership, based on a talk the reporters had had with Secretary of State Bryan. Bryan had begun to hold regular meetings with reporters at the State Department and to supply them with background material. These departmental briefings led to inconvenient newspaper stories when, as at the President's news conferences, the correspondents could not be limited in their questioning.[51]

In May 1913, Secretary of the Navy Daniels noted that Wilson was "greatly put out" to learn that an enterprising correspondent, Joseph K. Ohl, of the *New York Herald,* was asking well-informed questions about secret plans to send the Pacific fleet to the Far East in case of war with Japan.[52] By July 1913, only four months after his inauguration, leaks had become such a concern to Wilson that he told reporters that he was recalling Ambassador Henry Lane Wilson from Mexico to talk to him in person about the deteriorating situation there, "instead of through telegrams, which we feel may leak at any time."[53]

By the fall of 1913, Wilson's growing concern with leaks and his general unhappiness with the press was leading him to consider how he might assert greater presidential control over executive branch publicity. Congress, too, was concerned with the spread of agency press bureaus. In September 1913, the legislators approved a measure that forbade unauthorized executive branch hiring of "publicity experts." Asked at a press conference on 6 October 1913 about the congressional action, Wilson replied: "I am entirely against the way publicity agents have been used." Wilson then for the first time mentioned publicly the idea that it might be better to centralize government publicity in the White House.[54]

Before proposing so drastic a step, however, Wilson tried a variety of internal measures to stem the flow of leaks. He had planned originally to hold two Cabinet meetings a week to conduct expansive seminars on administration policy.[55] But, as the leaks continued, Wilson scheduled Cabinet meetings less frequently and limited the scope of their discussions. Ironically, Wilson's plan to limit Cabinet meetings was itself leaked to the press, which drew a prickly presidential response at a 9 October 1913 press conference. Wilson denied a *New York Sun* story that he was considering abolishing Cabinet meetings entirely, which he called "one of the most magnificent fictions that has been started."[56]

In December 1913, Wilson made a direct appeal at his Cabinet meeting to curb comments to the press. He asked Secretary of Agriculture David F. Houston to raise the issue of leaks, then took the opportunity to request the cooperation of all Cabinet members in allowing the President to determine what should remain confidential in their discussions. "Some things cannot be given publicity; at any rate, at once," Wilson said. "It is important to consider what shall be said, and how and when. I ought to have the privilege of determining this." Houston's account notes that the Cabinet quickly endorsed Wilson's request, although whether the President's appeal had any impact on the more talkative members is unclear.[57] By early 1914, Wilson found it more secure to deal with his Cabinet members individually or by letter.[58]

Wilson was especially concerned about newspaper stories on foreign affairs that he felt could wrongly influence public opinion. Throughout the winter of 1913–14, Wilson used his news conferences to characterize news accounts about problems with the Huerta regime in Mexico as "wrong" or "fake."[59] He warned reporters in January 1914 that speculative stories about foreign policy were embarrassing the government: "I do not think that the newspapers of the country have the right to embarrass their own country in the settlement of matters which have to be handled with delicacy and candor."[60]

Secretary of State Bryan, no doubt prompted by Wilson's concerns about leaks on foreign policy, made several attempts on his own to control the inquisitiveness of the correspondents. The State Department had taken an increasing interest in publicity since the Spanish-American War. During the Taft administration, the agency had been reorganized to include a Division of Information, which was headed by a former newspaperman,

Philip H. Patchin, of the *New York Sun,* who served as the agency's chief publicist. Taft's Secretary of State, Philander Knox, for a time had held regular briefings for correspondents.[61]

When Bryan reinstated these regular press briefings, he quickly ran into troublesome questions about foreign policy that he did not wish to answer. In July 1913, Bryan suggested that the State Department refuse to answer all correspondents' questions on policy announcements until the President decided it was appropriate to do. Later, in February 1915, Bryan, backed by Robert Lansing, then secretary of war, tried to persuade Wilson to try to bar correspondents entirely from the hallways of the State Department. Tumulty, however, warned Wilson that attempting such a move would alienate the correspondents.[62]

These concerns about unwelcome news stories from executive publicists, especially on foreign policy, underlay Wilson's continuing interest in creating a centralized "publicity bureau," which he described in a 1 June 1914 letter to Charles W. Eliot, former president of Harvard University. Wilson wanted to rein in publicity activity within the government, which he believed was wrongly influencing what the press was writing: "We have several times considered the possibility of having a publicity bureau which would handle the real facts as far as the government was aware of them, for all the departments. . . . Since I came here I have wondered how it ever happened that the public got a right impression regarding public affairs, particularly foreign affairs." Wilson acknowledged that centralizing executive publicity in the presidency was not a complete solution. "The real trouble is that the newspapers get the real facts but do not find them to their taste and do not use them as given them, and in some of the newspaper offices news is deliberately invented," he wrote.[63]

Wilson ultimately did not act on the proposal in his first term, presumably after objections by Tumulty, but his frustrations continued. In a 9 August 1915 letter to Edith Bolling Galt, Wilson wrote: "Always the newspapers! They make the normal and thorough conduct of the public business impossible."[64]

As United States involvement in the war in Europe, which had broken out in August 1914, became more likely, Wilson tried to assert more control over executive announcements, especially those dealing with foreign affairs. The President was himself adept at using leaks to place important pieces of information before the public that the administration could not openly endorse.[65] In December 1916, for instance, Wilson meticulously managed through the State Department the publicizing of a request to the warring European powers for acceptable peace terms. Keeping the diplomatic note secret in the White House, even from Tumulty, Wilson directed

Secretary of State Lansing, who had succeeded Bryan, to alert the correspondents at a morning briefing about an impending announcement, then to release it in the afternoon. When Lansing took it upon himself to interpret the President's note to reporters as an indication that the United States was drawing closer to war, an angry Wilson summoned Lansing to the White House and required him to issue a second statement retracting his earlier remarks. Wilson and Lansing carefully planned the leak, through the Associated Press, of the infamous Zimmermann note revealing Germany's imperial ambitions, which created a national sensation.[66]

Nevertheless, sensitive information continued to leak from the Cabinet to the press, despite Wilson's exhortations to his Cabinet and direct presidential intervention in executive announcements. After a Cabinet meeting on the afternoon of 21 March 1917, called to discuss a possible declaration of war against Germany, Wilson gave 50 waiting correspondents only a general statement. Later that evening, at least two Cabinet members revealed to reporters that Wilson intended to call Congress into special session within two weeks. White House aide Thomas W. Brahany named as the leakers Secretary of the Treasury McAdoo, by now Wilson's son-in-law, and Secretary of the Interior Lane.[67]

These first-term experiences formed an important context for Wilson's subsequent decisions to seek and to use wartime authority to establish stronger presidential controls over both the press and executive publicity practices. In his formative first term, he had reinvigorated the relationship between the president and the White House press corps that Taft had neglected. Despite Wilson's frustrations with the regularly scheduled presidential press conferences, the experiment represented an important step toward formalizing White House influence over the daily news from Washington, D.C.

However, Wilson's goal of speaking to the public on behalf of a unified administration had been frustrated by centrifugal developments in the executive branch, particularly the spreading use of press bureaus to advocate Cabinet and agency interests. Managing the press through handouts and other techniques of publicity was no longer the exclusive province of the White House. Despite presidential exhortations and congressional restrictions, publicists and press bureaus in the departments were establishing their own relationships with the press to generate news coverage.

These experiences taught Wilson that keeping sensitive information out of the newspapers was not only a matter of managing the correspondents at the White House. He needed greater authority over both the government and the press to persuade the public to support his war policies, beginning with the ability to centralize the flow of government information in the White House. From this perspective, Wilson's decision to create the Committee on Public Information in 1917 to mobilize the mass media to support the war effort was not a wartime aberration but an intensification of peacetime presidential initiatives to seek increased public support by managing the press.

CHAPTER SEVEN

PRESIDENTIAL PROPAGANDA IN WORLD WAR I

World War I was the first of the twentieth-century wars in which the federal government deployed recognizably modern techniques of mass persuasion to rally public support for the war effort. When the United States entered the war in April 1917, President Woodrow Wilson created the nation's first ministry of information, the Committee on Public Information (CPI), to appeal to citizens in their newspapers, magazines, theaters, libraries, schools, and homes. Under its assertive director, George Creel, the CPI launched an extraordinary promotional campaign, the legacy of which has been debated ever since.[1] At the same time, the Wilson administration vigorously wielded its wartime emergency powers to try to stifle the flow of sensitive information and to suppress dissenting views thought likely to undermine the war effort at home or on the battlefield.[2]

The result, according to Wilson's critics, was a threatening period of propaganda and censorship. The Committee on Public Information was surrounded by controversy from its creation in 1917 until Congress forced its liquidation two years later. The public reputations of Creel and others who joined in its wartime activities were tainted.[3] More than a dozen years later, critics of President Franklin D. Roosevelt warned that his key aides, including his press secretary, Stephen Early, and appointments secretary, Marvin McIntyre, had once worked for the CPI.[4]

However, the Committee on Public Information is only the best known of the presidential experiments in manipulating public opinion that took place during World War I. Wilson created several other presidential agencies that tried to use the mass media to guide public opinion toward his war policies. Prominent among these was the work of the U.S.

Food Administration, which launched a promotional campaign urging food conservation, whose intrusiveness into the nation's domestic life rivaled that of the CPI.

As pointed out in the previous chapter, these presidential campaigns to rally public support through mass persuasion were not wartime aberrations. Like much of the war effort, Wilson's information policies reflected an intensification of trends in government and society already under way at the turn of the century. Nevertheless, the wartime campaigns represented a significant expansion of presidential authority over the molding of public opinion through the press and other means of mass communications.[5]

The Wilson administration had experimented extensively with managing the press, both in the White House and executive agencies, to influence public opinion during the President's first term. The proliferation of government publicity had prompted Wilson to consider creating a "publicity bureau" in the White House to try to prevent or to control leaks that led to unwelcome stories in the press. Entry of the United States into the war in April 1917 gave him that opportunity. Creating the Committee on Public Information gave Wilson the institutional support that he hoped would enable him to control the flow of information from the executive branch more effectively, to manage press coverage more successfully, and, in doing so, to create public support for the war effort.

Launching the CPI followed months of discussion in the Wilson administration. After his reelection in November 1916, Wilson had become increasingly concerned with maintaining public support if the United States, as seemed increasingly likely, were to enter the war in Europe. To persuade the citizenry to send an army to Europe and to endure sacrifices at home, the President would need to convince Americans that the cause was just and that the hardships were necessary. Given the nation's isolationist past and the political turbulence of the progressive reform period, an extraordinary campaign of mass persuasion would be necessary.[6]

Wilson's first-term experiences had taught him that he could not rely on the press to inform the public appropriately, at least without guidance. The frequent failings of the newspapers reflected an inherent irresponsibility, in the President's view. Wilson declined to revive his first-term press conferences on a regular basis or even to grant the requests of friendly correspondents for interviews. He rejected pleas from his advisors to grant an interview to Roy Howard. of United Press, for instance, even though the owner of United Press, E. W. Scripps, had contributed significantly to the President's narrow reelection victory.[7]

Wilson was convinced, with some justification, that the press would reveal his confidential remarks or speculate in ways that could worsen the deteriorating international situation.[8] "In ordinary times, when our affairs are domestic affairs, we could exercise a great deal of freedom about that, but just now such—let me say excessive—importance is attached to the President's opinions that a thing offhand may have an effect that was not contemplated beforehand," he told correspondents in January 1917.[9] In a meeting with a British diplomat one week after the United States declared war on Germany, Wilson declared that American newspapers were wholly unreliable, ignorant, and prone to inventing stories that had no basis in fact.[10]

To provide needed guidance for the press and to shape popular opinion toward the war effort, Wilson had in mind an enlarged version of the "publicity bureau" that he considered creating in his first term. Creel, a former muckraking journalist and campaign worker who became director of the new Committee on Public Information, told Wilson that the CPI's primary focus should be on promoting the war effort by supplying uplifting information to the press and public, rather than by trying to suppress bad news through censorship. In a memorandum to the President, Creel wrote: "The suppressive features of the work must be so overlaid by the publicity policy that they will go unregarded and unresented. Administration activities must be dramatized and staged, and every energy exerted to arouse ardor and enthusiasm. Recruiting can be stimulated and public confidence gained, extortion can be exposed and praise given to the patriotism that abates its profits; and in the rush of generous feeling much that is evil and nagging will disappear."[11] When Wilson created the Committee on Public Information by executive order in April 1917, Creel told correspondents that the agency would emphasize publicity, not censorship.[12]

Nevertheless, Wilson believed that some censorship would be necessary to protect the war effort from damaging information in leaks or from destructive dissent. The President was opposed to "more than moderate" censorship, he told the Cabinet on 6 April 1917.[13] But when the proposed Espionage Act was submitted to Congress a week later, the administration asked for broad authority to exclude "treasonous" materials from public distribution, whether by the postal service or in the press. Despite strenuous objections from critics of the war, civil libertarians, and newspaper publishers, Wilson insisted that a president in wartime should be empowered to censor the press, if it became necessary. In a letter to the *New York Times* published on 23 May 1917, Wilson argued: "I have every confidence that the great majority of the newspapers of the country will observe a patriotic reticence about everything whose publication could be of injury, but in every country there are some persons in a position to do mischief in this field who cannot be relied upon and whose interests or desires will lead to actions on their party highly dangerous to the nation in the midst of a war. I want to say again that it seems to be imperative that powers of this sort be granted."[14]

After considerable debate, Congress refused the President's request for authority to censor the press, at least directly.[15] But Wilson was granted broad authority to suppress information by other means, not only in the Espionage Act, but in the Trading With the Enemy Act (1917) and the Sedition Act (1918). Wilson declined to intervene when his Cabinet members, especially Postmaster General Albert S. Burleson and Attorney General Thomas W. Gregory, used this authority vigorously to suppress dissent. Burleson moved quickly to revoke or to restrict the postal privileges of magazines that he deemed to be unpatriotic or disloyal to the war effort. Confronted with complaints from prominent reformers in July 1917, after Burleson revoked the mailing privileges of *The Masses* magazine and several smaller left-wing or anti-war publications, Wilson was sympathetic. But he did not act to reverse Burleson's actions.[16] Under Attorney General Gregory, the Justice Department moved to arrest and to jail Socialists, pacifists, German-Americans, and labor leaders, including the 1912 presidential candidate Eugene W. Debs, who was imprisoned for sedition. In 1919, after the Russian Revolution, Gregory's successor, A. Mitchell Palmer, launched a series of raids and arrests nationally against dissenters, which became known as the "Palmer raids," during a period described as the "Red Scare." To Wilson, civil liberties were important, but they were secondary to the primary goals of winning the war and maintaining order at home.[17]

Moreover, despite Creel's claims, the Committee on Public Information itself became involved in censorship. When Wilson created a Censorship Board in October 1917 to coordinate suppressive activities, Creel served on the board as the representative of the CPI.[18] Involvement in censorship, however peripheral, tarnished the reputations of both Creel and the agency, even though their main work focused on stimulating popular support for the war effort. The agency's official purpose was to create and to disseminate patriotic appeals through all available means of mass communications, including newspaper and magazine stories and advertisements, books, pamphlets, billboards, placards, speeches, and films. Creel avoided using the word "propaganda," previously a vaguely positive term that became associated during the war with heavy-handed emotional appeals and exaggerated atrocity claims. The word "has come to have an ominous clang in many minds," Harold Lasswell commented after the war.[19]

Creel argued in the CPI's privately published final report that "In all things, from first to last, without halt or change, it was a plain publicity proposition, a vast enterprise into salesmanship, the world's greatest adventure in advertising."[20] Mark Sullivan, the magazine columnist, observed that the techniques of "propaganda" often were little different from those known before the war as "publicity."[21]

However it was characterized, much of the promotional work of the CPI also resembled experiments in managing the press that had been conducted by presidents and executive administrators before the war. The CPI's earliest work consisted of publicizing and distributing copies of the President's speeches and statements supporting his war policies. Millions of pamphlets were sent to the citizenry, and newspapers and magazines frequently reprinted them.[22]

Creating the CPI allowed the President to delegate to Creel the frustrating chore of dealing with the press, a duty that had grown during Wilson's first term into an important and demanding White House assignment. Wilson became largely unavailable for press questioning during the war, and his secretary, Tumulty, suspended his daily briefings at the White House. The correspondents were sent instead to the press room of the CPI for information and briefings about the President's activities. Creel became, in effect, Wilson's wartime press secretary.[23]

At the heart of the CPI's relationship with the press was what Creel termed the "central information bureau," the Division of News, which relied partly on information gathered by peacetime newspaper correspondents who were recruited to "cover" the announcements of wartime agencies. Their job, Creel wrote, was to "'get the news,' to develop 'stories,' and to aid the department in an expert way to put the best foot forward."[24] One of the goals of the agency correspondence system was to try to coordinate the publicity activities of the major executive departments. Creel's 11 April 1917 memorandum to Wilson specified that the Cabinet departments of Agriculture, Labor, Commerce, Interior, Treasury, and Justice would be visited by CPI correspondents on a daily basis.[25] Three or four correspondents each were to be assigned to the war-related departments of State, War, and Navy, whose secretaries formed the supervising committee of the CPI.[26]

But Creel's plan to centralize the flow of executive branch war information in the CPI was complicated by the same institutional forces that frustrated Wilson's first-term attempts to control news from his Cabinet and agency press bureaus. The most prominent Cabinet holdout was Secretary of State Lansing, who refused to cooperate with Creel or the CPI, even though he was a member of its supervisory committee. The State Department already had its own division of information, which Lansing upgraded and expanded into a Division of Foreign Intelligence.[27] Lansing wanted to impose much stronger controls on the press, similar to those employed by the British, than did Creel. In addition, Lansing personally disliked and distrusted Creel, as he did Tumulty.[28] In an effort to persuade Lansing to cooperate, Wilson wrote a revealing letter to Breckenridge Long, an assistant secretary of state, which acknowledged that the CPI made mistakes early in the war. The President blamed them on "lawless" elements in the press, the "petty jealousy" of the correspondents, and, pointedly, at the lack of cooperation from the State Department: "It has been difficult to get one or two of the executive departments, notably the Department of State, to act through Mr. Creel's committee in the matter of publicity, and the embarrassments of lack of coordination and single management have been serious indeed."[29]

Despite Lansing's lack of cooperation, Creel had the support of Wilson, Tumulty, Secretary of the Navy Daniels, and Secretary of War Newton Baker. That gave the Committee on Public Information general control over most of the important war news.[30] From these and other sources, the Division of News sent approximately 6,000 news releases to the press in Washington and around the nation. The flood of news releases from the CPI and other wartime agencies went far to complete the institutionalization of the "handout" as a preferred form of communication between the government and the news media. Creel claimed that by December 1917, seven months into the war, every newspaper in California had received an average of six pounds of publicity materials from the government, enough to fill more than 1,200 newspaper columns.[31]

However, distribution of these handouts to the press did not guarantee that they would be published in the form desired by Wilson and Creel. Even in wartime, the press was under no constitutional obligation to reprint the handouts exactly as the Division of News had written them or even to use them at all. Many newspapers did, however. Journalists, like many other citizens, were caught up in the patriotic fervor, and the CPI was the only authoritative source of war news. But that did not prevent the press from speculating about, sensationalizing, or sometimes ignoring wartime announcements. In wartime, Wilson faced the same challenge that often frustrated his plans to lead public opinion in his first term: how to get the press to report responsibly on what the administration wanted to say.

Here, Wilson had a solution in mind: he long had envisioned a "national" newspaper to overcome the inherent localism of the U.S. press and to provide support for the president as national leader.[32] Creel credited Wilson with suggesting the creation of a government-operated "daily gazette" to publish a record of official acts and proceedings, as well as to provide an information link between the wartime agencies.[33] On 18 April 1917, Wilson sent a letter to Creel recommending the creation of a "national bulletin" to publish the government's notices and to answer anticipated public questions about government war policies. The letter was also signed by members of one of the President's new interagency groups, the War Trade Committee, made up of officials from the Justice, State, and Commerce Departments.[34]

Beginning on 10 May 1917, the CPI began to publish the administration's statements and announcements in the *Official Bulletin,* the nation's first official government-operated newspaper.[35] The newspaper, actually more of a newsletter, was published from May 1917 through March 1919. Circulation at one point reached 115,000 copies an issue. It was sent to public officials, newspapers, and war-related organizations, as well as posted in Post Offices and military camps. In addition to helping to centralize in the presidency the flow of official information, the *Official Bulletin* was useful in coordinating the wartime activities of various government programs, industry, the Red Cross, and wartime organizations.[36]

From Wilson's perspective, creation of the CPI and publication of the *Official Bulletin* provided at least partial solutions to the related problems of uncontrolled publicity within the executive branch and the inevitable distortion of sensitive information by an irresponsible press. For the first time, the flow of information from the government had been centralized institutionally under the President's control, and Wilson now had a reliable newspaper voice to appeal for public support for his policies.

But creation of a government newspaper, in addition to Wilson's request for authority to censor the press, alarmed the newspaper industry and the President's critics in Congress. Major newspapers attacked the *Official Bulletin* as a threat to freedom of the press and eventually prompted a congressional investigation into its activities.[37] The outspoken Creel created his own series of controversies, and Wilson had to defend him from demands in the press and in Congress to create a newspaper supervisory board for the CPI. When journalists spurred Wilson's critics in Congress to pursue the investigation of the CPI, Creel stopped sending copies of the *Official Bulletin* to the newspapers involved. After those editors objected to the loss of war news, he replied that they should "take it up with their congressmen." At one point, faced with congressional questions about his loyalty, Creel told reporters undiplomatically: "I don't like slumming, so I won't explore into the hearts of Congress for you."[38]

These controversies involving Creel tended to overshadow the President's role in guiding the wartime persuasion activities. The CPI was an institutional extension of the presidency, and Wilson closely oversaw its decision making. When Congressman Albert Johnson of Washington raised critical questions about the *Official Bulletin,* Wilson wrote: "I would suggest that the Committee on Public Information was created by me, that Mr. Creel is my personal representative, and that he feels constrained in the circumstances to refer all inquiries about the Committee and the work it is doing to me."[39] After reviewing Creel's first annual report in January 1918, Wilson wrote approvingly that "I have kept in touch with that work, piece by piece, as you know, in our several interviews, but had not realized its magnitude when assembled in a single statement."[40]

Wilson wanted to use the CPI to coordinate all of the government's wartime promotional campaigns. But as new war-related agencies and programs were launched, they often created their own press bureaus, sometimes over Creel's objections. Those that did so included the Food and Fuel Administrations, the Council of National Defense, the War Industries Board, and the War Trade Board. Eventually, an estimated 50 press bureaus were at work in the government in 1917–19, including the existing executive branch publicity offices. Some of them, especially the Food Administration, launched publicity campaigns that were nearly as extensive as those of the CPI.

The Food Administration, like the CPI, represented a significant presidential intrusion into the nation's domestic life to try to manipulate public opinion toward the war effort.[41] At its height, the Food Administration reached into the kitchens and dining rooms of tens of millions of homes. Diners in restaurants were asked to make sure that they and their neighbors minimized wastage by following the 12 rules of restaurant eating. Retailers were expected to require every purchaser of wheat to buy an equal amount of another cereal. At one time or another, the agency, using the mass media, told citizens when to kill hens; when to eat meat, wheat, or pork; and to eat only two pounds of meat apiece each week. Violators faced not only possible fines, but a kind of punishment by publicity: Food Administrator Herbert Hoover would announce a public "stamp of shame" for people or establishments thought to be wasting food and thereby hurting the war effort. By any measurement, the Food Administration constituted an extension of presidential persuasion into the press and into American home life.[42]

Wilson had not intended the Food Administration to be a propaganda agency, at least originally. Its primary policy goal was to resolve wartime shortages in food supplies. As the United States prepared to enter the war, in April 1917, Wilson had been told that two years of poor crops had reduced the nation's food surpluses. Years of war in Europe had devastated many of that continent's agricultural areas, and additional U.S. food shipments would be needed to support the troops and to prevent widespread civilian suffering. In addition, the prospect of wartime shortages of key commodities such as wheat and meat had triggered growing speculation and inflation.[43]

To take charge of the food situation, Wilson turned to Herbert Hoover, a successful mining engineer who had become an admired public figure in both Europe and the United States because of his relief work early in the war. Frustrated with the pace of food shipments to Belgium in 1914, Hoover launched a worldwide publicity campaign from his home in England. He wrote: "We have carried on, with the assistance of practically the whole of the American press, an enormous propaganda campaign on the subject of the Belgian people."[44] In four years, Hoover's commission was able to raise $1 billion to transport 5 million tons of food to Belgium and to France.[45] The success of the Belgian food relief campaign made Hoover a logical choice to be food administrator after the United States entered the war.

But the President needed congressional authority to control the production, distribution, marketing, and consumption of food products. When Wilson sent his request to Congress, critics accused him of seeking excessive power. Newspaper stories warned that Hoover would be a "food dictator," a characterization denied by both Wilson and Hoover. Both men tried to reassure Congress that emergency powers would be used only sparingly.[46]

But the controversy was only the first delay in the torturous legislative journey of the Lever bill, which contained the President's regulatory authority over the food industry. Wilson's critics seized on the bill to express their unhappiness with the war and with the President's conduct of it.[47] Farm state legislators objected to price controls. An amendment to prohibit consumption of alcoholic beverages as a wartime conservation measure provoked additional controversy and delay. Congressional debate dragged on through the summer of 1917, even though American involvement in the war was well under way. Finally, in August 1917, four months after declaring war, Congress granted the Food Administration farreaching controls over food production, manufacture, and distribution.[48]

In the meantime, lacking statutory authority to regulate the food industry, Wilson and Hoover turned to mass persuasion to try to get citizens to carry out the administration's food conservation goals. Hoover already had given some thought to appealing to the people whom he believed controlled the nation's food consumption: women, housewives in particular. In a speculative magazine interview, Hoover suggested that the war was an opportunity to increase nobility and self-sacrifice among citizens by appealing to them to curb their extravagances voluntarily. "Much can be done by national propaganda to limit extravagance in eating, in dress and display," Hoover said. "We could give much more energy to this matter by a central bureau in Washington, with subcommittees all over the United States. That is one where we could use our women to great advantage. We are good advertisers. A few phrases, too, would turn the trick—the world lives by phrases, and we most of all perhaps. . . . We need some phrase that puts the stamp of shame on wasteful eating, dressing and display of jewelry."[49]

Hoover's patronizing views notwithstanding, the suggestion of a highly visible role in the war effort for women had an immediate appeal to leaders of the long campaign for women's suffrage, which was then nearing its culmination. The National American Woman Suffrage Association, the largest group lobbying for the right to vote, had approved a resolution in March 1917 that supported U.S. entry into the war. The resolution also asked Wilson pointedly to establish employment bureaus to help women find war work.[50] Wilson had agreed to expand the Council of National Defense, a super Cabinet he created to coordinate the war effort, to include a Women's Committee, led by the suffragist Anna Howard Shaw.[51] Not all women supported the war or the tactics of the National American Woman Suffrage Association. But a variety of women's groups saw in Hoover's proposal an opportunity to show their patriotism and to keep pressure on Wilson to support suffrage.[52]

Frustrated by the congressional delay, Wilson on 20 May 1917 declared Hoover to be "Food Administrator" by executive order and ordered him to plan a propaganda campaign aimed at women.[53] In Hoover's acceptance statement, reprinted in the *New York Times,* he said: "It is my present idea to propose a plan to the American women by which we ask every woman in control of the household to join as an actual member of the Food Administration and give us a pledge that she will, so far as her means and circumstances permit, carry out the instructions which we will give her in detail from time to time."[54] Hoover's statement was endorsed by the Women's Committee of the Council of National Defense in a statement from the muckraker Ida Tarbell, one of several prominent reformers to join the food conservation campaign.[55]

One month later, with Congress still stalled over the Lever bill, Wilson told Hoover to go ahead with what became one of the largest domestic propaganda campaigns of the war. "The women of the nation are already earnestly seeking to do their part in this, our greatest struggle for the maintenance of our national goals, and in no direction can they so greatly assist as by enlisting in the service of the Food Administration and cheerfully accepting its directions and advice," Wilson announced.[56]

As a first step, Hoover set out to persuade the nation's householders to register with the Food Administration by filling out and sending in pledge forms. Once registered, householders were sent two cards, one to be placed in their front window and a second "home card," with food-saving instructions, to be placed in the kitchen. For ten cents, a pledge pin was also available. To publicize and to distribute the pledge forms, Hoover appealed to women's organizations, the Boy Scouts, business groups, and the press.[57]

The pledge campaign took place in two phases. During the first phrase, July–August 1917, Hoover relied primarily on publicity to persuade households to send in pledge forms. He asked newspapers and magazines to print the forms voluntarily, as well as to publish stories about better nutritional practices. Supportive sermons by the nation's ministers were timed to coincide with the official launch of the campaign on 1 July 1917.[58]

To stimulate national news coverage, correspondents were called to the White House to watch First Lady Edith Galt Wilson place a red, white, and blue food pledge card in one of the windows. Promoting food conservation was only one of the First Lady's wartime public activities. She arranged for sheep to graze on the White House lawn and for the wool to be auctioned to raise money for the Red Cross. She also sewed pajamas, pillowcases and blankets, and joined film stars to promote the sale of war bonds.[59]

Lou Henry Hoover, later First Lady, became the primary administration spokeswoman for food conservation. In her first public speech, she made a patriotic appeal to housewives, restaurants, and food wholesalers and retailers. She invited reporters into her home to show how she complied with "wheatless and meatless days" and cut sugar consumption.[60] Newspaper and magazine articles inspired by her speeches and other Food Administration announcements in her name appeared throughout the summer and fall of 1917, urging women to join the campaign.[61]

The pledge campaign was renewed, with local organizational support, in September–October 1917.[62] Assisted by volunteer Ray Lyman Wilbur, president of Stanford University, Hoover put together state-level committees and organizations with help from women's groups, churches, civic clubs, Boy Scouts, and local politicians. An estimated 500,000 volunteers joined in the door-to-door canvassing, which led to registration of nearly 14 million households.[63]

Throughout the war, these households were sent a series of instructions from the President and Hoover urging them to conserve scarce commodities by practices that became known collectively as "Hooverizing": observing "meatless Mondays," "wheatless Wednesdays," and a variety of other commodity-less days.[64] The Food Administration called upon the nation's home economists for advice on preparing and sending out numerous pamphlets, placards, and home cards that described, among other things, how to use nutritional substitutes, plan menus, and dry vegetables; in sum, to eat more efficiently while eating well. To oversee the preparation and distribution of these advisories, Hoover established a Home Conservation Division in the Food Administration under the direction of Sarah Field Splint, then editor of *Today's Housewife* magazine.[65]

Similar food conservation appeals were directed at restaurants and hotels, food dealers, and grocery stores. Libraries and schools were sent a curriculum on nutrition for home economics courses. Hoover wrote Wilson that "we feel that, by taking advantage of the war emotion, we here have an opportunity of introducing intelligibly into the minds of the children, not only fundamental data on nutrition, but also of being able to probably secure its permanent inclusion in school curricula, and therefore, feel that it is a matter of more than ordinary propaganda importance."[66]

To reach the largest audiences, those of the nation's newspapers and magazines, the Food Administration created a formidable publicity operation, the Education Division, run by Ben Allen, a former Associated Press newsman who earlier had promoted Hoover's Belgian relief effort. Allen oversaw creation of Hoover's "partnership" with the nation's newspapers and magazines, beginning with an appeal to 2,500 editors that "we must trust to the guidance of the press of the country to secure the awakening of the national conscience to the dominant idea of food administration. To guide the public mind in these channels, we are wholly and absolutely dependent upon the press. . . . If we do not receive this support, the problem is hopeless. If we do have it, it can be solved."[67]

Under Allen and staff members drawn from newspapers and magazines, the Education Division blanketed the nation's mass media with press releases. From May 1917 to April 1919, Allen and his staff sent out 1,870 press releases. About 1,400 went to the Washington press corps and another 470 to the rural press and through state administrators to other media.[68] The division created special offices that focused on the magazine and feature markets, farm journals, trade and technical journals, the religious press, and the Negro press, as well as on generalized services like illustrations, exhibits, and motion pictures.[69] Many of the general news releases were published first as presidential proclamations in the *Official Bulletin*. In January 1918, for example, Hoover prepared a statement in which Wilson proclaimed officially the designation of wheatless Mondays and Wednesdays, meatless Tuesdays, and porkless Saturdays.[70]

Hoover was particularly interested in the publicity potential of women's magazines, since their reading audiences were the primary targets of the Food Administration's persuasion campaigns. Several of the top women's magazine editors joined the Education Division. Gertrude B. Lane, editor of *Woman's Home Companion,* became chief of the Magazine and Feature Section, where she served for most of the war. Under Lane, the section produced five stories a week for women's magazines and newspaper sections, and they were sent to a list of 3,000 publications. An estimated 80 percent of the releases consisted of practical advice to housewives in the form of menus, recipes, verse, short articles, and special advice for holiday entertaining. Educational topics under the general theme of "Food Will Win the War" included conserving fats or particular commodities, drying vegetables, canning at home, reducing milk consumption, and planning gardens. Other articles included patriotic exhortations to encourage women to "cook the Kaiser's goose on their own stoves."[71]

Edward Bok, editor of the *Ladies Home Journal,* the nation's largest women's magazine, volunteered the magazine's services to Wilson early in 1917. The *Ladies Home Journal* printed numerous Food Administration–generated articles throughout the war. Bok also volunteered the use of the magazine's own food experts to help prepare nutritional advice.[72] The magazine in March 1918 published an article, "Dining with the Hoovers," that showed how Lou Henry Hoover fed her family and conserved food at the same time.[73]

As a wartime agency heavily involved in publicity, the Food Administration ostensibly was subject to oversight by Creel and the Committee on Public Information. However, Hoover viewed his agency as a "separate, independent" organization that reported directly to the President, not to Creel.[74] Hoover did not want Creel interfering in his affairs, and he also feared that the Food Administration would be harmed by the aura of censorship that surrounded the CPI. When Creel requested that all Food Administration publicity material be submitted to the CPI for review and censoring, Hoover refused to do so on the ground that saving food was too remote from military activity to be a security risk.[75] Hoover did agree to designate a staff member in each Food Administration division as a combination publicist-censor. Since there was little censoring to do, the action in effect created a publicity person in every office, a practice that Hoover continued as secretary of commerce in the 1920s.[76] Throughout the war, Hoover sent frequent memoranda, proposed announcements, speeches, handouts, and other advisories to Wilson directly, whether the President wanted to see them or not.[77]

On other issues, however, Hoover cooperated with Creel. He was willing to use some of the CPI's services to promote food conservation, such as the Four-Minute Men and the CPI's Advertising Division. But the Food Administration also appealed directly to the advertising industry for volunteers. Under the direction of C. E. Raymond, a vice president of the J. Walter Thompson agency, the agency's own Advertising Section sought voluntary display opportunities, from periodicals to catalogs to movie theaters. Appeals were made to advertisers to include Food Administration themes in their campaigns, and to all mass media to donate space for advertisements, signs, and posters. A special appeal was made to seek space on billboards. Under the direction of R. C. Maxwell, president of a large outdoor advertising firm, the agency erected an electric sign containing 3,000 lamps in Washington, D.C., and sought additional space on government buildings across the country. The Food Administration reported that advertising space valued at more than $19 million was donated for its appeals during the war.[78]

The Food Administration, like the Committee on Public Information, proved to be a magnet for journalists and reformers. Hundreds of press agents, advertising agents, and government and corporate publicists volunteered their services in the persuasion campaigns in both agencies.[79] Many of these volunteers found the work of stimulating patriotism to be a positive, even an inspiring, experience. In his final report, Hoover claimed that the Food Administration's work had resulted in increased food surpluses that allowed the United States to feed its citizens, its armies, and the citizens of Europe as well. Hoover wrote: "The basis of all the efforts of the Food Administration has been the educational work which has preceded and accompanied its measures of conservation and regulation."[80]

Hoover's volunteers, unlike many at the CPI, looked back with pride at their wartime persuasion campaigns. Ben Allen, the former newsman who was chief publicist for the Food Administration, wrote in his farewell message that "I believe I can say without conceit that we have participated together in the greatest propaganda campaign ever conducted in this country. It has been an inspiring thing which I shall treasure as the greatest experience in my life."[81] The journalist Will Irwin, who helped in several of Hoover's campaigns, agreed: "Never was there such an orgy of idealism and ballyhoo."[82]

Among the most enthusiastic of the volunteers had been publicists and members of the advertising trade, who found the experience to be a heady experiment in molding public opinion in a patriotic cause. The historian Stephen Fox attributes much of the "high tide and green grass" of the advertising industry in the 1920s to building on the wartime initiatives in mass persuasion.[83] Many journalists were also uplifted by the experience. A Pulitzer Prize in 1918 was awarded for an essay that praised Hoover and described how the nation's press had formed a "partnership" with the Wilson administration to win the war.[84] Many mainstream newspapers had helped to promote the war effort by publishing promotional public service advertising, even while complaining about the government's refusal to pay for it.[85]

However, it would be misleading to suggest that widespread enthusiasm about presidential management of the press and public opinion followed the wartime experiments in mass persuasion. Disillusionment with Wilson, Creel, propaganda, censorship, and the government's war policies followed swiftly after the Armistice in November 1918. The volunteers at the Committee on Public Information were not as uplifted at their wartime work as those at the Food Administration. As soon as they left the agency, many wrote influential articles critical of the CPI's role in spreading wartime propaganda.[86] Congress abruptly liquidated the CPI in June 1919, leaving Creel to scramble for storage space for its records. Lacking congressional approval to allow the Government Printing Office to publish the committee's final report, Creel was forced to arrange for its publication by a private publisher.[87]

Wilson's relationship with the press deteriorated after the Armistice; he spent much of following eight months in Paris, trying to negotiate the terms of the peace with his former wartime allies. The President took Creel with him to help him deal with the estimated 150 correspondents who also traveled to Europe. But Creel had little credibility left with the press because of his identification with censorship at the CPI. In Paris, Wilson enlisted another spokesman, the journalist Ray Stannard Baker.[88] Nevertheless, for a variety of reasons, the President was unable to generate news coverage back in the United States that was supportive of his role in the peace talks. Wilson had pledged to hold open peace negotiations; that he received considerable press criticism when he acquiesced to the demands of the other Allies to meet in secret should not have been surprising. The President remained reluctant to meet with correspondents personally and was not particularly forthcoming when he did so. Instead, the correspondents received conflicting and confusing statements from Wilson's advisors, official and unofficial spokesmen, the negotiators, and other interested sources. In Washington, Tumulty, left behind to run the White House in the President's absence, monitored the confusion of the correspondents by reading their newspaper stories. Tumulty tried repeatedly to warn Wilson about the tone of the domestic press coverage in a series of revealing cables and letters to the President and to Cary T. Grayson,

the White House physician. Tumulty urged Wilson to place more emphasis on managing the press in Paris if he expected stories that would help
win popular support for the peace agreement back home.[89]

Instead, the mixed coverage of the negotiations encouraged opposition
at home to the Treaty of Versailles and to U.S. membership in the League
of Nations. When Wilson returned to the United States, he launched a
strenuous cross-country speaking tour in support of Senate ratification of
the treaties that ended in September 1919 when he suffered an incapacitating stroke.[90] After the stroke, presidential communication with the press
largely ceased. Press attention shifted to the Senate, which defeated ratification of the treaties in November 1919. Through the remaining 18
months of Wilson's term, Capitol Hill, not the White House, became again
the center of Washington newsgathering. While the White House did not
return permanently to the relative isolation from the press that had marked
the Taft administration, the intensified relationship that Wilson had established with the press since 1913 was over.[91]

Nevertheless, both the presidency and the news media had been
changed substantially by the war. Before Wilson, presidential leadership of
public opinion through the new media of newspapers and magazines had
been an interesting adjunct to executive governance. McKinley and
Theodore Roosevelt sought the assistance of the press to help build public support for the immediate challenges of war and reform. Taft had
demonstrated that aloofness from the press was no longer advisable if a
president wished to maintain public support for his governing authority.

But to Wilson, using the press to guide public opinion was not just a
useful tool of executive leadership; it had been the cornerstone of a
strengthened presidency. In peace and in war, Wilson had sought public
support for greater presidential authority by experimenting with all available means to manage the press and the mass media. The White House had
sought to shape information reaching the public in peacetime by establishing a stronger presidential relationship with the Washington correspondents through such devices as regular press conferences and intensive
personal lobbying by the President's staff.

During World War I, Wilson had deployed the full range of presidential
authority over mass communications to persuade or to command press and
public support for the war effort. Maintaining presidential control over the
press and public opinion after the war was neither allowable nor acceptable. But the wartime experience had gone far to promote popular familiarity with the president as chief of state and leader of national opinion.
Many journalists and much of the public had accepted, more or less will-

ingly, stronger presidential involvement in guiding press and public sentiment, at least for a patriotic cause during wartime.

Furthermore, the CPI, the Food Administration, and other wartime
agencies of persuasion had given new institutional impetus to government
adoption of the techniques of publicity to shape public opinion. Even
though the agencies themselves were dismantled, their legacy encouraged
an expansion of press bureaus and publicity practices throughout the government in the 1920s. Herbert Hoover, whose reputation so benefited
from his wartime work that he became a presidential candidate in 1920,
went on to create in the Department of Commerce a publicity organization that was widely copied by New Deal programs in the 1930s.[92]

The Wilson administration, in peace and in war, had laid the ground-
work for a permanent relationship between the executive and the news
media. White House leadership of public opinion through the press was
becoming an institutionalized form of presidential leadership. No
twentieth-century president who followed Wilson tried to return the
White House to the pre–World War I aloofness from the press exemplified
by William Howard Taft.

CHAPTER EIGHT

HARDING AND COOLIDGE: EMERGENCE OF THE MEDIA PRESIDENCY

The 1920s often have been viewed as something of an interlude in the twentieth-century expansion of presidential management of public opinion through the news media. Republican candidate Warren G. Harding pledged in 1920 to lead the nation "back to normalcy" and away from the turmoil of World War I and the Wilson years.[1] To correspondent Fletcher Knebel, they were the "placid twenties," stretching generously from the end of the war to the excitement of the New Deal in the 1930s.[2] The political scientist Elmer C. Cornwell Jr. referred to the Harding and Coolidge administrations as periods of "consolidation" in presidential leadership of public opinion, and to the unhappy single term of Herbert Hoover, who took office in 1929, as a "retrogression."[3] Among historians, the presidencies of the 1920s were diminished in hindsight by that of Franklin D. Roosevelt, whose well-documented impact on executive leadership of public opinion through the mass media overshadowed those who preceded him as well as those who followed him.[4]

Yet this dismissiveness seems overstated. Returning to normalcy under Harding and Coolidge did not mean a return to the laissez-faire approach to the press and public opinion preferred by the last prewar president, William Howard Taft. Historians who consider Harding one of the nation's worst presidents because of the scandals in his administration nevertheless acknowledge his popularity with the press.[5] As for Coolidge, Charles Willis Thompson, a veteran *New York Times* correspondent, claimed in 1927 that the taciturn Vermonter was no less successful at publicity than Theodore Roosevelt had been.[6]

Under Harding and Coolidge, the presidential press conference became a routine White House practice, and both presidents were quick to take advantage of the developing technologies of photography, film, and radio.[7] In addition, Hoover, who served as secretary of commerce to both presidents, created a sophisticated publicity operation in the Department of Commerce that was cited as a model for New Deal agencies a decade later.[8] It is also significant that by the late 1920s, Washington correspondents had begun to complain publicly about the proliferation of government publicity activity. In 1927, for example, J. Frederick Essary, of the *Baltimore Sun*, wrote that "Washington has become the great generator of propaganda in this country." He added: "In almost every department there is a chief of a 'bureau of information' which is merely a title for an official press agent."[9]

Frequent, predictable access to the president encouraged a parallel professionalization of Washington journalism.[10] By the late 1920s, the correspondents had come to regard the White House as a permanently prominent source of news and were shifting their primary newsgathering focus from Congress to the presidency.[11]

Wilson and his information agencies had accelerated this transformation, which had been under way since the turn of the century. But the wartime expansion of presidential publicity that helped to turn Washington into a world news capital had waned by 1920. The Committee on Public Information, the Food Administration, and the other wartime agencies had been dismantled. Wilson's postwar relationship with the press deteriorated after the Armistice and largely ceased after his incapacitating stroke. The Senate, where the Versailles and League of Nations treaties were defeated, became once again the center of Washington newsgathering.[12]

Harding, however, found the correspondents to be receptive when he set out to reestablish the White House as a leading source of news. During his 29 months as president, from March 1921 to August 1923, Harding instituted or restored publicity practices that were continued by his successor, Coolidge, and by subsequent twentieth-century presidents. These included frequent, regularly scheduled presidential press conferences with established rules of attendance and conduct; expansion of the resident's personal and professional relationships with the correspondents, their clubs, and industry trade associations; and the encouragement of parallel publicity activity in Cabinet agencies to support the administration's policies.

Harding had several advantages in reestablishing a close presidential relationship with the press. Unlike Wilson, he was a Republican, still a significant consideration in 1920s political journalism. Newspaper partisanship, although declining, affected the careers and judgments of the correspondents.[13] Although many newspapers had declared themselves to be officially "independent" of the political parties, Frank R. Kent, a *Baltimore Sun* correspondent, estimated that three-fourths of them remained partisan in practice, especially those in smaller communities.[14] Most of the major daily newspapers in New York and Washington were Republican in orientation, and their correspondents were expected to respect their employers' allegiances.

Moreover, Harding, unlike Wilson, was familiar with the ways of the press long before he became president. Harding had been a newspaper publisher, and he understood how news was produced, at least at the *Marion (Ohio) Star*. As a U.S. senator, he had seen the Washington press in action and gained the support of influential publishers, especially Ned McLean, of the *Washington Post*. Harding's publicity advisors in the 1920 presidential campaign included Will H. Hays, chairman of the Republican National Committee; Scott C. Bone, an editor of the *Washington Post,* and Judson C. Welliver, a former correspondent and aide to Theodore Roosevelt. Welliver remained a publicist and speechwriter both to Harding and to Coolidge.[15]

Perhaps most importantly, Harding had the advice and direction of Florence Kling De Wolfe Harding, one of the century's most knowledgeable first ladies in dealing with the press. Florence Harding had worked for 14 years at the family newspaper in Marion, Ohio. She was a key advisor and public spokeswoman in advancing her husband's political career. At the Republican National Convention in June 1920, Florence Harding sought out correspondents, as well as delegates, to lobby. She surprised them by allowing herself to be interviewed as an on-the-record source promoting his candidacy. In November 1920, the first presidential election that followed enactment of women's suffrage, photographers were invited to take a picture of Florence Harding voting with her husband.[16]

The new President also genuinely liked newspapermen, a significant change from Taft and Wilson. He befriended the correspondents who moved to Marion in 1920 for his "front porch" presidential campaign. The correspondents, whose most recent experiences with presidents had been with an aloof Taft and a magisterial Wilson, responded warmly. About a dozen of the Republican correspondents formed an insiders' group, the "Order of the Elephant," to socialize with Harding during the campaign. Later, the group became the nucleus of a revitalized and expanded White House press corps.[17]

When the President-elect greeted 50 correspondents in his hotel suite on the eve of his inauguration, he assured them, "I am just a newspaperman myself."[18] To demonstrate his willingness to be helpful to the press after his inauguration, he came out of the White House after midnight to tell correspondents the outcome of his first presidential conference with congressional leaders.[19]

The most visible evidence of Harding's campaign to form a closer working relationship with the press was the reestablishment of frequent, regularly scheduled, presidential press conferences open to all correspondents. Wilson had experimented extensively with similar press conferences during his first term, but none had been held at the White House on a regular schedule for nearly six years. Before taking office in March 1921, Harding received a memorandum on the subject from Gus J. Karger, of the *Cincinnati Times-Star,* a veteran correspondent who had served as an unofficial liaison between the press and the last Republican president, Taft. In the memorandum, Karger suggested that both Harding and his Cabinet officers make themselves readily available for questioning by correspondents and hold frequent, regularly scheduled news conferences. "The newspapermen want the news. . . . Everything that is done to make it easy for them in their legitimate requirements will help them and assist the Administration," Karger wrote. He also suggested rules of conduct under which the President could be questioned openly but not quoted directly or indirectly without his consent. Harding seems to have followed Karger's advice. He announced that press conferences would be held twice a week, Tuesdays and Fridays, following his Cabinet meetings, and that individual Cabinet members would hold regular press conferences as well.[20]

At Harding's first post-inaugural press conference, he greeted the correspondents warmly, shook hands with each one, and then talked candidly about the Cabinet meeting he had just left. Edward G. Lowry, the magazine writer, compared the welcoming atmosphere with Wilson's chilly first press conference eight years earlier. Unlike Wilson, Harding did not lecture to the correspondents or take offense at their questions. Instead, according to Lowry, Harding "did not wait for questions, but began to talk, an easy, gossipy chat about the first Cabinet meeting of his administration. He knew the professional interests of his hearers. He told them 'the story' of what they came to hear."[21]

Harding's candid remarks at these twice-weekly conferences made news, even if he could not be identified as the source. He also gave the correspondents human-interest tips on how to make their stories more interesting to read. "He knows what is news and has an attractive way of communicating it to the press," wrote Richard V. Oulahan, Washington bureau chief of the *New York Times.* "He has the news sense, the nose for news, and frequently goes out of his way to give them the sidelights on government affairs more interesting than important and having a human touch that makes attractive reading matter."[22]

After being shunned or barely tolerated by Taft and Wilson, the correspondents were attracted to these frequent, predictable opportunities to question the President openly and to receive useful replies, even if most of them were off the record.[23] Instead of diminishing in novelty after Harding's inauguration, the press conferences drew crowds of 50 or more correspondents and hangers-on, prompting the President to seek a revival of the White House Correspondents Association to screen out the noncorrespondents and to try to enforce the rules of confidentiality.[24]

However, as press attention to the President's statements increased, so did the consequences of newspaper stories based on Harding's injudicious or erroneous remarks. Florence Harding helped to write and to edit her husband's formal speeches, but she could not control his off-the-cuff remarks. By the fall of 1921, after more than one misstatement found its way into print, Harding decreed that all questions must be submitted in advance in writing.[25] The correspondents grumbled at the inconvenience, but their attraction to the President's press conferences was undiminished. "The correspondents still attend in unprecedented numbers Mr. Harding's bi-weekly audiences," Edward G. Lowry wrote. "They find these meetings useful. They get news. These contacts are reproduced in a thousand places. The President is presented as he presents himself with all his native kindliness and appealing qualities to the fore."[26]

Harding's campaign to appeal for public support through the mass media went well beyond reestablishing and maintaining regular press conferences. He was the first president to take full advantage of the increasing use of still photographs by newspapers and magazines and of newsreels. Taft and Wilson had regarded posing for photographers as burdensome and submitted to it without enthusiasm. Taft complained about the "sacrifice of dignity" involved.[27] Wilson appreciated the propaganda possibilities, but denied repeated pleas by his advisers to appear personally in a wartime promotional film on conserving food.[28]

In the 1920 campaign, however, posed photographs of the Hardings, both Warren and Florence, were made available to the press in Marion and distributed nationally by Republican headquarters in an effort to "picturize" the couple. Florence Harding made a special point of cultivating newsreel cameramen, as well as still photographers and correspondents.[29]

At the White House, Harding walked out readily into the garden to be photographed or filmed with the visitors of the day, whether they were Boy Scouts, Girl Scouts, golfers, printers, public officials, delegations from service clubs, Hollywood film stars, or even Albert Einstein.

The handsome, smiling President took a good picture, and many of them were reproduced in newspaper rotogravure sections. For example, the 3 April 1921 picture section of the *New York Times* Sunday edition contained five photographs of Harding, including two from the White House Easter egg roll; one of the President playing with his photogenic airedale, "Laddie"; one of him posing with former President Taft; and one with a delegation from the National Disabled Citizens' League.

"It is effective publicity and quite legitimate," Lowry wrote. "The people who are taken with the Presidents and their friends like the pictures. The newspapers print them because they are news and because they interest readers."[30] The success of these "photo opportunities" drew crowds of photographers to the White House, and in June 1921 the White House News Photographers Association was organized to limit access only to those who were properly accredited.[31]

Contributing to the President's popularity with the correspondents was the continuing assistance of Florence Harding, now First Lady. In the White House, she developed her own contacts with both male and female reporters. She sympathized with women reporters in the man's world of newspapering and held informal press conferences for "us girls," at which she answered political questions as well as inquiries about social activities. Some women reporters even were invited to interview her in her bedroom. Correspondents who wrote positive stories received thank-you notes and, at times, flowers.[32]

Florence Harding also spoke to public gatherings on political issues like women's suffrage.[33] She accepted an honorary membership in the National Women's Party and made public statements of support for other women's political groups. Her public activity was so extensive that she was the first First Lady to request the assignment of a Secret Service agent for protection.[34]

The President, too, sought publicity and support in the mass media beyond the White House. Harding made an intensive effort to lobby correspondents socially and also to appeal to media owners and editors through their growing professional and trade associations. In Washington, Harding chatted with the correspondents, played in their golf tournaments, and frequently attended the social and professional gatherings of the White House Correspondents Association, the Gridiron Club, and the National Press Club.[35] He chose the National Press Club's annual "Hobby Party" as the forum for his first formal speech after his inauguration.[36] In 1922, Harding again chose the National Press Club as the site for a formal report on his first year in office, which included praise for the press and a request for its continued support. Press Club members presented the President with a birthday cake with one candle and reportedly gave him an ovation.[37]

Harding also attended or sent formal messages to the annual meetings of industry associations, such as the board of directors of the Associated Press and the American Newspaper Publishers Association. Previous presidents occasionally attended these trade conventions, but few contributed such lavish statements of praise and good fellowship to influential publishers and editors.[38] In 1923, however, after press reports had begun to appear that suggested possible corruption in his administration, Harding appeared before the American Society of Newspaper Editors to endorse their consideration of a code of ethics for journalists.[39]

The Harding administration has become notorious among historians for corruption and presidential misbehavior. The President valued loyalty above all else in his appointments, and several members of what critics called the "Ohio gang" were accused of influence peddling. Charles R. Forbes, whom Harding had appointed to head the Veterans' Bureau, resigned before a Senate committee began to investigate allegations of fraud. Forbes's chief assistant, Charles F. Cramer, committed suicide, and Forbes himself later went to prison. In late May 1923, Jess Smith, a close associate of Attorney General Harry M. Daugherty, also committed suicide while under pressure in a complex deal involving the disposal of $6.5 million in Liberty bonds. Some of the money ended up in a political fund managed by the Attorney General, who eventually was dismissed by Coolidge and tried twice on charges of fraud, although not convicted. In the best known of the Harding scandals, Secretary of the Interior Albert B. Fall leased drilling rights at naval petroleum reserves at Teapot Dome, Wyoming, and Elk Hills, California, to oil men and speculators who made general "loans" to Fall.[40]

Harding's personal life also set a standard of sorts for presidential misbehavior in the twentieth century. As Carl Sferrazza Anthony documents in his 1998 biography of Florence Harding, the president was a compulsive adulterer throughout his public career, he served and drank alcohol in the White House when it was illegal to do so during Prohibition, and he gambled with speculators and other favor-seekers.[41]

At least the outlines of the major scandals were known to many Washington correspondents during Harding's presidency, as were his personal failings. Yet little appeared in the newspapers before his death in August 1923. Once congressional hearings into the scandals began two months later, however, the resulting headlines and stories helped to make "Teapot Dome" a twentieth-century synonym for political corruption.[42] The relative absence of news coverage prior to the President's death reveals a great deal about the limitations of Washington journalism in the 1920s and the tenuous nature of the relationship that was developing between the White House and the correspondents.

Even though the full range of influence-peddling scandals did not become known until late 1923, conservationists and other critics of Secretary Fall had been trying to persuade the press to look into his activities at the Interior Department for the past two years. Some of these pleas came from the peripatetic conservationist, reformer, and publicist Gifford Pinchot, whose leaks to the press had undermined Taft's secretary of the interior, Richard A. Ballinger, a dozen years earlier. The parallels between Pinchot's publicity campaign against Ballinger in 1909 and his efforts against Fall are striking.

Pinchot had not been in the government since 1910, when he was fired as chief of the U.S. Forest Service by Taft. But he remained active in Republican and progressive politics. Pinchot loyally supported the party's nominee for president in 1920, despite misgivings about Harding's views on conservation. He kept a close watch on conservation issues through Harry A. Slattery, a Washington attorney and activist who had worked for Pinchot's National Conservation Commission under Theodore Roosevelt. Slattery alerted Pinchot in 1921 that Secretary Fall, a wealthy New Mexico rancher, developer, and former U.S. senator, wanted to gain control of public resources, including those lands supervised by the U.S. Forest Service, by having them transferred into Fall's jurisdiction at the Interior Department.[43] Beginning in late 1921, Pinchot launched a publicity campaign against Fall's activities, in much the same way that he tried to thwart Ballinger's actions as secretary of the interior in 1909. Stories defending the Forest Service subsequently appeared in the *Christian Science Monitor* and other newspapers. By March 1922, the American Forestry Association was able to present Harding and the congressional leadership with bundles of newspaper clippings opposing the transfer of the Forest Service to Fall's Interior Department. Fall fought back, also in the press, by attacking "Pinchotism" and "propaganda."[44]

Pinchot was able to stimulate enough news coverage to head off Fall's plan to gain control of the Forest Service. But he was less successful in leaking reports of possible corruption in Fall's plans for the petroleum reserves, which were transferred to the Interior Department from the navy. In 1909, Pinchot had been able to ignite a press frenzy by planting reports that Secretary Ballinger was linked to corrupt activity involving public coal lands in Alaska. The allegations were never proven, but sensational coverage by newspapers and muckraking magazines undermined Ballinger's policies and drove him from Taft's Cabinet. In 1922, however, when Pinchot tried to suggest wrongdoing in the proposed sale of drilling rights in the Teapot Dome and Elk Hills reserves, press reaction was limited, even though his warning was proven later to be well founded. Frustrated at the lack of interest in the press, Pinchot turned his attentions to his campaign to be elected governor of Pennsylvania. Slattery then appealed to another reformer and publicist, Sen. Robert M. La Follette of Wisconsin, who persuaded the Senate to launch an investigation. But despite La Follette's speeches, public statements, news events, leaks, and other attempts at publicity, only a handful of stories about Fall and Teapot Dome had appeared by the end of 1922. Fall left Harding's Cabinet in March 1923 with his public reputation more or less intact. It was not until six months later, after Harding's death, that the scandal broke in the Congress and in the press.[45]

The limited response of the press to the campaign of allegations against Fall is suggestive of changes in the president's relationship to the press and in newsgathering practices between Taft and Harding, even though the parallels with the Ballinger conflict are imperfect. Pinchot in 1909 had been able to present the press with an on-the-record accuser against Ballinger, the whistle-blower Louis Glavis. Available evidence against Fall in 1921 and 1922 was only inferential. And Fall, unlike Ballinger and Taft, had defended himself vigorously to the correspondents. Just as importantly, under Harding the White House had become a more valuable source of news to the correspondents than it had been under Taft. Access to a popular president, not exposure, was regarded as essential to maintaining an increasingly productive relationship. "The curious thing about President Harding was that everyone loved him in spite of the horrible debacle of his administration," commented Olive Ewing Clapper, wife of the United Press White House correspondent, Raymond Clapper.[46] Instead of pursuing rumors of possible corruption, some prominent correspondents discussed ways of protecting Harding from the misdeeds of his associates.

In early 1923, Harding's defenders suggested that he appoint a "director of administrative publicity" to better advertise the President's positive achievements. Some of the most prominent correspondents publicly endorsed the idea. Richard V. Oulahan, the dean of the press corps, wrote in the *New York Times* that many newspapermen agreed with a comment by Secretary of Labor James J. Davis that Harding was "the poorest advertiser in the United States." Oulahan wrote that "on many occasions they (the correspondents) have found the President reluctant to furnish enlightenment on acts of his administration, with the result that they have had to obtain information from other and possibly less well informed quarters."[47] Harding's problem, Oulahan wrote in his memoirs, was not that he was corrupt personally but that he was simply too modest: "He will not shout loud in a loud shouting age."[48] Harding quickly disavowed the proposal to hire an official White House publicist, as did its purported author, the advertising executive Albert Lasker. But some correspondents, including

Oulahan, remained sympathetic to the idea and defended the President until his death.[49]

If news coverage of possible corruption in the Harding administration was limited, published reports of the President's personal misconduct were all but nonexistent. Newspaper stories about Harding's adultery did not appear until 1927, when Nan Britton, one of his mistresses, published a disputed memoir, *The President's Daughter,* which claimed that Harding was her lover and the father of her child.[50] Yet, as Anthony's biography of Florence Harding documents, prominent journalists knew of Harding's womanizing, drinking, and gambling in the White House. Some were active participants, especially Ned McLean, publisher of the *Washington Post.* The *Post* carried no stories about Harding's adulteries, although McLean and some of his editors were aware of them. Indeed, McLean helped to investigate and to settle blackmail claims against the President. In addition, some of the correspondents sent to Marion, Ohio, for the 1920 presidential campaign, had attended a lawn party hosted by one long-time mistress, Carrie Phillips. Others were present at a private party at the National Press club, where Harding reportedly confided that "I can't say no."[51] As far as illegal drinking was concerned, Harding served and drank alcohol routinely with correspondents as a candidate and as President, even though he was publicly a "dry," a supporter of Prohibition. Not only did the correspondents not write about Harding's personal failings, they acquiesced with a decree by Florence Harding that the President should never be portrayed as smoking tobacco.[52]

The lack of contemporary news coverage of the President's personal failings is unsurprising in this time period. Washington journalists well into the twentieth century generally respected the privacy of public officials, particularly the president. Although both Theodore Roosevelt and Wilson had complained about press intrusion into their family lives, the photographs and stories in mainstream newspapers and magazines about them and their families were almost always admiring. As long as the president was carrying out his official duties, no respectable news organization was likely to publish a story suggesting personal misconduct without some sort of public record to base it on. Even the tabloid *New York Daily News,* which begin publication in 1919, restricted its coverage of celebrity scandals or love affairs to divorce cases, where there was a court record available. For a more traditional newspaper to publish any story that referred openly to adultery or sexuality in the early 1920s likely would have been condemned by local ministers as an immoral act. Most community newspapers at the time were reluctant to publish even something as inoffensive as the notice of an impending birth.[53]

As far as alcohol consumption was concerned, for a Washington correspondent to be allowed to drink with the president was more likely to be regarded as a symbol of professional advancement than as an opportunity to embarrass the White House for breaking the law. Most newspaper correspondents, along with millions of other Americans, saw nothing wrong with drinking illegally during Prohibition.[54]

Despite whatever misgivings the correspondents may have held about Harding and his administration, the President's two-year "honeymoon" with the press, as William Allen White described it, continued until his death in August 1923 and was reflected in the fulsome editorial tributes that followed.[55] "No President has ever maintained more mutually frank and satisfactory contacts with the reporters; none, of the many more gifted in making Page One news, has been more highly esteemed," editorialized *Editor and Publisher.*[56] The Standing Committee of Correspondents, which controlled congressional press accreditation, adopted a similarly worded resolution: "No finer contact of genuine understanding and sympathy ever was established between an American president and the newspapermen than that which governed the relations of President Warren G. Harding and the writers of the Capitol." The Standing Committee selected an escort of correspondents who had covered Harding during his career to march in the President's funeral procession.[57]

Harding's successor, Vice President Coolidge, became the first president to embrace fully his predecessor's methods of appealing for public support through the mass media. This continuity between the Harding and Coolidge administrations marked an important transition from the episodic initiatives of individual presidents to a permanent relationship between the president and the press. Between August 1923 and March 1929, Coolidge continued, and helped to make permanent, Harding's practices of appealing to public opinion through the press. He met with the correspondents frequently and attended the meetings of their social and trade associations. Coolidge also made himself readily available for photographs and films, and he experimented extensively with the new mass medium of radio. He also kept on the payroll Harding's publicist, Judson C. Welliver. In a June 1925 listing of White House staff members, Welliver was described as a "special employee," whose $7,500-a-year salary equaled that of Everett Sanders, who was then Coolidge's secretary, or chief of staff.[58]

The significance of this transition was underscored by anxiety among the correspondents, who feared that Coolidge might discontinue the presidential press conferences that Harding had revived and popularized. The correspondents had been drawn increasingly to the White House to attend the conferences and to benefit from access to Harding's comments. In

March 1921, only two dozen correspondents constituted the White House "clan" photographed with the President after Harding's first presidential press conference.[59] In August 1923, an estimated 150 correspondents attended President Coolidge's first press conference. When Coolidge assured them that he would continue to hold press conferences twice a week, the relieved correspondents applauded and, while posing for a group photograph afterwards, gave the new President three cheers of support.[60] Coolidge wrote in his autobiography that the welcoming applause of the correspondents was one of his most pleasant memories of the presidency.[61]

Frederic William Wile, a correspondent for the *Christian Science Monitor* and other newspapers, prepared a ceremonial transcript of the first Coolidge presidential press conference that described the "spontaneous and hearty burst of applause" as "a token of gratitude to Mr. Coolidge and an expression of the satisfaction in which the 'entente' between President and press had been inaugurated." Wile wrote to the new President that "you know, of course, the unqualified satisfaction of our fraternity with our initial contact with you and of the prevalent confidence that the relationship is destined to grow more delightful as time goes on."[62]

However, while Coolidge continued to hold the Tuesday and Friday press conferences, the new President was neither as gregarious nor as outspoken as Harding. Coolidge's newsworthy remarks were infrequent and carefully chosen, even off the record. Coolidge was well aware that his remarks were likely to turn up in print, regardless of the ground rules of anonymity.[63] "Everything that the President does potentially at least is of such great importance that he must be constantly on guard," the cautious Coolidge observed.[64] Fragmentary records in the Coolidge Papers suggest that the President went to the press conferences with note cards containing the typed questions submitted by the correspondents and one- or two-sentence replies prepared to read if he chose to do so.[65]

Coolidge could be talkative, even garrulous at times, but he said little at the press conferences that the correspondents found useful. Nor did he volunteer background information to help them interpret the events of the day.[66] The correspondents, who had become accustomed under Harding to sending stories about the president to their publications on a regular basis, were left without their customary supply of White House news and guidance. Two months after Coolidge became president, some correspondents were being transferred to more productive assignments. Puzzled editors and publishers started to drop by Coolidge's press conferences themselves to discover what had stopped the flow of news, according to a report in *Editor and Publisher*.[67] An account of one Coolidge press conference, published in May 1924, described the President flipping quickly through the written questions submitted by the correspondents, answering each one negatively; sidestepping a single spoken question; and ending the meeting 12 minutes after it began.[68]

The correspondents also grew increasingly frustrated by the ground rules that allowed the president to make announcements or to float trial balloons anonymously. Coolidge was by no means the first president to take advantage of the rules of anonymity, which limited the correspondents to attributing any quotable statements to sources "close to the president" or, increasingly, to the "White House spokesman." But public grumbling from the correspondents increased as Coolidge used the disguise repeatedly to make newsworthy suggestions and then to disavow them if they turned out to be erroneous or controversial. To protect his deniability, Coolidge refused to allow the correspondent David Lawrence to bring along his own stenographer to record the President's remarks.[69] As the disagreement dragged on, some correspondents began to write sarcastically about the "White House spokesman" who was short and wore a blue suit, just like the President; sat in the President's chair at the President's desk; and was intimately familiar with the President's thinking.[70] The correspondents were particularly miffed in 1926 when Coolidge granted a rare on-the-record interview to a non-journalist, the advertising executive Bruce Barton, and the subsequent transcript was distributed by the Associated Press.[71]

Despite these complaints, as Raymond Clapper, chief of the United Press White House Bureau, acknowledged, the correspondents "are willing to endure occasional irritations rather than give up a good source of news."[72] In fact, the correspondents had little choice but to comply with Coolidge's ground rules if they wished to maintain the press conferences.[73] Herbert Hoover promised to end the "spokesman" system after he was elected president in 1928, but it was curtailed significantly only under Franklin D. Roosevelt.

Coolidge lacked Harding's charm and a common journalistic bond, but he nevertheless tried to reach out to the correspondents socially and professionally. Coolidge regularly attended the dinners of the White House Correspondents Association and the Gridiron Club.[74] He spoke at the ceremony in 1926 at which the cornerstone was laid for the National Press Club building and took the occasion to make a major foreign policy statement.[75] After the 1924 presidential election, in which he won a full four-year term, Coolidge invited selected editors and prominent correspondents to take a Potomac River cruise on the presidential yacht, the *Mayflower*. Coolidge further flattered his guests by allowing the sailing to be filmed for a newsreel.[76]

David Lawrence, one of the correspondents invited on the Potomac cruise, wrote later that Coolidge went further than previous presidents in his solicitousness toward the working press. While it was not uncommon for editors to be greeted as social equals, yachting with the President was a heady experience for the correspondents.[77] When Coolidge invited the correspondents and spouses covering his summer vacation in Massachusetts to take a similar cruise, an account of the voyage made the front page of the *New York Times*.[78]

Coolidge continued and expanded Harding's practice of attending or sending supportive messages to meetings of media industry and trade associations. These included, at various times, the American Newspaper Publishers Association, the Southern Newspaper Publishers Association, the Associated Press, the American Society of Newspaper Editors, the National Editorial Association, and the Pan American Congress of Journalists.[79] Although United Press correspondents found Coolidge largely uncommunicative at the White House, the President was welcomed warmly when he made a major policy address at the news service's twentieth anniversary dinner in New York City.[80] In addition to the indirect benefits of cultivating media trade associations, Coolidge was interested in the industry as a business to be encouraged. He believed that advertising was essential to economic prosperity. In 1926, he became the first president to speak to a convention of the American Association of Advertising Agencies.[81]

Coolidge, like Harding, was intrigued by the possibilities of appealing to the public through emerging technologies of mass communication, especially photographs and newsreels. His calculated approach to photo opportunities may have lacked Harding's cheerfulness and seeming spontaneity, but Coolidge was more than willing to pose. Whether carrying a sap bucket to collect maple syrup, displaying a pet raccoon, throwing out the first ball at baseball games, going fishing, or wearing funny hats, Coolidge and the First Lady, Grace Goodhue Coolidge, appeared frequently in newspapers, magazines, and newsreels. In the picture section of the *New York Times* Sunday edition on 8 November 1925, for example, Grace Coolidge was posed with a "typical boy" visiting the White House. Another picture showed her pinning a Red Cross button on the President.[82]

The vivacious First Lady drew press attention in part because of the contrast with her dour husband. In addition to being a frequent subject for photographs, she was profiled flatteringly in magazines.[83] As a spokeswoman for the administration, however, Grace Coolidge was often seen but seldom heard. She made twice as many appearances as Florence Harding had and became a frequent focus of "goodwill" pictures in newspapers and magazines. Unlike Florence Harding, however, she did not speak out on policy issues. The President did not allow it. But her upbeat disposition and willingness to be photographed made her an effective public symbol for the administration.[84]

Coolidge was the first president to experiment extensively with the new medium of radio. A network of 11 stations was organized to broadcast the President's April 1924 speech to the Associated Press directors in New York, although reception around the country was marred by static and bad weather.[85] Another network of radio stations was created to broadcast the 1924 national political conventions, and Coolidge used it to deliver several short speeches during the fall campaign.[86] His inauguration speech, in March 1925, was the first to be broadcast over radio. It was broadcast by a coalition of radio companies to a potential audience of 25 million Americans.[87] Coolidge turned out to have a good voice for radio, and his dry wit went over well. The broadcasts of formal speeches were well received, and the President arranged to speak informally to radio audiences at least once a month.[88]

Coolidge proved to be so successful at promoting himself through the press that the political scientist Lindsay Rodgers, an advocate of Senate supremacy, warned that White House use of the extraconstitutional power of publicity was making the President "the most powerful elected ruler in the world." Coolidge, Rogers wrote, was able to launch his views anonymously in the newspapers on Wednesdays and Saturdays by holding press conferences on Tuesdays and Fridays. "It is government by favorable publicity," Rogers warned, and Congress lacked the means to reply.[89]

Congress was not the only institution in the polity affected by the increased prominence of the presidency in the press. Routine access to the president helped to accelerate the expansion of Washington journalism that had been under way since the early 1900s. The number of accredited correspondents for daily newspapers increased substantially in the 1920s, to 327 in 1929 from 215 in 1920.[90] Emergence of the president as a routinely productive source of news bound many of these correspondents to the White House occupationally. Frequent presidential press conferences allowed the correspondents to meet the expectations of their editors for daily stories. Furthermore, association with the president increased the prestige and legitimacy of the correspondents themselves. Not surprisingly, the correspondents followed the president's wishes in establishing formal and informal procedures and practices to advance their mutual interest in making news. For those correspondents assigned to the White House, their professional success was tied to that of their chief news source, the president. Underscoring this allegiance, the correspondents reacted protectively under both Harding and Coolidge when their chief source was threatened or the supply of news was restricted.

Under Coolidge, the correspondents were confronted not with charges of corruption that might endanger their First Source but by a lack of news from the taciturn President. In the absence of newsworthy presidential actions or announcements, some correspondents began a more or less open conspiracy to turn Coolidge's silences into stories about his "character." "It really was a miracle," wrote former United Press correspondent Thomas L. Stokes. "He said nothing. Newspapers must have copy. So we grasped at little incidents to build up human interest and we created a character. He kept his counsel. Therefore, he was a strong and silent man. . . . Then, in time, as the country found out that he was not a superman, neither strong nor silent, they emphasized his little witticisms, his dry wit, and we had a national character—'Cal.'"[91]

Coolidge shrewdly encouraged the creation of "Silent Cal" by contributing homespun stories and New England rusticisms. Several correspondents wrote in their memoirs about this invention of a presidential "character" to make up for the lack of news at the Coolidge White House.[92] Only Frank R. Kent, a columnist for the Democratic *Baltimore Sun,* publicly denounced his colleagues for going along with a deception that he said concealed the unfitness of Coolidge to be president.[93]

These protective reactions under Harding and Coolidge were indicators of the mutual dependency of the relationship that had become established between the presidents and the correspondents. Just as the president relied on the correspondents to carry his messages to the citizenry for public support, the correspondents needed access to the president for news that would meet the professional expectations of their employers. Both the president and the press corps needed the continuing cooperation of the other to accomplish their mutual goal of making news. When accusations against Harding seemed to threaten the productive relationship that he had developed with the press, the correspondents had an interest in protecting him. When Coolidge failed to produce enough news at his press conferences, the correspondents helped out by writing about his "character." An enduring, if uneasy, alliance had been formed between the president and the White House correspondents both to make news and to maintain their mutually productive relationship.

The Harding and Coolidge administrations formed a critical link between Wilson, World War I, and subsequent twentieth-century media presidencies. Between 1921 and 1929, Harding and Coolidge made routine many of the practices of appealing to the public through the press that had been experiments by previous presidents. Frequent, regularly scheduled presidential press conferences, once occasional novelties, were now institutionalized, a foundation of the White House relationship with the press. Both the president and the correspondents had adjusted their work habits and their expectations to accommodate this mutually rewarding relationship and, at times, to protect it.

By 1929, presidential guidance of public opinion through the mass media was no longer a set of experiments by particularly innovative presidents or a wartime emergency measure. Practices once considered novel, such as the press conferences, were now presumed to be permanent and to follow complex rules and customs that assumed the continuing existence of the practices themselves. That these changes took place in the "placid twenties," rather than during wartime or national crisis, suggests that managing the press had become a permanent element of presidential leadership.

Nor was this development limited to the presidency. Encouraged by Harding and Coolidge, executive administrators in the 1920s, especially Secretary of Commerce Hoover, reorganized the major agencies of the executive branch to make publicity a routine element in departmental governance as well.

CHAPTER NINE

HERBERT HOOVER
AND CABINET PUBLICITY
IN THE 1920S

Publicity practices adopted by the White House to promote public support for the president's policies spread widely in the executive branch in the 1920s. Cabinet officers and agency directors applied many of the promotional techniques used during World War I to try to increase public and congressional support for their programs. Press conferences, press bureaus, handouts, and other tactics of publicity were used to promote news coverage of agency activities in much the same way that the presidents since McKinley appealed for public support for themselves and their policies through the news at the White House.

World War I accelerated the experiments with agency publicity that had been under way since the turn of the century, when Gifford Pinchot found that newspaper coverage was a more effective way to appeal for public support than were government pamphlets. Wilson's wartime information agencies had dramatized how publicity could be used administratively to raise awareness of, and compliance with, government policies. But agency publicity largely was still in its infancy in 1921. The volunteer propagandists who had joined the Committee on Public Information and other wartime agency campaigns largely had left the government, although press bureaus remained in the major permanent departments.

At the White House, presidents since Theodore Roosevelt had found the growth of agency publicity to be both an opportunity and a challenge to their own attempts to attract public support by managing the press. When all went well, executive branch publicists could assist the White House by providing additional support in the press for the president's policies. But publicity from outside the White House also could divert the press from the president's own agenda. Or, as Pinchot had demonstrated under William Howard Taft, leaks to the press could undermine public support for the administration's policies or for the president himself. Wilson had tried repeatedly in both peace and war to restrict or to coordinate the publicity activity of his appointees, whether by personal appeals to his Cabinet members or by creating an information ministry in the form of the Committee on Public Information.

Harding, however, chose to take the opposite approach. Rather than try to exercise presidential authority over executive branch publicity activities, Harding decided to encourage them. Emerging from his first Cabinet meeting, in March 1921, the new President announced that he had instructed his department heads to hold their own regularly scheduled press conferences and to speak to journalists on behalf of themselves and, presumably, on behalf of the administration.[1] In making his decision, Harding followed closely the suggestions of a veteran Washington correspondent, Gus J. Karger, of the *Cincinnati Times-Star,* who recommended that Cabinet members, as well as the president, be in contact with reporters frequently, twice a day if necessary, and in person, rather than through press agents.[2]

Harding's announcement pleased the correspondents, who looked forward to having more opportunities to get newsworthy information from high-ranking official sources. Whether the Harding presidency benefited from having multiple voices speaking on behalf of the administration to the press and public is debatable. But the decision effectively gave the president's blessing to widespread adoption of publicity practices by administrative agencies across the executive branch.

Harding's decision to encourage his Cabinet members to speak independently to the press was based on at least two questionable assumptions. First, it assumed that what his Cabinet members told the press for public consumption would be consistent with the President's policies and those of the other Cabinet members. Second, it assumed that the Cabinet members and department heads were familiar enough with the techniques of managing the press to be able to generate supportive news stories from their remarks to reporters. Neither assumption proved to be well founded.

Cabinet appointments traditionally went to semiautonomous party elders or to representatives of important constituencies, such as farmers. Those appointees often were useful in advising the president on policy, but they did not necessarily feel obligated to carry out his orders. Wilson had struggled to persuade the diverse members of his Cabinet to reflect his views in their comments to the press, as well as in their policies. Harding, on the other hand, believed that encouraging his Cabinet members to speak out individually would showcase the "best minds" that he had attracted to his administration.[3]

What Harding discovered, however, was that the "best minds" often disagreed, both among themselves and with him. His appointees reflected diverse and often conflicting personalities and constituencies. Instead of being able to coordinate the voices of a generally unified administration, Harding often was forced to be an unwilling referee.[4] In addition to Herbert Hoover, whom Richard V. Oulahan, of the *New York Times,* termed admiringly the "handy man of the Administration," Harding had appointed several other strong personalities to the Cabinet.[5] Those included Secretary of State Charles Evans Hughes, Secretary of the Treasury Andrew W. Mellon, and Secretary of Agriculture Henry C. Wallace. Some of Harding's other appointments were less successful, notably Ohio crony Harry Daugherty as attorney general and Sen. Albert B. Fall as secretary of the interior. Both were later disgraced in the various Harding administration scandals, as noted in the previous chapter.[6]

Despite their policy disagreements, most of Harding's Cabinet members were willing to comply with the President's instructions to meet with the press. But since they also differed in their prior experiences with publicity, the results of their encounters with correspondents were mixed.[7] The initial responses to Harding's exhortation to seek publicity on the administration's behalf varied considerably.

Secretary of Agriculture Wallace was well acquainted with the press and its ways. Wallace was the outspoken editor of an Iowa farm journal, *Wallace's Farmer.* Moreover, the Agriculture Department long had been a pioneer among the Cabinet departments in disseminating information to its various constituencies, whether through official government publications or through the press.[8] The gregarious Attorney General Daugherty, borrowed cigarettes from the correspondents who attended his news conferences and joked about his poker bets with the President.[9] In contrast, Secretary of the Treasury Mellon was a reserved financier who had little experience with reporters. Mellon found dealing with them puzzling and occasionally troublesome. Thomas L. Stokes, a onetime United Press correspondent, described Mellon as bemused that a one-word answer to a reporter's question, yes or no, could result in a lengthy newspaper story the next day. Few reporters attended Mellon's press conferences, and those who did found that he little to say that was usable as news.[10]

Secretary of State Hughes, sometimes described as the first among equals in the Harding Cabinet, was a dignified former governor of New York who had been the Republican presidential candidate in 1916. He also had gained a reputation for regarding newspaper correspondents as "a cross between public nuisances and unapprehended criminals," according to one writer.[11] The State Department had been involved in publicity since at least the Spanish-American War, as presidents beginning with William McKinley sought public support for military actions outside the United States. But the conduct of diplomacy itself was regarded as a necessarily confidential process, not to be discussed in the press. During World War I, Secretary Robert Lansing kept the State Department's information office separate from the Committee on Public Information to try to prevent leaks of diplomatic information.[12]

However, the Harding administration's active foreign policy, combined with the President's pledge of Cabinet publicity, had increased the expectations of the correspondents. Hughes at first found dealing with the Washington press problematic.[13] When he tried to stop the correspondents from writing stories about diplomatic notes, stories appeared that he was withholding information.[14] Hughes proved to be a quick study in adapting to the techniques of publicity, however. The Secretary reorganized the State Department press information structure and placed Henry Suydam, a popular war correspondent, in charge of the Division of Current Information.[15] He held press briefings as often as twice a day and tried to cultivate the correspondents with humor and charm.[16] In 1922, after the Washington Conference on naval disarmament, the correspondents presented the "new Hughes" with a birthday cake and a large pair of shears to cut through the symbolic knots of diplomacy.[17] A flattering *New York Times* profile of Hughes at the end of Harding's first year in the White House described him as second only to the President in importance.[18]

No Cabinet member in the Harding and Coolidge administrations was more aggressive in seeking publicity than Herbert Hoover, who was secretary of commerce to both presidents and who became, not coincidentally, the Republican candidate for president in 1928.[19] Hoover's brief but spectacular public career before becoming secretary of commerce had been characterized by an extraordinary emphasis on public appeals to promote and to accomplish his largely humanitarian works. John Lee Mahim, one of the many public relations and advertising executives with whom Hoover consulted regularly, commented in 1922: "Your publicity was probably as an important feature of your work as any other phase of it."[20]

As food administrator for Wilson during World War I, Hoover directed one of the war's largest domestic propaganda campaigns. Wartime appeals to conserve food made Hoover, literally, a household word. After the war, he organized and led a series of highly publicized relief campaigns to send food to starving children in war-ravaged Europe and to Russia.[21] Hoover's admirers regarded him as one of the few American leaders to emerge from the war as a hero. His popularity in 1920 was such that both major political parties sought to enlist him as a presidential candidate.[22] Hoover's campaign for the Republican nomination was unsuccessful, however, and he ended up supporting the party's candidate, Harding. After the election, Harding sought out Hoover to add luster to his Cabinet.[23]

The Department of Commerce that Hoover took over in 1921 was a disorganized collection of obscure and unrelated government offices that lacked a central administrative purpose or direction.[24] In his *Memoirs*, Hoover recounted that Wilson's secretary of commerce, Oscar Straus, told him that the job would require no more than two hours a day of his time.[25] But Hoover's goals were much more ambitious. By reorganizing and revitalizing the various bureaus, offices, and programs, Hoover intended to create a Commerce Department that would stimulate a national economic revival.[26] Hoover had plans to make available commercial and financial information to businesses; to encourage cooperation rather than competition in industry;[27] to urge more standardization and efficiency in manufacturing; and to raise public spirits by sending out encouraging economic messages.[28] Overall, Hoover hoped to use the Commerce Department to transform the uneven national economy of the 1920s into one that was stable and prosperous.[29]

To generate public support for these ambitious goals, Hoover brought to the job his wartime enthusiasm for leading public opinion through mass persuasion. He assembled at the Department of Commerce the most elaborate publicity apparatus yet established in the executive branch in peacetime.

Hoover brought together publicists and advertising experts from private industry; former newspapermen and wartime propagandists; and departmental employees with a flair for publicity. These included, at one time or another from 1921 to 1927, Christian A. Herter, who had done publicity work for Hoover's European relief projects; Harold Phelps Stokes, a veteran reporter for the *New York Evening Post* and the *Washington Evening Post;* George Akerson, formerly Washington correspondent for the *Minneapolis Tribune;* and Edward Eyre Hunt, a former editor of *American Magazine* and war correspondent.[30] These and numerous other publicists, employed either by the Department of Commerce or by Hoover personally, worked to promote an estimated 250 major Hoover policy initiatives, including industrial conferences, publicity campaigns for businesses and consumers, promotions and advisories on improving business practices, and programs to provide statistical support for economic activities.[31]

Hoover's reorganization of the department and its publicity work began with an upgrading of its largest internal agency, the Bureau of Foreign and

Domestic Commerce. Under Julius Klein, a Harvard professor and former commercial attaché to Argentina, the bureau was reorganized into commodity divisions to better promote international trade. Klein also established an information service in the bureau that became the central publicity coordinating office for the rest of the Commerce Department.[32]

Paul J. Croghan, a government employee in the Bureau of Foreign and Domestic Commerce, became the coordinator of publicity operations for all the Commerce Department bureaus and an important link between Hoover and the Washington correspondents. Croghan reported both to Klein and to Hoover's numerous personal publicists, called "personal assistants," who worked out of the Secretary's office. In a May 1921 memorandum to one of those publicists, Frederick Feiker, Croghan reported that he was beginning to receive publicity material from the other major agencies in the department.[33]

Croghan prepared comprehensive daily reports on the department's successes in managing its press coverage, based on his analysis of returns from newspaper subscriptions and clipping services. Throughout his six years as secretary of commerce, Hoover received lengthy, detailed, daily advisories from various publicists on the successes or failures of his publicity initiatives and a comparative analysis of the press coverage of other Cabinet departments.

"Publicity is booming. We are receiving clippings by the armful," Croghan wrote to Christian A. Herter in April 1921. Croghan listed newspaper coverage of Hoover speeches on departmental reorganization, railroad rates, and the postwar economy. "I understand the Secretary does not want more than one clipping on each subject and I have been endeavoring to do this. In some cases, we receive 50 or more duplicates from various papers," Croghan wrote.[34] In August 1924, Klein informed Hoover that the Commerce Department's news releases filled 168 column inches in the 28 July issue of the *New York Journal of Commerce* (later the *Wall Street Journal*) compared with only 79 column inches from all other federal agencies combined.[35]

In addition to seeking press coverage through daily news releases, Klein and Croghan worked to expand the department's official publications, which were sent to various constituency groups. The most prominent of these publications was *Commerce Reports*. Originally a daily newsletter with limited circulation, the publication was transformed into a weekly collection of reports on foreign trade opportunities, based on consular cables; summaries of stock and commodity trading; a compilation of news releases issued during the week, and other information intended to promote economic development.[36]

At first mailed only to businesses and other agency constituents, *Commerce Reports* was offered to daily newspapers on an experimental basis for possible use in business news sections. An encouraging response from newspaper editors led Hoover's publicists to launch an advance edition as a full-page supplement to weekend newspaper editions. The package of official reports, including news releases, was made available to editors on Thursdays for weekend publication.[37] This "Financial News" page from the Department of Commerce was quickly adopted by daily newspapers to fill out Sunday business sections. Two additional employees were set to work preparing the section. Within a few months, more than 200 daily newspapers were carrying it, according to departmental memoranda.[38]

Once a large-scale publicity operation was launched to promote the work of the Bureau of Foreign and Domestic Commerce, Hoover set out to establish similar programs in the department's other major bureaus. At the Food Administration, Hoover had discovered the advantages of designating a publicist in every major office to forward potentially newsworthy ideas up through the departmental chain of command to a central press office. The central office could then generate and coordinate publicity activity for the entire agency, as well as advise the bureaus on how better to make news to showcase their activities.

Croghan, acting as publicity coordinator for the overall Commerce Department, advised the Bureau of the Census to announce the results of the 1920 census at earlier dates than in previous decades and to do so immediately through press releases, rather than to wait for the official version to be printed in government publications. The Census Bureau subsequently reported that 6,218 copies of handouts were sent to the press that announced results by states, counties, and cities based on various census indexes, including sex, nationality, age, school attendance, literacy, and employment; commercially useful statistics on agriculture, irrigation, drainage, manufacturing, and mining were highlighted.[39]

Hoover's attempt to increase the publicity activity of another major bureau, the Bureau of Standards, is revealing because of the lack of enthusiasm among its employees, who were primarily scientists, for the notion of popularizing their technical studies and findings for newspaper use. In early 1922, Hoover assigned one of his personal publicists, Donald Wilhelm, a veteran magazine writer, to publicize the contributions of the Bureau of Standards to key Hoover campaigns on simplification and standardization in manufacturing. Wilhelm proposed to prepare an extensive series of magazine articles that would showcase the bureau's work.[40]

However, Dr. S. W. Stratton, director of the Bureau of Standards, resisted Wilhelm's suggestion that the bureau hire its own publicist to assist in preparing the articles. The Director's reluctance to comply with the demands of publicity became the subject of a series of meetings and memoranda involving Wilhelm, Stratton, and Croghan. In a long memorandum in March 1922, Wilhelm tried to persuade Stratton that promoting the bureau's work in popular publications, as well as in technical ones, was necessary to enlarge its influence and to increase public and congressional support for it. His memorandum illustrates how publicity was becoming important to governance at the administrative level in the federal government, as well as in the presidency.

In the memorandum, Wilhelm wrote: "Of course, it is perfectly possible for a governmental agency intrinsically to fail on a given job and still seem to succeed, by use of the best possible presentation of its case; and, conversely, it is perfectly possible for a governmental agency to succeed gloriously and yet seem to fail. Of course, in this thought one has to consider not only the public, but Congress as well. And the more I see of the bureau, the fine personnel you have, and the enormous accomplishments you make, it seems to me from every point of view desirable that you should have a much larger share of recognition."[41]

Finally, in November 1922, Stratton agreed to hire a former newspaperman to prepare news releases, which then would be routed to the press through Croghan. Wilhelm also would receive the publicist's help in preparing magazine articles. A memorandum of agreement stressed the importance of impressing outsiders, especially members of Congress, with news about the bureau's work. The agreement stated: "The public is entitled to know what is going on in the bureau; that a Congressman who reads a statement about some accomplishment of the bureau is more impressed than by two hours of talking; and that the news end should be developed and strengthened greatly."[42]

As a result of Hoover's centralization of departmental publicity, newsworthy information began to flow to the Secretary's office not only from the existing bureaus, such as Foreign and Interstate Commerce, Census, Standards, Fisheries, and Mines, but also from new Commerce Department offices created in the 1920s to oversee additional administrative responsibilities, such as regulation of radio and aviation. These offices, too, were directed to publicize their activities.[43] The result was to transform the Department of Commerce into an agency in which thinking of ways to promote departmental activity in the press was a routine responsibility in every significant bureau or office.[44]

One of the primary purposes of trying to centralize the flow of departmental publicity material in one office was to provide the Secretary with a daily supply of handouts to give to the press: releases based on trade statistics, census reports, investment opportunities, consular reports from overseas, and progress reports from various Hoover campaigns against unemployment, waste, duplication, farm problems, and inefficiencies in business.

To help to manage the increasing flow of handouts and other statements through the Secretary's office to the Washington correspondents and, thereby, to shape news coverage of the department's activities, Croghan established the first peacetime agency "press room" at Commerce Department headquarters. The primary purpose of the departmental press room was to serve as a convenient distribution point to make available to correspondents the daily supply of news releases. The press room also contained a telephone, typewriters, and working space to attract journalists. Because of the regular supply of handouts and the Commerce Department's convenient location, near "Newspaper Row" on Pennsylvania Avenue between the White House and the Capitol, the press room quickly became a popular gathering spot for the correspondents to work and to socialize. Correspondents began to mention the Commerce Department press room in their stories, and some wrote fondly about it in their memoirs. Other departments soon created their own press rooms to attract correspondents and to try to increase their news coverage.[45]

The large supply of handouts and other newsworthy information from the Commerce Department led to a belief among the correspondents that the once-obscure department and its various bureaus had become among the most important sources of news in Washington. When David Lawrence proposed in 1925 to establish a newspaper of government, the *United States Daily News* (later *U.S. News and World Report*), he estimated that three full-time reporters would be needed at the Commerce Department "to cover this important branch of the service." That was more than Lawrence thought would be necessary to report on newsworthy activities at the State, Treasury, Justice, War and Navy, or Interior Departments.[46]

The convenient availability of news releases and other story materials from the Commerce Department and its bureaus, as well as Hoover's reputation for candor, contributed to the popularity of the Secretary's press conferences, which were held on the twice-weekly schedule that Harding had recommended. "As Secretary of Commerce, Mr. Hoover was the best news source in Washington," one correspondent wrote.[47] Paul Y. Anderson, a critic of President Hoover's relations with the press at the White House, nevertheless recalled that as secretary of commerce, Hoover "was the best 'grapevine' in Washington, and a perfect gold mine of the 'graveyard' stuff."[48]

Records of Hoover's news conferences at the Commerce Department confirm their popularity. Two dozen correspondents attended a routine

Hoover news conference on 18 April 1921, according to a Croghan advisory.[49] In 1923, a list prepared by Croghan of the correspondents who regularly attended Hoover's press conferences contained nearly 40 names. "I think the above covers most of our regular callers," Croghan wrote, "although I think practically every newspaper man in this city has attended the Secretary's press conferences at some time."[50]

Those attending Hoover's news conferences included not only correspondents from the mainstream news services and newspapers but also from specialized publications like *Shoe Recorder, Textile World, Metal Trade Review, Petroleum News,* and the *American Mining Congress Journal.* These specialized correspondents reflected not only the department's diverse constituencies, but also Hoover's efforts to appeal to them through the business press.[51]

Hoover recognized that the mass media had become more diverse than traditional general-circulation newspapers and magazines. He sought to reach the audiences of specialized publications because of the important constituencies that they represented. At the Food Administration, Hoover had targeted women's magazines, which were read by the "house managers" who he believed controlled the nation's food consumption. At the Commerce Department, Hoover was interested in business leaders, the readers of business and industrial publications. Shortly after his appointment to Harding's Cabinet, Hoover met with the editors of numerous trade publications to discuss how to furnish them with departmental information that was appropriate to their particular interests. Hoover established a close working relationship with McGraw-Hill and other specialized publishers.[52] Along with the presidents he served in the 1920s, Hoover maintained an active schedule of lobbying publishers, editors, and advertisers in person and through their trade and industrial associations.[53]

Hoover's popularity with the press and the extraordinary flow of publicity material from the Commerce Department resulted in news coverage that sometimes overshadowed the other Cabinet members or the presidents that he served in the 1920s. Public inquiries seeking information from the Department of Commerce grew from 700 calls a day in 1921 to 8,000 by mid-1925.[54] "Hoover Emerges as a One-Man Cabinet," was the headline on a 1926 *New York Times* profile that suggested Hoover as a presidential candidate in 1928.[55]

Not everyone in the Harding and Coolidge administrations was pleased with Hoover's success at gaining the daily attention of the press. Harding remained a strong supporter of Hoover's activities, although he almost certainly was startled when Louis Rothschild, a reporter for a trade publication, told the President that he should not hold press conferences on Tuesday mornings "because it conflicts with Secretary Hoover's."[56]

Coolidge, who inherited Harding's Cabinet in 1923, was less enthusiastic about having Hoover as secretary of commerce. The new President rebuffed Hoover's attempts to draw the White House into cooperative publicity activities.[57] Mindful of Hoover's popularity with the press, however, Coolidge decided not to try to replace him after the 1924 election. The Coolidge White House didn't interfere openly with Hoover's publicity campaigns, but the President let it be known when he was displeased at the volume of news coverage that Hoover received.[58]

In 1927, Hoover received national publicity by leading the government's relief efforts to cope with the devastating Mississippi River flood. Hoover spent three months traveling in the region by train to direct the work of thousands of volunteers and government workers. Using the newly formed National Broadcasting Company radio network, Hoover described the devastation to the nation and outlined the relief measures under way.[59]

The radio broadcasts and weeks of news reports about the flood emphasized Hoover's role, leading to enthusiastic stories and books about his works by admiring journalists.[60] Coolidge, however, speaking anonymously at a press conference, referred acerbically to the "wonder boy" and "miracle worker," which provoked days of newspaper stories containing responses from Hoover's defenders.[61]

Hoover's tactics in managing the press from the Commerce Department also contributed to changing patterns of Washington journalism. The popularity of Hoover's departmental press conferences led to problems in maintaining order among the crowds of correspondents and hangers-on. Lack of an accreditation system sometimes left Hoover, like the presidents he served, unable to distinguish between the legitimate correspondents and the spectators and stock speculators who attended his press conferences. Hoover also was concerned about protecting the confidentiality of his off-the-record remarks in such a diverse and highly competitive group.

Harding's solution had been to encourage a revival of the White House Correspondents Association to screen correspondents and to attempt to discipline wayward ones. Later, the White House applied the same solution to regulate the number of photographers. Hoover took a similar approach. After one of the Secretary's supposedly confidential comments appeared in a newspaper story in April 1921, Hoover suggested at his next press conference that the correspondents who regularly covered the Commerce Department organize themselves to deal with these "leaks" and the problem of unauthorized guests. A conference of correspondents was held the following weekend to organize what became the first departmental press association, modeled after the White House Correspondents Association and the Standing Committee of the Congressional Press Gallery.

The meeting that Hoover sought was attended by correspondents who regularly covered the Departments of Commerce, Justice, and Treasury. They agreed to create a five-member committee to "pass on the eligibility of men who desire to attend newspaper conferences held in all departments except State, War and Navy, and the White House," according to a Croghan advisory to Hoover. The screening committee included representatives from the Federal Trade Information Service, the *New York Herald,* the *New York Sun,* International News Service, and the Associated Press. In addition to setting up an accreditation system, the committee was authorized to "take steps to correct those who wander from the path of fair play in publishing material gathered at the conferences with Cabinet officers," Croghan wrote.[62]

The association proved to be more successful as an accrediting service than as a disciplinary one, despite Hoover's frequent complaints about his news coverage. Like Wilson, Hoover was notably sensitive to criticism of any sort and was an exacting reader of the articles that he saw in newspapers and magazines. Louis W. Liebovich calculated that Hoover and his assistants wrote 2,000 complaining letters to editors and publishers during his six years as secretary of commerce.[63]

Between 1921 and 1927, Hoover made routine the hiring of publicists throughout the Department of Commerce, the centralization of departmental publicity in the Secretary's office, and the distribution of publicity material promoting the department's activities to specialized press constituencies, as well as to general newspapers and magazines. By accommodating the occupational needs of the press through frequent press conferences, handouts, and the creation of a popular press room where correspondents gathered to work and to socialize, Hoover transformed the Commerce Department into one of the major Washington news centers, along with the White House and the congressional press galleries. The political scientist James L. McCamy, author of the first systematic study of departmental publicity, wrote in 1939 that "administrative publicity in its contemporary scope is generally said to have reached its maturity in the Department of Commerce under the secretaryship of Mr. Herbert Hoover."[64]

Hoover may have been the most aggressive of the Cabinet publicists under Harding and Coolidge, but the Commerce Department was only one of many administrative agencies to try to seek news coverage in the

1920s. One indicator of the growth of departmental publicity was increased public grumbling about the "handout habit" among Washington journalists.[65] J. Frederick Essary, of the *Baltimore Sun,* complained that on a typical day in 1931 he received 96 handouts, mostly from departmental publicists. "Taken together, this mass production of 'educational' literature distinguishes the federal government as the greatest propaganda establishment in the world," Essary wrote.[66] Nevertheless, the correspondents were more than willing to take advantage of the growing numbers of handouts, briefings, press rooms, press conferences, and other newsmaking opportunities created by Hoover and other departmental publicists.

Harding's exhortation to his Cabinet members may not have helped him to project the image of a unified presidency in the press, but it encouraged a major expansion of the publicity activity in executive branch departments in the 1920s. By giving presidential blessings to increased executive contacts with the press, Harding and his successor, Coolidge, contributed to the adoption of such practices at the administrative level of government, as well as in the presidency. Administrators sought increasingly to generate public support for their policies by creating or expanding departmental press offices, hiring additional publicists, centralizing departmental publicity work, and making the promotion of department activities in the press a routine part of agency administration. Appeals for public support through the mass media were becoming part of the routine practice of executive governance across the government, not only in the White House.

Widespread adoption of publicity techniques to appeal for popular support had important long-term consequences for the agencies, for the presidency, and for Washington journalism. One immediate outcome was to advance the political career of Herbert Hoover. Throughout his public life, Hoover often seemed ambivalent about seeking publicity for himself. He relished public acclaim but resisted "press agentry." As secretary of commerce, he had ordered that information about the department's work be disseminated as widely as possible by all available means of mass communication. At the same time, Hoover instructed Croghan not to use his name in press releases except where the subject referred directly to him. Otherwise, Hoover wrote, "Where practicable, announcements should be made on the authority of the Department of Commerce . . . ," according to a 1925 memorandum.[67]

Regardless of Hoover's ambivalence about promoting himself personally, nearly 15 years of headlines and stories based on his humanitarian work, underscored by his numerous government publicity campaigns, made Hoover one of the most popular political figures in the nation by the late 1920s.[68] When Coolidge chose, in August 1927, not to run for reelection, Hoover became a candidate for president at the peak of his popularity in the press and, consequently, with the public, at least partly because of his success at promoting his work through the most advanced techniques of publicity.

CHAPTER TEN

HOOVER: THE PRESS AND PRESIDENTIAL FAILURE

The disastrous single term of Herbert Hoover has become synonymous with presidential failure in the political history of the twentieth century. Hoover carried 40 of the 48 states in the 1928 election as the nation's "master of emergencies," a humane, hard-working, efficient public official. Four years later, Hoover was a figure of public ridicule, the subject of scornful jokes and partisan attacks about his inability to end the country's economic collapse. Hoover was easily defeated by Franklin D. Roosevelt when he sought reelection in 1932, and the image of Hoover's failed presidency has been carried forward by generations of historians.[1]

Ironically, considering Hoover's previous successes at managing the press to publicize his work during World War I and as secretary of commerce under Harding and Coolidge, his presidential collapse has been blamed, in part, on his difficulties with the press at the White House.[2] The contrast between Secretary Hoover, the expert publicist, and President Hoover, the butt of the White House press corps, has been the subject of considerable comment by historians. One explanation for the reversal is that Hoover's publicity campaigns oversold him as a "great humanitarian," "super businessman," "great salesman," and "omniscient economist." The result was a superhuman image that collapsed when Hoover could not cure the nation's economic depression.[3] Other scholars focus on Hoover's personality, arguing that Hoover's Quaker upbringing may have left him ambivalent about using publicity to promote himself personally.[4] Another theory is that Hoover, who was unusually shy for a public official, used publicity to avoid human contact and was incapable of dealing with the intrusiveness of the press at the White House.[5]

However, the most comprehensive study of Hoover and the press at the White House points out that it is unlikely any president between 1929 and 1933 could have escaped blame for the nation's economic crisis.[6] Six months after Hoover's inauguration, in October 1929, the speculative bubble that had sustained the soaring stock market of the 1920s collapsed. Hoover announced an emergency tax cut and exhorted industry and business leaders to support the stock market. The stock market rallied in early 1930, but fell again in June 1930 and continued to fall. None of the optimistic statements or resuscitative measures that Hoover tried could reverse the collapse. The gross national product fell by one-third between 1929 and 1933. Millions of Americans lost their jobs and homes. The stock market hit bottom in June 1932, just months before Hoover's defeat in the presidential election.[7]

Still, the extent of Hoover's problems with the press at the White House is surprising, even considering the collapse of the economy. Hoover's years of humanitarian work, underscored by constant publicity, led many prominent journalists to join his presidential campaign in 1928. But once he was in the White House, his relations with the correspondents soured. By late 1931, they had "reached a stage of unpleasantness without a parallel during the present century," according to critic Paul Y. Anderson, a correspondent for the *St. Louis Post-Dispatch* and the *Nation* magazine.[8] Anderson and other correspondents wrote extensively about Hoover's rocky relations with the press. The result was to create a literature of complaint that has been cited by scholars as additional evidence of Hoover's failure as president.

This chapter suggests that Hoover's problems with the press were related to the fundamental changes in presidential leadership and in Washington newsgathering that had taken place over the previous 30 years. Increased association with presidents had encouraged a desire for more independence among the correspondents, based partly on the professional rewards of being able to provide their editors with a reliable flow of news from the White House. The ability of the correspondents to deliver those stories was based on expectations about the White House publicity practices that recent presidents had adopted to appeal to public opinion through the press.

By the late 1920s, those expectations included frequent presidential news conferences open to all correspondents, regardless of party affiliation; the convenient availability of the president or his surrogates to respond to questions; a dependable supply of newsworthy information in one form or another to meet the correspondents' daily occupational needs; and some recognition of the correspondents' emerging professional status. When those expectations were not met satisfactorily, the correspondents displayed an increasing willingness to go public with their complaints about presidential behavior toward the press in articles written for newspapers, magazines, and trade journals.

This literature of complaint is often cited by historians as evidence of Hoover's failings as president. But it also was an indicator of changes in the media presidency. By the late 1920s, the press corps that presidents since McKinley had relied upon to carry their appeals to the citizenry was sufficiently organized and self-assured to begin to assert publicly its own professional interests and expectations about White House behavior.

Several developments contributed to professionalization of the correspondents in the 1920s. World War I had transformed Washington into the nation's news capital and elevated the importance of those who transmitted wartime information. The volume of news from Washington declined somewhat after the war, but it remained the second most frequent dateline for news on the Associated Press wires, after New York. The greater volume of news stories, compared to the prewar period, also reflected an increase in the number of correspondents who had been hired to write them. By 1929, daily newspapers in 138 cities employed Washington correspondents. The number registered with the congressional press galleries had climbed to nearly 300, more than double the number of those registered 30 years earlier.[9]

Furthermore, a growing number of the correspondents worked for newspaper chains, such as the Hearst and Scripps organizations, which usually provided relatively stable, year-round, salaried employment, rather than the freelancing on space rates that characterized Washington journalism at the turn of the century. In a study of the correspondents between 1864 and 1932, Samuel Kernell noted that job turnover dropped significantly after World War I. More correspondents were beginning to look on news work as a career, rather than as a stepping-stone to becoming a managing editor, a press agent, or a politician.[10]

In addition, the correspondents' freedom to make independent judgments on news, although limited, had been enhanced by the increasing preference of editors for "objective" or mildly interpretive reporting, in contrast to partisan commentary that followed the directives of their publishers or political patrons. Official partisanship had been in decline since the late nineteenth century. By 1931, 41 percent of the nation's daily newspapers, representing more than half of the daily circulation, had declared themselves editorially "independent" of the political parties.[11] Michael Schudson notes that correspondents who reported on Hoover's Message to Congress in 1930 did not hesitate to interpret what the President said, as well as what he didn't say.[12] Walter Lippmann, who described the more autonomous approach as "objectivity," argued in 1931 that it was the key to the emergence of journalism as a profession.[13]

Within the Washington press corps, expanded news coverage of the White House and Cabinet agencies, in addition to the traditional focus on Congress, had contributed to specialization, another indicator of professionalism. As secretary of commerce, Hoover successfully had appealed to the growing trade and business press to promote the work of the Commerce Department. Differentiation of roles also was apparent in the work of the mainstream press corps. In 1928, Raymond G. Carroll, of the *Philadelphia Public Ledger*, suggested three functional divisions among mainstream journalists in Washington: those correspondents who worked for press associations such as the Associated Press and United Press, which emphasized news on deadline; the bureau reporters from the largest newspapers or newspaper chains, who were more likely to write interpretive stories and features; and a declining proportion of "old-school" freelance correspondents for locally oriented or partisan newspapers around the country.[14] The bureau reporters, the fastest-growing category, were less dependent directly on the good will of the president for daily access than the permanently assigned White House correspondents, who tended to work for the press associations.[15]

Even more independent was an emerging fourth group, the syndicated political columnists. These new pundits, including David Lawrence, Frank R. Kent, Mark Sullivan, and, after 1931, Walter Lippmann, represented the beginnings of an elite class of correspondents who were less constrained by dependence on particular political leaders or editors. While few of the regular reporters enjoyed this sort of independence, the columnists symbolized a new kind of professional aspiration.[16]

Within this larger, more diverse, and somewhat more independent press corps, reporting on the White House had become a prestigious subspecialty with its own professional organization, the White House Correspondents Association. Harding and Coolidge had encouraged the development of the association, first organized under Wilson, to assist the White House with accreditation of correspondents, to screen attendance at press conferences, and, to some extent, to regulate the rules of engagement between presidents and the press.[17] In 1925, for example, an emergency meeting of the association was called to consider a new rule after Coolidge was offended when wire service correspondents dashed out of the President's news conference to file breaking stories.[18]

The association primarily had been a social group at Harding's inauguration in 1921. By the late 1920s, it had grown into an influential professional organization. More than 100 correspondents, one-third of the total registered with the congressional press galleries, voted in the group's election of officers in 1929, when Wilbur Forrest, of the *New York Herald-Tribune,* defeated Ralph E. Collins, of the *New York Sun,* for its presidency.[19] The association's annual dinners had become increasingly elaborate, and the president and other political leaders were obligated to attend. In 1930, those present included an estimated 350 correspondents and guests, including members of the Cabinet and Congress, plus radio and show business entertainers, such as Ginger Rogers.[20] In 1932, an estimated 500 people attended the White House Correspondents Association's tenth annual dinner, including President Hoover, Cabinet and congressional leaders, plus radio, stage, and film entertainers.[21]

Outside of Washington, one indicator of professionalization among the White House correspondents was the growing number of newspaper and magazine articles they were writing about their relationship with the president. Some of the articles were self-absorbed and more than a little self-glorifying.[22] But others complained that the White House did not meet the correspondents' expectations in providing the news necessary for them to do their jobs. This willingness to complain to reading audiences and, at least potentially, to risk White House disapproval, reflected a self-assurance that was in itself an indicator of professionalization.

Grumbling among the correspondents about their treatment at the White House was far from new, at least within the privacy of the press corps. The correspondents' access to the president and other executive leaders had increased substantially since the turn of the century. But these encounters, however useful in producing news, often were marked by condescension, favoritism, and overt manipulation. Theodore Roosevelt invited only a dozen or so favored correspondents to his informal news conferences and then dictated what they should write. Taft tried to ignore the correspondents almost completely. Wilson at times lectured them like wayward students and was sharply critical of what they wrote. Yet, prior to World War I, few correspondents dared to complain publicly in the press about how they were manipulated by presidents or other public officials. A review of publication indexes between 1890 and 1918 turned up only a handful of articles that focused on relations between presidents and the press. Most articles that did appear praised presidents for their generosity in seeing correspondents and pleaded for greater access.[23]

The absence of public complaints by correspondents prior to the 1920s is unsurprising. Gathering news at the White House still was a marginal assignment, and access to the president was tenuous. Press conferences were experiments, not a routine presidential practice, and attending them was a privilege, not an expectation. The penalty for displeasing the president was loss of access and, potentially, loss of a job, if the White House complained directly to editors or publishers. Theodore Roosevelt, in particular, did not hesitate to banish correspondents who displeased him.[24] Yet few critical articles by correspondents were published until the Coolidge administration, when the literature of complaint about presidential behavior toward the press began to appear.[25]

Coolidge, after Harding's death in 1923, continued Harding's practice of twice-weekly press conferences, which drew increasing numbers of reporters to the White House. Unlike the gregarious and outspoken Harding, however, Coolidge said little that was helpful to the correspondents in making news. Hugh Baillie, later president of United Press, said of Coolidge's first press conference: "We didn't get much out of him; in fact, we never got much out of him."[26] What Coolidge did say that was newsworthy often was cloaked in the official anonymity of the "White House spokesman," which the President used shrewdly to deflect responsibility for his remarks. Frustrated at the lack of news, some correspondents promoted the mythology of "Silent Cal," the stoic president from New England, as described in an earlier chapter. Other correspondents, however, went public with their complaints.

In a revealing article in 1924, Frank R. Kent, of the Democratic *Baltimore Sun,* one of the first independent political columnists, denounced the "curious conspiracy among newspaper reporters to keep from the people the facts about public men." Writing in the iconoclastic *American Mercury,* Kent publicly described and deplored the self-censorship practiced by White House correspondents to protect their access to the president:

> For one thing, [writing the truth] would be regarded as unclubby by the other correspondents, as a serious breach of etiquette if not an actual breach of confidence, as cruel, unethical, bolshevistic. Besides, these fellows have become so accustomed to a certain sort of soft pedaling that the presentation of a White House situation exactly as it is would seem to them exaggerated, justified and untrue. Then, too, it is the natural desire of every Washington correspondent to have a good personal standing at the White House. He is flattered if the President knows him by name. He wants to be well regarded by the presidential secretary, the White House staff, the Secret Service men, the members of the Cabinet. Their ill will, he thinks, is a liability to be avoided. Accordingly, his interests as well as his instinct, regardless of the politics of his paper, make him treat the White House statements and stories in a way to impress the White House with his friendliness, fairness and good feeling.

Although deference toward presidents by the correspondents was nothing new, Kent argued that Coolidge, whom he regarded as unfit to be president, was especially dependent on uncritical news coverage: "It has been literally amazing that a man could be so long, so consistently and unqualifiedly dull. But that is not the picture the country gets. That cannot be written. It is not news."[27]

Kent's sharply worded criticisms of Coolidge and an acquiescent press corps made public a set of complaints that other correspondents had voiced privately, anonymously, or in the limited circulation of trade journals.[28] More articles complaining about the treatment of correspondents at the Coolidge White House appeared in general circulation magazines in 1925, after the "White House spokesman" further frustrated the press corps by repudiating stories that were based on his anonymous comments. Coolidge refused to allow the correspondent David Lawrence to bring a stenographer into a press conference to produce a defensible transcript of the President's off-the-record remarks.[29] Lawrence, along with other prominent columnists and correspondents, followed Kent in publishing critical articles about Coolidge's relations with the press.[30]

Oswald Garrison Villard, editor of the *Nation* magazine, blamed Theodore Roosevelt for beginning the corruption of Washington correspondents by instituting press conferences in the first place. "Curiously, he made the position of Washington more important while also undermining the integrity and independence of the writers," Villard wrote in *Century* magazine.[31] *New York World* correspondent Charles Merz, writing in the *New Republic* in 1926, complained that "no ruler in history ever had such a magnificent propaganda machine as Mr. Coolidge; and certainly it would be impossible for anybody to use it more assiduously. The unanimity with which the press supports him is one of the major phenomena of our time."[32]

Some of the articles complaining about press relations at the White House came from correspondents whose publications were inclined to be critical of Coolidge for partisan or ideological reasons. The *New York World*, the *Nation*, and the *New Republic*, for example, leaned Democratic.[33] But others were written by correspondents without obvious partisan affiliation, such as Raymond Clapper, White House bureau chief of United Press.[34] In one month in 1927, critical articles by leading correspondents appeared in three major general-circulation magazines: the *Saturday Evening Post*, the *Atlantic Monthly*, and the *New York Times* Sunday magazine. The authors also chided their fellow correspondents for failing to resist Coolidge's manipulations more strongly.[35]

Interestingly, these public complaints by the correspondents followed a significant expansion of their access to the presidency. Coolidge had kept up the twice-weekly schedule of press conferences that Harding had established and was available generally for photo opportunities. Further-more, unlike, say, Theodore Roosevelt or Wilson, Coolidge refrained from trying to dictate the correspondents' stories. He simply overlooked those stories he disliked, and he didn't try to retaliate against offending reporters. Yet increasing familiarity with presidents and the dependable frequency of press conferences had changed the qualitative expectations of the correspondents. These expectations were not grandiose or adver-sarial. The correspondents only wanted Coolidge to provide them with news more regularly and to be less overtly manipulative.[36] What was sig-nificant was that the correspondents were willing to assert these expec-tations publicly and to criticize the White House when they were not met, despite the potential risk of losing access by displeasing the Presi-dent. This reflected a new level of professional self-assurance.

When Hoover succeeded Coolidge as president in 1929, then, he en-countered a White House press corps that was larger, more organized, more financially secure, more accustomed to associating with presidents, and considerably more self-assured than that faced by Wilson only a dozen years before. Moreover, at least some of its members were willing to com-plain publicly when their expectations of presidential behavior toward the press were not met.

It would be an exaggeration to describe the press corps that Hoover faced as adversarial, at least by the standards of the late twentieth century. Aside from a handful of columnists and Democratic correspondents, it was a group whose professional status was based on cooperation, not con-frontation, with the White House. Indeed, most of the correspondents looked forward to working with Hoover, who had been one of their best news sources in the Harding and Coolidge administrations. Some of the most prominent correspondents had worked in Hoover's presidential cam-paign. Furthermore, Hoover had promised that he would improve relations with the press at the White House.[37] All of which makes surprising the ex-tent of the correspondents' subsequent disillusionment.

Shortly after his inauguration, in March 1929, President Hoover met with about 200 correspondents and requested that the White House Cor-respondents Association form a committee to negotiate liberalized guide-lines for his press conferences.[38] The result was encouraging to the correspondents: an agreement that Hoover would continue Coolidge's practice of twice-weekly press conferences, but, for the first time, allow di-rect quotation of some of the president's comments.[39] In addition, Hoover designated George Akerson, a popular former newspaperman, to serve as the first official presidential press secretary, an institutional recognition of the increased status of press relations in the Hoover White House. Akerson was empowered with the authority to speak for the President, another first, and he held his own twice-daily briefings with the correspondents.[40]

Outside the White House, Hoover extended vigorously Coolidge's practice of lobbying newspaper and magazine owners and editors, as well as socializing with them. In the first weeks of his presidency, Hoover attended the spring meeting of the Gridiron Club; spoke to the annual luncheon of the Associated Press board of directors; hosted touring foreign editors; helped to dedicate a new printing plant for the *Chicago Daily News;* and met individually with various newspaper editors.[41]

Hoover's initiatives toward the press at first pleased the correspondents, including some of his partisan critics, and they said so publicly. Ray T. Tucker, of the *New York Telegram,* which had not supported Hoover's election, praised the new White House relationship with the press in an article in the *North American Review.*[42] Another critic, Paul Y. Anderson, of the *Nation,* praised Hoover grudgingly in an article that also ridiculed the "Hoover boys" in the press corps. "Not since the days of the worshiping Woodrovians (Wilson) has personal idolatry attained such a virulent form among Washington correspondents. . . . Hoover, already a hero, promises to become a saint before his administration is a month old," Anderson complained. Still, Anderson supported the new rules for presidential press conferences: "From every standpoint of frankness, honesty and practicality, the new system is a vast improvement over the one it supplanted."[43]

During Hoover's first few months in office, he expanded, or at least maintained, the routines of presidential press relations that had become established under Harding and Coolidge. Those included frequent news conferences; increased access to the President and his official surrogate, Akerson; liberalized rules on quoting the President; a greater flow of handouts and announcements; and recognition in the form of presidential support for professional and trade associations.[44] In addition, in late 1929, White House press facilities were renovated to allow each correspondent a mahogany desk and a typewriter in a carpeted press room, described as the "best press room that Washington correspondents ever had in the executive offices."[45]

Indeed, Hoover maintained much of this framework of routines throughout his presidency, even as his popularity with the press corps declined. Hoover held press conferences more often than nearly any other president: 79 in his first year, 87 in his second, and 69 in his third. Although the number of formally designated press conferences declined sharply in 1932, Hoover still held them more often over four years than any other twentieth-century president except Coolidge and Franklin D. Roosevelt.[46]

Moreover, Hoover continued the routine publicity practices that had been so well received by the press at the Commerce Department: high-profile, news-generating conferences on national economic issues, backed up with reams of mimeographed handouts with presidential statements and reports. He met frequently with leading publishers, editors, and influential and supportive columnists and correspondents. He maintained an extensive correspondence with others. Some were frequent guests at the White House or, more rarely, at the President's weekend retreat. Yet, even before the crash of the stock market in October 1929, complaints about Hoover's treatment of the press had begun to appear.

Once past the opening months of Hoover's presidency, the correspondents found that his press conferences actually generated little news, despite the liberalized rules.[47] Like Coolidge, Hoover required the correspondents to submit their questions in advance in writing. Also like Coolidge, Hoover chose to answer only some of the questions, reading from prepared statements. Others were ignored or discarded. Moreover, beginning in September 1929, Hoover canceled press conferences on short notice if he was too busy or had nothing to say, even if the correspondents were already waiting for him. At other press conferences, he would appear only to announce abruptly that he had no news.[48] Eighteen months after the promised liberalization of press conference rules, Hoover said less and less at them that the correspondents found newsworthy, and attendance at the conferences was in decline.[49] News and film photographers also were frustrated when Hoover, unhappy about leaked stories from publicity-seeking visitors to the White House, stopped the casual meetings with citizen delegations, local politicians, and celebrities that had served as frequent photo opportunities under Harding and Coolidge.[50]

Hoover also strongly resisted press intrusion into his private life for "human interest" features. Coolidge had taken advantage of this occupational inquisitiveness to regale the correspondents with New England yarns and to pose for photographers wearing hats and headdresses. Hoover, however, resented what he regarded as the press's fixation on trivialities.[51] This included inquiries about the First Lady, Lou Henry Hoover. She was active as a public speaker, appealing to women to help solve the problems of economic depression. She spoke frequently on radio, addressing upbeat messages to women and to children across the country. But these remarks were not aimed at the Washington correspondents. Like her husband, she also was regarded as uncooperative with the press in the White House by the correspondents. She refused to allow either interviews or casual photographs of herself or the family. The couple's children and grandchildren were strictly off limits. The dearth of personal information led one correspondent, Bess Furman of the Associated Press, to pose as a Girl Scout Christmas caroler to gain entrance to the White House family quarters for an article on how the First Family celebrated Christmas.[52]

Especially irksome to the correspondents was the President's refusal to grant them general access to Rapidan, the fishing retreat the Hoovers had constructed in rural Virginia. Not only were correspondents barred from coming within miles of the camp, except by invitation, but the White House also refused to notify the press when the presidential motorcade was scheduled to or from the camp. The result was a series of hurried and dangerous pursuits on rural roads, in which cars were wrecked and correspondents and family members seriously injured.[53]

In July 1931, Hoover reportedly was infuriated at a story in the *New York Times* that reported that the President's motorcade was forced to exceed the speed limit while returning from Rapidan to Washington for an international conference on war debts.[54] Hoover ordered an investigation into news leaks about the trip, as he had into the sources of other "human interest" stories that he found to be offensive. Those included a story that the President had been disturbed by the noise of a carpenter repairing a White House attic, and that a patch on a White House shower curtain reflected a Hoover economy drive.[55]

Even by the thin-skinned standards of the presidency, Hoover was notably sensitive to press coverage of any sort.[56] As he had at the Commerce Department, Hoover as president complained continually to editors about real or presumed slights, and he aggressively pursued the sources of unwanted stories. Olive Ewing Clapper, wife of Raymond Clapper, of United Press, wrote that "newspapermen tore their hair over the many fights they had with President Hoover and his press secretaries. Ray was constantly in hot water over stories written by his staff, to which the White House or some government official objected. Every newspaper office had similar trouble."[57] Hoover was blamed for the firings of at least two reporters, Robert S. Allen from the *Christian Science Monitor* and Drew Pearson from the *Baltimore Sun,* after their gossipy book, *Washington Merry-Go-Round,* became a best-seller in 1931.[58]

At the same time, Hoover openly favored those columnists and reporters who were his friends and sympathizers. He invited them, as well as selected editors and publishers, to be personal guests at both the White House and at Rapidan. Those privileged correspondents often took the opportunity to write exclusive stories about presidential activities, which angered the rest of the press corps. Presidential favoritism toward the press was nothing new. Theodore Roosevelt practiced it routinely. But the practice had become less overt with the decline of newspaper partisanship and the frequency of open press conferences. Partly out of necessity, Wilson, a Democrat, invited all correspondents, not just his partisans, to attend his press conferences. Harding, who was a Republican but liked correspondents generally, continued the open invitation, as did Coolidge. Nor did Coolidge display much personal favoritism, perhaps because he had few close friends in the press corps to favor.[59]

Hoover, however, preferred to deal with favored correspondents individually, rather than in mixed groups. He met frequently with those correspondents socially and in private audiences. But the practice was no longer as acceptable to a press corps that had become accustomed to more or less equal access to the president at press conferences. Presidential favoritism quickly became a theme in the literature of complaint. The articles focused less on criticizing the president than the correspondents who benefited the most from Hoover's favors, especially Richard V. Oulahan, of the *New York Times,* the dignified dean of the press corps, and Mark Sullivan, a columnist who breakfasted frequently with Hoover and was part of his "medicine ball" cabinet.[60]

Robert S. Allen, one of the authors of *Washington Merry-Go-Round,* characterized the White House correspondents as "reactionary and subservient" and labeled Oulahan "a willing vehicle for presidential propaganda."[61] Oulahan, a correspondent in Washington since the Cleveland administration, defended himself, also in print. Oulahan was proud of his close relations with presidents, which lent authority to his stories in the *New York Times.* He also observed that the increasing penchant for self-criticism among the correspondents was an indicator that the Washington press corps "has become a public institution."[62]

Hoover's favoritism toward a handful of correspondents, his frequent complaints about news coverage, his dour demeanor, and his occasionally abrupt behavior at press conferences contributed to an increasingly personal antagonism toward him on the part of some correspondents. Even Richard L. Strout, the *New Republic* columnist TRB, who was a frequent critic of Hoover's policies, remarked at the president's personal unpopularity with the press. "Yet Hoover has treated the correspondents much more squarely than did the good Calvin (Coolidge), has made infinitely more news, talks to them with much freedom, force and intelligence," he wrote as TRB. "Notwithstanding this, they do not like him—and one evidence is the way in which small White House happenings are played up to Mr. Hoover's embarrassment, whereas they were played up the other way for Calvin."[63]

Hoover's deteriorating relationship with the correspondents presented an opportunity to the President's political opponents, who launched a publicity campaign to try to turn news coverage against the White House. When correspondents lacking a presidential news story needed a source of information, they could count on Charles Michelson, a former *New York World* correspondent who proved to be a talented opposition publicist for the Democratic National Committee.[64] Michelson was more than willing to supply anti-Hoover information and to make available Democratic sources who would speak against Hoover without any restrictions on their direct quotation. Michelson also cleverly shaped Democratic criticism of Hoover's economic policies in quotable phrases about "Hoovervilles" and the "Hoover flag," an empty pocket turned inside out.[65]

In addition, the Hoover White House damaged its own credibility among the correspondents by a series of blunders in making important announcements. One was Akerson's erroneous announcement in 1930 that Hoover had nominated Justice Harlan F. Stone to be chief justice of the U.S. Supreme Court. Akerson then had to read a statement that the President had actually nominated Charles Evans Hughes. In early 1931, the White House issued a misleading summary of the long-anticipated Wickersham Commission report on the problems of Prohibition. The White House version of the commission's conclusion contradicted that of its members. Correspondents at first were confused, then angered at what they saw as a deliberate attempt at deception.[66] When the two largest press associations, Associated Press and United Press, rated their top stories for the world in 1931, both listed the controversy involving the Wickersham report as among the top ten. The worldwide economic depression, of course, led both lists.[67]

Public complaints about Hoover's press relations reached a peak in late 1931, when *Editor and Publisher* launched a series of broadly worded, weekly assaults on the administration's "subtle censorship" and "news stifling."[68] Hoover's new and unpopular press secretary, Theodore Joslin, chose that inopportune moment to lecture the correspondents on their responsibility to consider the impact of negative news stories on a citizenry battered by economic collapse. The President considered the economic crisis the equivalent of a wartime emergency, Joslin said. He suggested that correspondents consult with his office before writing stories about it. The correspondents interpreted Joslin's remarks as a request for voluntary censorship, as practiced in World War I. Joslin denied later that was what he meant. But a National Press Club petition in protest quickly gathered 100 signatures.[69]

By 1932, the tone of the President's press relations had become bitter, at least in the literature of complaint. Elliott Thurston, writing in *Scribner's,* said that "except for a few favorites who cling to the White House

or to the Rapidan camp, Mr. Hoover has scarcely a friend or defender
among the hundreds of working newspaper men of Washington."[70] Ray
T. Tucker, who now regretted his earlier praise of Hoover, wrote that four
years before, "almost all the young and idealistic members of the Washington corps of correspondents were his valiants. Hardly a handful have
faith in him now."[71]

Still, despite the economic collapse and the rancor of the correspondents' literature of complaint, news coverage of Hoover's presidency remained restrained and frequently supportive, at least until late in his term.
Louis Liebovich's survey of newspapers around the nation found that the
administration's press coverage remained generally favorable during
Hoover's first 18 months in the White House. Nor did Hoover himself
seem overly concerned about the correspondents' complaints, at least in
comparison with the other problems facing his presidency. No extraordinary effort was made to win back the correspondents and editors who
were abandoning his administration, even after Democratic victories in the
congressional elections in 1930 resulted in new, vigorous criticism of
Hoover's economic policies.[72]

Some of Hoover's supporters blamed his problems on a hostile, preda-
tory press corps. Herbert Corey, writing in George Lorimer's *Saturday
Evening Post,* said that Hoover, lulled by his earlier publicity successes, did
not realize that many of the correspondents "were hostile to him politically and that all of them, broadly speaking, viewed him as a potential
source of news which might sometimes be satisfyingly sensational."[73] But
there is little evidence in the news coverage of the Hoover administration
to support the notion of an adversary press. Even at the lowest point of the
Hoover presidency, in mid-1932, overall news coverage did not reflect, at
least overtly, negative attitudes among the correspondents. Press coverage
of the tragic Bonus March in the summer of 1932, once thought to be the
final publicity blow to Hoover's reelection, was surprisingly supportive.
Liebovich's analysis of newspaper coverage found that most stories characterized the marchers as troublemakers and did not criticize Hoover's decision to call in federal troops to rout the marchers with tanks and tear gas.[74]

Nevertheless, the correspondents' public complaints about Hoover
and the press reflected a significant development in the evolution of the
media presidency. The press corps attracted to the White House to carry
the president's views to the public was now sufficiently self-assured to
complain publicly when a president did not meet their expectations of
making news. The issue was not whether it was appropriate for a president to try to reach the public by managing the press. Rather, it was how
well a president met the expectations and occupational requirements of

the correspondents who had been drawn to the White House to receive news on a regular basis.

When the correspondents went public with their complaints, they created a documentary record that became one of the criteria by which Hoover's presidency was evaluated, both at the time and by subsequent historians. Walter Millis, writing in the *Atlantic Monthly* in 1932, said that Hoover's failure to accommodate the press properly at the White House was indicative of Hoover's larger failings in policymaking.[75] The White House's relationship with the press, a secondary aspect of presidential leadership 35 years before, had become a basis for evaluating overall presidential success or failure.

The literature of complaint about Hoover was also an indicator that while the relationship between presidents and the press had become institutionalized, it was not necessarily stable. Just as executive governance had been changed by presidents who appealed increasingly for public support, so had the patterns of Washington journalism. To maintain access to the nation's news pages to appeal for popular support, a president needed to keep adapting to the shifting expectations of an increasingly independent press corps.

CHAPTER ELEVEN

CONCLUSION:
THE MEDIA PRESIDENCY

Between 1897 and 1933, seven presidents experimented with managing the press to appeal for popular support through "new media" created by advances in communications technologies and the explosive growth of commercial newspapers and magazines. The "old media" of sponsored publications were in decline in the late nineteenth century, along with the political parties that had supported them. Advertising-supported newspapers, popular magazines, and, by the 1920s, radio offered new opportunities for presidential leadership. These new forms of mass communication were capable of transmitting the president's appeals to increasingly larger audiences of citizens. News stories, images, and broadcasts could project the appearance of presidential authority to the farthest corners of the country. The prominence of these messages in the press could leave an impression of popular support in an era before systematic measurement of public opinion.

When the presidents of a century ago tried to appeal to the public through these new media, however, they found that access was not necessarily available on demand or in the form that the White House desired. Lacking the leverage of government controls or economic sponsorship, and with party allegiance weakening, presidents who wished to appeal to media audiences found that a new form of leadership was required. The gatekeepers of these increasingly independent media—owners, editors, producers, and journalists—needed to be persuaded to allow space and time for the president's messages in their pages and, later, in their broadcasts. Presidents who wished to receive news coverage had to compete for access and prominence with the daily round of events, sensations, features, and human-interest stories, as well as with similar efforts at publicity by other political leaders.

In various ways, presidents from William G. McKinley to Herbert Hoover tried to reach these media audiences by adapting to the shifting technological, organizational, and ideological requirements of making news. Their cumulative successes and failures in adopting the priorities and techniques of publicity transformed both the presidency and the way that Americans viewed their national leaders for much of the twentieth century.

The durability of the relationship established between the executive and the gatekeepers of the news media between 1897 and 1933 has obscured the experimental nature of that transformation, as well as some of its implications for presidential leadership in the twenty-first century. Managing the press to achieve public support was as much a challenge to the presidency as an opportunity. There were presidential failures as well as successes, and potential benefits came with costs. Presidents who wanted to receive favorable news coverage had to learn how to lobby the press, just as presidents who wished to achieve legislative success needed to lobby Congress. Some presidents, especially William Howard Taft, were unwilling to sacrifice the time and dignity involved. But other presidents, especially those who followed Woodrow Wilson, viewed managing the press as a necessary tool to maintain or to expand public support for their governing authority.

To learn the techniques of publicity and to carry them out successfully required increasing amounts of the president's time and that of his limited staff. In the late nineteenth century, when managing the press was not among the president's highest priorities, chiefs of staff such as Secretaries Daniel S. Lamont and George Cortelyou could handle press inquiries as part of their regular duties. But when presidents began to meet with correspondents more regularly and more purposefully, additional staff support was necessary. Theodore Roosevelt reached beyond the White House for help from Gifford Pinchot's "press bureau" in the U.S. Forest Service. Woodrow Wilson in World War I created an information ministry, the Committee on Public Information, to assist him in promoting public support for the war effort. Under Warren G. Harding and Calvin Coolidge, a full-time White House assistant was employed to work with the press. Only after Hoover was inaugurated in 1929 was the position acknowledged institutionally by the designation of an official press secretary.

The potential of reaching of mass media audiences appealed also to many other government leaders who watched the president's successes. Executive branch officials and administrators began to hire their own publicists and to seek publicity for their own purposes, which were not necessarily those of the White House. Presidents in turn were faced with distracting leaks to the press and increased competition for the correspondents' attention from these other public officials and their press agents. Theodore Roosevelt encouraged executive branch publicity activity when it served his purposes and tried to suppress its leaks when it did not. By bringing Pinchot's campaign for government conservation into the White House, Roosevelt both benefited from its publicity and gained some control over a potential distraction to the President's own newsmaking. When Roosevelt's successor, Taft, tried to scale back his conservation policies, the disenchanted Pinchot demonstrated that uncontrolled and unanswered leaks to the press from competing agency publicists could undermine Taft's secretary of the interior, Richard A. Ballinger, and the President himself.

Wilson in his first term considered the creation of a presidential "publicity bureau" to try to stop leaks and to centralize executive publicity activity in the White House, an effort reflected institutionally during World War I by the President's creation of the Committee on Public Information. But White House influence over executive branch publicity declined after the CPI was dismantled at the end of the war. In 1921, Warren G. Harding inadvertently encouraged the centrifugal development of executive branch publicity activity by directing his Cabinet members to speak to the press on their own, based on the questionable assumption that they would speak with one voice on the administration's behalf. Under Harding's policy of encouraging Cabinet publicity, carried forward by Calvin Coolidge, Herbert Hoover created a press office in every major bureau in the Department of Commerce, a departmental publicity structure that was widely copied by New Deal agencies a decade later. It also assisted Hoover in creating a base of popular support for his successful campaign for president in 1928.

Presidential attempts to stimulate public support through the mass media affected other institutions in the polity. Just as news stories around the nation created the appearance of public support for the president, those published by the major newspapers and magazines in Washington and New York carried the president's messages to other centers of national governance. Managing the press was a means by which the president could transmit publicly his views to other government officials, as well to the citizenry. Prominence in the press was not only an indicator of White House influence on public opinion. It was an amplifier of the president's views into the discourse of national policymaking.

Congress had been the dominant branch of government in the late nineteenth century, and the main focus of Washington newsgathering. Presidential attempts to appeal to the public through the press constituted a visible challenge to Capitol Hill supremacy in both policymaking and newsmaking. Between 1897 and 1933, the presidency proved eventually to be more successful than Congress at making news in Washington and in the nation. The correspondents found the president to be a convenient single source or subject for news stories about federal policymaking. With its diffused leadership structure and inherent localism, Congress was slow to respond institutionally to the challenge of the media presidency. Individual members of Congress were concerned at first more with their regional newspapers than with stories published in faraway Washington or New York. Significantly, congressional attempts to restrict the spread of executive branch publicity activity began as a response to news coverage of Theodore Roosevelt's conservation policies in western, rather than in national, newspapers.

The president's demonstrated ability to upstage Congress in the press encouraged similar attempts across the executive branch. Publicity from administrative agencies posed a potential challenge to congressional committee control over agency budgets and operations. Pinchot, who had created the first "press bureau" in the U.S. Forest Service in 1905, recognized that the "free" publicity in newspapers and magazines offered a means to circumvent congressional restraints on the use of official government publications. Pinchot and his imitators were able to use the press to appeal for support among agency clients, other power centers in the polity, and from the public at large, all without congressional permission.

Congress tried unsuccessfully in 1913 to stop the creation of agency press bureaus and to bar the executive hiring of "publicity experts." But experiments in managing the press were already under way in numerous executive publicity offices, which sent a growing flow of "handouts" and "press bulletins" to receptive newspapers and news services. Government adoption of publicity practices was accelerated during World War I by Wilson's creation of wartime propaganda agencies, including the Committee on Public Information and the Food Administration. In the 1920s, Secretary of Commerce Hoover encouraged major bureaus in the Department of Commerce to develop publicity strategies to promote recognition of their activities by the public and by Congress. By the end of the 1920s, despite congressional resistance, publicists and publicity offices were widespread in major executive agencies.

Presidential attempts to appeal to the public through the news also had a substantial effect on the "fourth branch of government": the press. Adoption of publicity practices by the White House and executive agencies played a formative role in the professionalization of national political journalism. Covering the presidency and the executive branch prior to 1897 had been a secondary activity by junior members of an entrepreneurial press corps based in the congressional press galleries. Under McKinley and, particularly, under Theodore Roosevelt, covering the president became a more attractive assignment for favored correspondents. Roosevelt made the White House a daily source of news, and he inadvertently invited increased press attention to his family life.

Wilson encouraged the emergence of the presidency as a primary focus of Washington newsgathering by experimenting at length with press conferences open to all correspondents, not just those of the president's political party. During World War I, Wilson's wartime agencies had a near monopoly on the war information available to the press. The Senate reasserted congressional dominance of the Washington news agenda with the defeat of Wilson's postwar treaties in 1919. But, beginning in 1921, Harding and Coolidge re-invigorated the presidential press conference and drew the correspondents back to the White House, this time more or less permanently. Congress remained the central focus of the news from Washington until the New Deal. But the shift in leadership of public opinion to the White House already was under way.

Once drawn to the White House, the correspondents found that growing access to the president increased their occupational status, as it did the amount of news that they were able to provide to their employers. From a small group of favored correspondents affiliated with sympathetic or partisan newspapers, the White House press corps expanded to include hundreds of correspondents and photographers by the 1930s. Continuing association with presidents encouraged an increased self-regard among the correspondents, whose professional stature also was enhanced by more stable employment, salaried compensation, specialization, declining newspaper partisanship, greater leeway in interpreting events, and the development of a journalistic elite, the syndicated columnists. By 1933, covering the White House had become a prestigious assignment with its own professional organizations, particularly the White House Correspondents Association.

From the standpoint of the presidency, however, the professionalization of journalism and other changes in the practices and institutions of mass communications made reaching media audiences as much of a moving target as a reliable means of influencing public opinion. McKinley and Theodore Roosevelt usually could count on selected correspondents to transmit what they wished to say when they wished to say it. But the outcomes became less predictable as the number of correspondents invited to the White House grew and became more diverse politically and occupationally. Even Theodore Roosevelt could not prevent the correspondents, once invited to form a more personal relationship with the President, from inquiring into his family life. Wilson's open press conferences drew Republican as well as Democratic correspondents, and also those who were more interested in human interest stories about the President's daughters than with Wilson's policy proclamations.

In the 1920s, growing self-assurance among the correspondents also took the form of a literature of complaint about the relationship that had been established with the White House. Frequent access to the president for newsworthy information had brought the correspondents increased professional success and prestige. But it also left them dependent on the President and his publicists for news stories to meet the daily requirements of their employers. The correspondents reacted protectively when Harding's presidency was threatened by reports of corruption and imaginatively when Coolidge was not sufficiently forthcoming in furnishing them with newsworthy information. When the correspondents felt that Coolidge, and then Hoover, did not meet satisfactorily the correspondents' expectations of making news, they complained publicly about the quality of their access to the president and the restrictive rules of engagement that had been established between the press and the White House.

The correspondents' complaints about the press relations of Coolidge and Hoover did not reflect an emerging adversary press, at least by late-twentieth-century standards. With important exceptions, notably the columnist and theorist Walter Lippmann, the correspondents of the 1920s and early 1930s were concerned more with receiving a regular supply of news than with articulating global arguments about press freedom or the need to inform citizens of a democratic society. But these public tensions reflected the dynamic nature of the relationship that had formed between the White House and the news media. For a president to manage the press successfully, an ongoing process of persuasion was required, not just the following of established practices and routines. To maintain access to the public through an independent mass media, presidents had to continue to adapt to their changing values and processes, as well as to changes in ownership and in technologies.

Franklin D. Roosevelt, who was inaugurated in 1933, succeeded where Hoover was believed to have failed in adapting to these changes. Restoring public confidence in the economy and stimulating public support for New Deal recovery programs were central to Roosevelt's presidency. Managing the press to achieve that public support was one of his highest priorities. The second Roosevelt reestablished twice-weekly press conferences, which had lapsed in Hoover's last year, and dropped the most irksome of the rules of engagement: the requirement that the correspondents submit their questions in advance in writing. Unlike the defensive

Hoover, FDR found journalists to be a bully audience, as had his cousin Theodore, 30 years before. The new President supplied the correspondents regularly with newsworthy information, and direct quotations were available in typed form. The result was to defuse the correspondents' complaints while reasserting presidential influence over newsmaking.[1] Roosevelt, like Wilson, also tried to centralize executive branch publicity activities in the White House: he created a National Emergency Council to monitor and to attempt to influence public opinion regionally as well as nationally, and he arranged for the radio networks to broadcast his views without interruption or editing. He also authorized the launching of an ambitious program of government documentary films to be shown in theaters.[2] Not all of Roosevelt's publicity initiatives were successful, and he could not eliminate the inherent tensions between the institutions of the press and the presidency. But he gained a long press "honeymoon" in the critical early years of his administration and established a standard for leadership of public opinion through the press against which subsequent twentieth-century presidents have been measured.

Since the 1930s, the ability of the president to create and to maintain public support through mass communications has been recognized as a primary determinant of presidential success or failure, even as the underlying relationship between the president and the news media deteriorated late in the century. Re-examination of the formative years between 1897 and 1933 suggests some observations.

First, although the media presidency has endured for most of the twentieth century, it is not necessarily a permanent form of presidential leadership. The modern relationship between the president and the news media has its roots in the decline of political parties and the commercialization of mass communications in the late nineteenth century, rather than in the directives of the nation's Founders. Just as there is no specific language in the Constitution to support a rhetorical presidency whose governing authority is based on appeals for popular support, neither is there a constitutional requirement that the president communicate with the citizenry through the press. Presidents of the twentieth century have found the news media, in one form or another, to be an expedient and frequently effective means of seeking public support. But no constitutional obligation exists for them to do so.

The media presidency has endured because the relationship between the president and the press has been, for the most part, mutually beneficial to both institutions. Since early in the century, both the White House and the news media have adapted to accommodate and, until recently, to perpetuate this relationship. From the perspective of the White House, managing the press has been a primary requirement for a successful presidency, not an optional activity. Failure to persuade the gatekeepers of the media to present the president's views to their audiences is a potential threat to popular support for the chief executive's governing authority. Complaints that one twentieth-century president or another has manipulated the press excessively or intruded on press freedom are important, but they need to be considered in the context of the institutional imperatives of the media presidency. Maintaining public support through available means of mass communications is as important to presidential authority in the late twentieth century as negotiating with Congress, directing administrative bureaucracies, or conducting foreign policy.

Despite their complaints, the news media, too, have benefited from the relationship, both individually and institutionally. Many of the newsgathering practices of modern Washington journalism are based on the acceptance of a certain amount of "management" by the president, his advisors, and other official sources. The news media have gained primacy in the governing process by being messengers of authoritative information to and among the institutions of the polity, as well as to the public. Since television made possible the live broadcast of presidential press conferences, the White House correspondents in particular have become visible symbols of freedom of the press in the nation's living rooms. However, presidential experiments with other forms of "new media" in the 1990s pose a potential threat to their prominence and prestige, as well as to that of news organizations that employ them.

Second, the search for a "new media" to better project the president's appeals to the public has been a characteristic of the media presidency since its earliest days. The transformation of the presidency that began late in the nineteenth century was based, in part, on the ability of successive presidents to take advantage of new ways to appeal for popular support. The White House continually sought seek out new forms of communication that promised larger audiences or fewer distortions than "old media" could provide. Each new communications technology or format, whether based on the telegraph, the telephone, photography, newsreels, or radio, was tried at one time or another between 1897 and 1933 by presidents unhappy with newspaper partisanship, politically ambitious editors, sensationalism, muckraking magazines, tabloid newspapers, or irresponsible correspondents. Some of the new technologies and formats, notably radio and, later, television news, proved to be more effective vehicles for presidential communication than others. But none was more successful at projecting a credible message to the public than managing the press at the White House, at least until late in the century.

Given the onrush of new communications formats and technologies in the 1990s, however, it seems likely that a future president will become more successful at communicating to the public through some "new media" than the "old media" that gathered at the White House early in the century. Repeated "feeding frenzies" and other adversarial behavior in the news media of the 1990s provided additional incentive for the White House to continue to seek other, less distorted, ways to appeal to the public for popular support. Nothing here suggests that the "old media" of newspapers, news services, and broadcast networks will cease to be influential gatekeepers and interpreters of the presidency. The institutional foundations of their relationship make a complete break unlikely, despite the hopes or fears of both parties. But the news media's role as exclusive intermediaries between the president and the citizenry is likely to continue to decline. Considering that many of the values and practices of twentieth-century political journalism developed in conjunction with the media presidency, the potential displacement of the press in this relationship raises significant questions that need to be addressed about the relevance and the future of the journalistic filtering process through which Americans have viewed the presidency for much of the century.

Finally, the influence that the media presidency has had on patterns of executive leadership, the polity, and political journalism since early in the twentieth century suggests that any future transformation in presidential communications will have an impact well beyond the institutions involved. Whatever form a "communications presidency" takes in the twenty-first century will present new challenges and opportunities, not only for presidential leadership, but for how the nation is governed, for the range of political ideas represented in the mass media, and for how Americans learn about their leaders in a democratic society.

NOTES

Introduction

1. On the formidable mythology of the Watergate experience, see Michael Schudson, *The Power of News* (Cambridge, Mass: Harvard University Press, 1995), 143–65.

2. Adam Gropkin, "Read All About It," *New Yorker,* 12 December 1994, 84–102. Samuel Kernell, *Going Public: New Strategies of Presidential Leadership,* 2nd ed. (Washington, D.C.: CQ Press, 1993), 55–64, 192–6.

3. Michael Baruch Grossman and Martha Joynt Kumar, *Portraying the President: The White House and the News Media* (Baltimore, Md: Johns Hopkins University Press, 1981), 19–28. See also Stephen Hess, *The Government-Press Connection* (Washington, D.C.: Brookings, 1984).

4. Kenneth T Walsh, *Feeding the Beast: The White House versus the Press* (New York: Random House, 1996), 6–7.

5. Thomas E. Patterson, "Legitimate Beef: The Presidency and a Carnivorous Press," *Media Studies Journal* 8 (No. 2, Spring 1994): 21–6.

6. See, among others, Robert Entman, *Democracy without Citizens: Media and the Decay of American Politics* (New York: Oxford, 1989), James Fallows, *Breaking the News* (New York: Pantheon, 1996), and Thomas E. Patterson, *Out of Order* (New York: Vintage, 1994).

7. Larry J. Sabato, *Feeding Frenzy: How Attack Journalism Has Transformed Politics* (New York: Free Press, 1991) is credited with popularizing use of the phrase.

8. See, generally, John Anthony Maltese, *Spin Control: The White House Office of Communications and the Management of Presidential News,* 2nd ed. (Chapel Hill: University of North Carolina Press, 1994).

9. Jennifer Waber, "Secrecy and Control: Reporters Committee says Clinton Administration's dealings with the press have become more antagonistic," *Editor and Publisher,* 24 May 1997, 10–13, 33–4.

10. Sidney Blumenthal, "The Syndicated Presidency," *New Yorker,* 5 April 1993, 42–7.

11. Patricia I. Dooley and Paul Grosswiler, "'Turf Wars': Journalists, New Media and the Struggle for Control of Political News," *Press/Politics* 2 (No. 3, Summer 1997): 31–51.

12. James B. Lemert, "Adapting to Clinton and the New Media Reality," *Media Studies Journal* 8 (No. 2, Spring 1994): 53–8.

13. On scandal coverage in the Clinton administration and the presidential response, see Howard Kurtz, *Spin Cycle: Inside the Clinton Propaganda Machine* (New York: Free Press, 1998).

14. David Domke, et al., "News Media, Candidates and Issues, and Public Opinion in the 1996 Presidential Campaign," *Journalism and Mass Communications Quarterly* 74 (No. 4, Winter 1997): 718–37.

15. Schudson, *The Power of News,* 53–71.

16. The quotations are from Douglass Cater, *The Fourth Branch of Government* (New York: Vintage Books, 1959), 25.

17. *The Federalist Papers,* Clinton Rossiter, ed. (New York: Mentor, 1961), 517.

18. For overviews of the evolution of president-press relationship, see James E. Pollard, *The Presidents and the Press* (New York: Macmillan, 1947), and John Tebbel and Sarah Miles Watts, *The Press and the Presidency* (New York: Oxford University Press, 1985).

19. William David Sloan, "The Early Party Press: The Newspaper in American Politics, 1789–1812," *Journalism History* 9 (1982): 19. On the details of government patronage, see Culver H. Smith, *The Press, Politics and Patronage: The American Government's Use of Newspapers* (Athens: University of Georgia Press, 1977).

20. The quotation is from Frank Luther Mott, *American Journalism: A History of Newspapers in the United States through 140 Years: 1690–1940* (New York: Macmillan, 1949), 169. On the Jacksonian press, see Gerald J. Baldasty, "The Press and Politics in the Age of Jackson," *Journalism Monographs* 89 (August 1984).

21. The citation is from Jeffrey Rutenbeck, "The Stagnation and Decline of Partisan Journalism in Late Nineteenth-Century America," *American Journalism* 10 (Nos. 1–2, Winter-Spring 1993): 38–60.

22. See generally, Carol Sue Humphrey, *The Press of the Young Republic, 1783–1833* (Westport, Conn: Greenwood Press, 1996).

23. For a recent overview of communications history research into this transition, see Timothy E. Cook, *Governing with the News: The News Media as a Political Institution* (Chicago: University of Chicago Press, 1998), 20–60. Cook makes a useful distinction between direct government "sponsorship" of the press and indirect "subsidies," such as lower postal rates.

24. For influential works that place the beginnings of this transition in the press to the 1830s and 1840s, see Michael Schudson, *Discovering the News* (New York: Basic Books, 1978), and Dan Schiller, *Objectivity and the News* (Philadelphia: University of Pennsylvania Press, 1981).

25. For a comprehensive overview, see Gerald J. Baldasty, *The Commercialization of News in the Nineteenth Century* (Madison: University of Wisconsin Press, 1992).

26. On the scholarly debate, see Michael Schudson, "Toward a Troubleshooting Manual for Journalism History," *Journalism and Mass Communication Quarterly* 74 (No. 3, Autumn 1997): 463–76.

27. George Juergens, *Joseph Pulitzer and the New York World* (Princeton, N.J.: Princeton University Press, 1966), 16, points out that Pulitzer seemed to overlook the possibility that reliance on advertisers also might restrict newspaper independence.

28. Jeffrey B. Rutenbeck, "Newspaper Trends in the 1870s: Proliferation, Popularization, and Political Independence," *Journalism Quarterly* 72 (Summer 1995): 361–75. Gerald J. Baldasty and Jeffrey Rutenbeck, "Money, Politics and Newspapers: The Business Environment of Press Partisanship in the Late Nineteenth Century," *Journalism History* 13 (Summer-Autumn 1989): 60–9.

29. Michael E. McGerr, *The Decline of Popular Politics* (New York: Oxford University Press, 1986), 42–68.

30. McGerr, *The Decline of Popular Politics,* 3–11.

31. Richard L. Kaplan, "The Economics and Politics of Nineteenth-Century Newspapers: The Search for Markets in Detroit, 1865–1900," *American Journalism* 10 (Nos. 1–2, Winter-Spring 1993): 84–101.

32. Mark Wahlgren Summers, *The Press Gang: Newspapers and Politics, 1865–1878* (Chapel Hill: University of North Carolina Press, 1994), 2–6.

33. William David Sloan and James D. Startt, eds., *The Media in America: A History,* 3rd ed. (Northport, Ala: Vision Press, 1996), 210–13. Tebbel and Watts, *The Press and the Presidency,* 168–98.

34. Martha Joynt Kumar, "The White House Beat at the Century Mark," *Press/Politics* 2 (No. 3, Summer 1997), 10–13, documents that presidential contact with the press in this period was more extensive than the isolation claimed by earlier scholars.

35. On the mythology of the Price anecdote, see Rodger Streitmatter, "William W. Price: First White House Correspondent and Emblem of an Era," *Journalism History* 16 (Spring-Summer 1989): 32–41.

36. Lewis L. Gould, *The Presidency of William McKinley* (Lawrence, Kans.: Regents Press of Kansas, 1980), vii, argues that McKinley revitalized the office to become the first modern president.

37. See George Juergens, *News from the White House: The Presidential-Press Relationship in the Progressive Era* (Chicago: University of Chicago Press, 1981), and Robert C. Hilderbrand, *Power and the People: Executive Management of Public Opinion in Foreign Affairs, 1897–1921* (Chapel Hill: University of North Carolina Press, 1981). On World War I propaganda, see Stephen Vaughn, *Holding Fast the Inner Lines: Democracy, Nationalism and the Committee on Public Information* (Chapel Hill: University of North Carolina Press, 1980).

38. The quotation is from J. Frederick Essary, *Covering Washington: Government Reflected to the Public in the Press* (Boston: Houghton Mifflin, 1927), 18. See

also Essary, "Uncle Sam's Ballyhoo Men," *American Mercury* 23 (August 1931): 419–28.

39. For a formative work on this theme, see Elmer C. Cornwell Jr., *Presidential Leadership of Public Opinion* (Westport, Conn.: Greenwood Press, 1979 [1965]). See also George Edwards III, *The Public Presidency: The Pursuit of Popular Support* (New York: St. Martin's Press, 1983), and Betty Houchen Winfield, *FDR and the News Media* (Urbana: University of Illinois Press, 1990).

40. Jeffrey K. Tulis, "The Two Constitutional Presidencies," in Michael Nelson, ed., *The Presidency and the Political System,* 3rd ed. (Washington, D.C.: Congressional Quarterly, 1990), 85–115. Tulis, *The Rhetorical Presidency* (Princeton, N.J.: Princeton University Press, 1987), 182, 186. Mary Stuckey, "The Rhetorical Presidency: A Nexus for Scholarship," *PRG Report* 20 (No. 2, Fall 1997): 6–8.

41. See generally the works of Richard Neustadt, *Presidential Power* (New York: John Wiley and Sons, 1980).

42. On this aspect of progressivism, see Robert H. Wiebe, *The Search for Order* (New York: Hill and Wang, 1967).

43. Charles O. Jones, *The Presidency in a Separated System* (Washington, D.C.: Brookings, 1994), 2–3.

44. William J. Ridings Jr. and Stuart B. McIver, "1990s Presidential Poll," *Presidential Studies Quarterly* 25 (Spring 1995): 375–7.

Chapter 1.
McKinley and the First White House Press Corps

1. Arthur M. Schlesinger Jr., *The Imperial Presidency* (Boston: Houghton Mifflin Co., 1973), 82–90.

2. Hilderbrand, *Power and the People,* 3–4.

3. W. Dale Nelson, *Who Speaks for the President? The White House Press Secretary from Cleveland to Clinton* (Syracuse, N.Y.: Syracuse University Press, 1998), argues that Cortelyou was the first modern press secretary.

4. See Richard V. Oulahan, unpublished memoirs, "Early Newspaper Experiences," Chapter 2, Box 1, Richard V. Oulahan Papers, Herbert Hoover Presidential Library.

5. Leonard D. White, *The Republican Era: 1869–1901* (New York: Macmillan, 1958), 1–12.

6. Pollard, *The Presidents and the Press,* 541–5.

7. Ritchie, *Press Gallery,* 181–4. See also Ritchie, "'The Loyalty of the Senate': Washington Correspondents in the Progressive Era," *Historian* 50 (August 1989): 574–91.

8. Harold W. Stanley and Richard G. Niemi, *Vital Statistics on American Politics* (Washington, D.C.: CQ Press, 1988), 48.

9. Jean Folkerts and Dwight L. Teeter Jr., *Voices of a Nation: A History of Mass Media in the United States,* 3rd ed. (Boston: Allyn and Bacon, 1998), 246–7.

10. Lincoln Steffens, "The Business of a Newspaper," *Scribner's* 22 (October 1897): 446–67.

11. The quotation is from Woodrow Wilson, *Congressional Government* (Boston: Houghton Mifflin, 1885), 321.

12. Summers, *The Press Gang,* 160–70.

13. Ritchie, *Press Gallery,* 73–130.

14. Ritchie, *Press Gallery,* 131–144.

15. Richard E. Welch Jr., *The Presidencies of Grover Cleveland* (Lawrence, Kans.: University Press of Kansas, 1988) 35–41, 51, 222–3.

16. Joseph Bucklin Bishop, "Newspaper Espionage," *Forum* 1 (1886): 528–37. Betty Boyd Caroli, *First Ladies,* exp. ed. (New York: Oxford University Press, 1995), 319–20. The incident is summarized in Pollard, *The Presidents and the Press,* 503–11, and in Tebbel and Watts, *The Press and the Presidency,* 272–6.

17. Carl Sferrzza Anthony, *First Ladies: The Saga of the President's Wives and their Power, 1789–1961* (New York: William Morrow, 1992), 253–67.

18. The quotation is from Oulahan, unpublished memoirs, "Cleveland," Chapter 11, Box 1, Oulahan Papers, Herbert Hoover Presidential Library.

19. Oulahan, unpublished memoirs, "Presidential Messages," Chapter 5, Box 1, Oulahan Papers, Herbert Hoover Presidential Library.

20. George F. Parker, *Recollections of Grover Cleveland* (New York: Century, 1911), 375.

21. See generally, Pollard, *The Presidents and the Press,* 499–551, and Tebbel and Watts, *The Press and the Presidency,* 256–94.

22. The quotation is from W. W. Price, "Secretaries to the Presidents," *Cosmopolitan* 30 (March 1901): 491.

23. The quotation is from David S. Barry, "News-Getting at the Capitol," *Chautauquan* 26 (December 1897): 282.

24. Kumar, "The White House Beat at the Century Mark," 20–1.

25. The incident is described by David S. Barry, *Forty Years in Washington* (Boston: Little, Brown, 1924), 219–21, and Arthur Wallace Dunn, *From Harrison to Harding,* 2 vols. (New York: G. P. Putnam's Sons, 1922), 1:87–97.

26. Michael Schudson, "The Politics of Narrative Form: The Emergence of News Conventions in Print and Television," *Daedalus* 3 (Fall 1982): 101–2.

27. McKinley's preference for privacy extended to his views about the press, which are rarely discussed in his correspondence or, except in general terms, in his public remarks. See William G. McKinley Papers, Library of Congress.

28. For brief discussions about McKinley and the press by McKinley's principal biographers, see Gould, *The Presidency of William McKinley,* 241; Margaret Leech, *In the Days of McKinley* (New York: Harper and Brothers, 1959), 230–1, and H. Wayne Morgan, *William McKinley and his America* (Syracuse: Syracuse University Press, 1963), 322–3. On McKinley's congressional career, see Wilfred E. Binkley, *President and Congress,* 3d rev. ed. (New York: Vintage Books, 1962), 228–9.

29. Arthur Wallace Dunn, *Gridiron Nights* (New York: Frederick A. Stokes, 1915), 18, 30–4.

30. "McKinley was a Guest," *Washington Post,* 28 March 1897. Gould, *The Presidency of William McKinley,* 38. Dunn, *Gridiron Nights,* 61.

31. Kumar, "The White House Beat at the Century Mark," 25–6.

32. "Porter's Urbanity: The Kind Treatment of Newspapermen by the President's Private Secretary," *The Newspaper Maker,* 2 April 1897. Streitmatter, "William W. Price," 36. Morgan, *William McKinley and His America,* 322–3.

33. *Washington Post,* 11 June 1897.

34. See clippings, 14 June 1897 to 17 June 1897, in "Current Comment," scrapbooks, McKinley Papers, Library of Congress.

35. The quotation is from Barry, "News-Getting at the Capitol," 286.

36. "The President and the Press," *Ohio State Journal,* 30 November 1897, in "Current Comment," McKinley Papers.

37. Anthony, *First Ladies,* 268–94.

38. The quotation is from "Washington Gossip," *New York Mail and Express,* 2 July 1898.

39. Frank W. Carpenter, "At the President's Door," *New York Dispatch,* undated 1897, a clipping in the "Current Comment" scrapbooks, McKinley Papers.

40. Kumar, "The White House Beat at the Century Mark," 20.

41. Cortelyou memorandum, "The Work of the President's Office," 20 February 1903, Box 34, George B. Cortelyou Papers, Library of Congress.

42. Charles Willis Thompson, "Coolidge has Learned the Art of Publicity," *New York Times,* 7 August 1927.

43. Gould, *The Presidency of William McKinley,* 66–73; Hilderbrand, *Power and the People,* 13–7.

44. See the *Post* generally, 27 February 1898 to 10 April 1898.

45. Hilderbrand, *Power and the People,* 18–21.

46. See "White House Statement," *Washington Post,* 2 April 1898, 1, and "The President's Reply," *Washington Post,* 8 April 1898, 1.

47. See stories emanating from the Executive Mansion in the *Post* on 2 March 1898; 3 March 1898; 7 March 1898; 24 March 1898, and 30 March 1898, among others.

48. See entries in the Cortelyou Diary from 29 March 1898 to 6 April 1898, Box 52, Cortelyou Papers.

49. For examples, see "Report Not Yet Made," *Washington Post,* 4 March 1898, 1; "To Arrive Saturday," *Washington Post,* 18 March 1898, 1; "Report Not Yet Here," *Washington Post,* 20 March 1898, 1; "Awaits the Report," *Washington Post,* 21 March 1898, 1, among others.

50. See "Report on Maine Disaster," *Washington Post,* 28 March 1898, 1.

51. For Cortelyou's views on the report and the leak, see his diary entries of 22 March, 25 March, 26 March, 28 March 1898.

52. Cortelyou Diary, 25 April 1898.

53. The *Washington Post* noted on 21 March 1898 that the President was keeping his employees on duty "far beyond the usual hour. . . . Secretaries and clerks were on duty all day, some of them remaining until after midnight."

54. The quotation is from Barry, *Forty Years in Washington*, 253–4.

55. For accounts of McKinley and Cortelyou working out the wording of these statements, see Cortelyou Diary entries for 26 July and 30 July 1898.

56. Hilderbrand, *Power and the People*, 19. Cortelyou Diary, 17 March 1898; 20 March 1898.

57. The quotations are from the Cortelyou Diary, 16 April 1898.

58. Gould, *The Presidency of William McKinley*, 91–121, and Hilderbrand, *Power and the People*, 30–51. See also William Eleroy Curtis, "President McKinley and the War," *Chicago Record-Herald*, undated, scrapbooks, McKinley Papers.

59. Cortelyou Diary, 30 July 1898.

60. The quotation is from Ida Tarbell, "President McKinley in War Times," *McClure's* 21 (July 1898): 214.

61. Cortelyou Diary, 12 August 1898. Hilderbrand, *Power and the People*, 36.

62. Hilderbrand, *Power and the People*, 18, 50.

63. Cortelyou Diary, 8 August 1898.

64. Price, "Secretaries to the Presidents," 492.

65. The quotation is from Albert Halstead, "The President at Work—a Character Sketch," *Independent* 53 (5 September 1901): 2081.

66. See Edward G. Lowry, *Washington Closeups: Intimate Views of Some Public Figures* (Boston: Houghton Mifflin, 1921), 127–9.

67. Gould, *The Presidency of William McKinley*, 127–8.

68. For letters turning down local press applications to join the train, see Cortelyou to Henry T. Scott, and Cortelyou to George G. Bain, both 3 April 1900, McKinley Papers.

69. See, for example, "The War as a Text: President Addresses Big Crowds En Route to Omaha," *Washington Post*, 12 October 1898, 1.

70. For an example of Cortelyou's notes of his conversations with reporters, see the Cortelyou Diary, 13 December 1898.

71. The quotation is from David S. Barry, "George Bruce Cortelyou," *World's Work* 5 (April 1903): 3337–40. See also Leech, *In the Days of McKinley*, 230.

72. These dispatches, among others, are reprinted in the *Washington Post*, 12 October 1898, 11.

73. For examples of invitations to correspondents to join the December 1898 southern trip and their responses, see correspondence between John Addison Porter and Barry, *New York Sun;* A. S. Ayres, Scripps-McRae Press Association; Charles Boynton, Associated Press; Robert M. Larner, *Savannah (Georgia) Morning News*, and J. K. Ohl, *Atlanta Constitution*, all in the McKinley Papers, 8 December 1898 to 10 December 1898. Morgan, *William McKinley and His America*, 323.

74. Kumar, "The White House Beat at the Century Mark," 16.

75. For a description of the technological limitations involved, see Melville E. Stone, *Fifty Years a Journalist* (Garden City, N.Y.: Doubleday, Page, 1921), 313–4.

76. Parker, *Recollections of Grover Cleveland,* 126.

77. Charles Boynton to John Addison Porter, 6 December 1898, McKinley Papers.

78. J. B. Shale to John Addison Porter, 30 August 1899. Shale to George B. Cortelyou, 4 September 1899. Cortelyou to Melville E. Stone, 6 September 1899. All in McKinley Papers.

79. The process is described by Cortelyou in "The Work of the President's Office," 10–11, Box 34, Cortelyou Papers. Signing the agreement in December 1899 besides the AP were the *New York Sun* Press Association, *Outlook,* Publishers Press Association, Union Associated Press, Scripps-McRae Press Association, the *Washington Post,* and the *Washington Times.* The agreements are in correspondence with Cortelyou and Porter, 4 December 1899, McKinley Papers.

80. The quotation is from Isaac F. Marcosson, *Adventures in Interviewing* (New York: John Lane, 1919), 18.

81. The quotation is from Barry, "George Bruce Cortelyou," 3340.

82. The quotation is from Halstead, "The President at Work—a Character Sketch," 2081. See also Price, "Secretaries to the Presidents," 487–92.

83. O. O. Stealey, *Twenty Years in the Press Gallery* (Stealey, 1906), 34–5.

84. Gould, *The Presidency of William McKinley,* 247–8.

85. The quotation is from Dunn, *From Harrison to Harding,* 1:328.

86. The quotations is from Frances E. Leupp, "The President—and Mr. Wilson," *Independent* 77 (27 November 1913): 394.

87. Gould, *The Presidency of William McKinley,* 247–8. R. H. Dunn to Cortelyou, 22 April 1901, McKinley Papers. For a roster of the traveling press corps and documentation of the extensive press arrangements for the trip, see Cortelyou's correspondence in April 1901. For the press statements regarding Ida McKinley's illness, see correspondence beginning 11 May 1901, all in McKinley papers.

88. Cortelyou Diary, 10 June 1901, Box 53, Cortelyou Papers.

89. W. W. Price, "How the Work of Gathering White House News Has Changed," *Washington Evening Star,* 16 December 1902, and Gilson Gardner, "Inside the Quotes," *Editor and Publisher* 5 (March 1906): 1.

Chapter 2.
Theodore Roosevelt: Publicity! Publicity! Publicity!

1. See, among others, Lewis L. Gould, *The Presidency of Theodore Roosevelt* (Lawrence, Kans.: University Press of Kansas, 1991), 20–1; 153–4; Hilderbrand, *Power and the People,* 52–71, and Juergens, *News from the White House,* 14–90.

2. John Orman, "Covering the American Presidency: Valenced Reporting in the Periodical Press," *Presidential Studies Quarterly* 14 (Summer 1984): 381–90.

3. The quotation is from Archie Butt to Mrs. Lewis F. B. Butt, 28 March 1909, in Lawrence F. Abbott, ed., *Taft and Roosevelt: The Intimate Letters of Archie Butt*, 2 vols. (New York: Doubleday, Doran, 1930), 1:28–32.

4. William Allen White, *Masks in a Pageant* (New York: Macmillan, 1928), 309.

5. Willis J. Abbot, *Watching the World Go By* (Boston: Little, Brown, 1924), 244.

6. Victor Proud (Richard V. Oulahan), "Roosevelt, the Politician," *Saturday Evening Post*, 21 September 1907, 6–7, 31. Copy in Box 2, Richard V. Oulahan Papers, Herbert Hoover Presidential Library.

7. Mark Sullivan, *Our Times*, 7 vols. (New York: Charles Scribner's Sons, 1926), 1:74–5.

8. Edmund Morris, *The Rise of Theodore Roosevelt* (New York: Coward, McCann and Geoghegan, 1979), 159–97, 227–40. David McCullough, *Mornings on Horseback* (New York: Simon and Schuster, 1981), 246, 256–7, 275.

9. Henry F. Pringle, *Theodore Roosevelt: A Biography* (New York: Harcourt, Brace., 1931), 69–71.

10. Elting S. Morison, ed., *The Letters of Theodore Roosevelt*, 10 vols. (Cambridge, Mass.: Harvard University Press, 1951), 1:447.

11. Joseph Bucklin Bishop, *Theodore Roosevelt and His Time; Shown in His Own Letters*, 2 vols. (New York: Charles Scribner's Sons, 1920), 1:59–60.

12. Theodore Roosevelt, *An Autobiography* (New York: Macmillan, 1914), 177.

13. William B. Gatewood Jr., *Theodore Roosevelt and the Art of Controversy* (Baton Rouge: Louisiana State University Press, 1970).

14. The meeting is described in Lincoln Steffens, *The Autobiography of Lincoln Steffens*, 2 vols. (New York: Harcourt, Brace, 1931), 1:256–7.

15. The articles, which originally appeared in *McClure's* magazine, are collected in Lincoln Steffens, *The Shame of the Cities*, Louis Joughin, ed. (New York: Hill and Wang, 1966).

16. Jacob Riis, *How the Other Half Lives* (New York: Charles Scribner's Sons, 1907 [1890]).

17. Roosevelt to Horace Elisha Scudder, 6 August 1895, in Morison, *The Letters of Theodore Roosevelt*, I: 573.

18. Steffens, *The Autobiography of Lincoln Steffens*, 1:289–91.

19. The quotation is from Roosevelt to Lodge, 23 December 1895, in Morison, *The Letters of Theodore Roosevelt*, 1:605.

20. Roosevelt, *An Autobiography*, 210.

21. Roosevelt to Paul Dana, 16 August 1897, in Morison, *The Letters of Theodore Roosevelt*, 1:778. See also Roosevelt to Jacob Riis, who apparently was miffed at not being invited, 2 September 1897, 1:797.

22. See Oulahan, "How the Rough Riders were Named," 1–4, Box 3, Oulahan Papers. For a discussion of how Roosevelt persuaded newspaper

correspondents in Cuba to record his exploits, see Brown, *The Correspondent's War,* 205, 273–4.

23. The "round robin" episode is described by Pringle, *Theodore Roosevelt,* 171–98, and by Roosevelt, *An Autobiography,* 251–2.

24. The quotation is from Roosevelt, *An Autobiography,* 289–91.

25. Pollard, *The Presidents and the Press,* 570.

26. Roosevelt to Edward Cary, 2 April 1900, in Morison, *The Letters of Theodore Roosevelt,* 2:1590.

27. Roosevelt to Joseph Bucklin Bishop, 11 April 1900, in Morison, *The Letters of Theodore Roosevelt,* 2:1609. Roosevelt wrote again the next day to expand on his grievances against the *Tribune* and the *New York Evening Post,* which he saw as controlled by editors hostile to him. See Morison, 2:1610.

28. The quoted phrase is from Roosevelt, *An Autobiography,* 369.

29. Richard Hofstadter, *The Age of Reform* (New York: Vintage Books, 1995), 198–214.

30. Henry C. Adams, "What is Publicity?" *North American Review* 175 (December 1902): 894. Other examples include J. Allen Smith, *The Spirit of American Government* (Cambridge, Mass.: Harvard University Press, 1965 [1909]), 373–4; Arthur T. Vance, "The Value of Publicity in Reform," *Annals* 29 (January 1907): 87–92, and Henry Bruere, "Government and Publicity," *Independent* 63 (12 December 1907): 1422–6.

31. Edward Bellamy, *Looking Backward from the Year 2000* (New York: New American Library, 1960 [1888]), 119.

32. Hilderbrand, *Power and the People,* 54–5, also points out that Roosevelt saw no contradiction in placing his faith in the public to reach the right decisions while also believing that public opinion was too important to be left unguided.

33. Edward Alysworth Ross, *Sin and Society* (Boston: Houghton Mifflin Co., 1907, 23–4). Roosevelt to Ross, 19 September 1907, in Morison, *The Letters of Theodore Roosevelt,* 5:4448.

34. Oliver K. Gramling, *AP: The Story of News* (New York: Farrar and Rinehart, 1940), 156–7, 190.

35. Ritchie, "'The Loyalty of the Senate': Washington Correspondents in the Progressive Era," 574–91.

36. Stephen Ponder, "E. W. Scripps and the Progressive Movement, 1908–1912," in *A Celebration of the Legacies of E. W. Scripps* (Athens: Ohio University, 1990).

37. The meeting is described in Barry, *Forty Years in Washington,* 267–72. The quotation is from 270–1. See also Juergens, *News from the White House,* 4–11.

38. Ritchie, *Press Gallery,* 179–86.

39. The quotation is from Will Irwin, *The American Newspaper* (Ames: Iowa State University Press, 1966 [1911]), 18.

40. The transient nature of reporting as a craft in this period is documented by Ted Curtis Smythe, "The Reporter, 1880–1900: Working Conditions and Their Influence on News," *Journalism History* 7 (1980): 1–10.

41. Gardner, "Between the Quotes," *Editor and Publisher* 5 (31 March 1906): 1.

42. The quotations are from Louis Brownlow, *A Passion for Politics*, 2 vols. (Chicago: University of Chicago Press, 1955), I:399.

43. The quotation is from Oulahan, unpublished memoirs, "Roosevelt's Methods," 5, Box 2, Oulahan Papers.

44. Walter E. Clark to Erastus Brainerd, undated 1902, Box 2, Erastus Brainerd Papers, University of Washington.

45. Nicholas Roosevelt, *The Man as I Knew Him* (New York: Dodd, Mead, 1967), 39.

46. Oulahan, unpublished memoirs, "Presidents and Publicity," 4, Box 1, Oulahan Papers.

47. J. J. Dickinson, "Theodore Roosevelt, Press Agent: And What His Newspaper 'Cuckoos' have done for Him," *Harper's Weekly* 51 (28 September 1907): 1410.

48. Walter E. Clark to Erastus Brainerd, 26 January 1906, Box 2, Brainerd Papers.

49. Walter E. Clark to Erastus Brainerd, 30 October 1903, Box 2, Brainerd Papers.

50. Oscar King Davis, *Released for Publication: Some Inside Political History of Theodore Roosevelt and His Times* (Boston: Houghton Mifflin, 1925), 123–4.

51. Oulahan, unpublished memoirs, "Presidents and Publicity," 4, Box 1, Oulahan Papers.

52. Henry L. Stoddard, *As I Knew Them: Presidents and Politics from Grant to Coolidge* (New York: Harper and Brothers, 1927), 373.

53. Marcosson, *Adventures in Interviewing*, 87.

54. The quotation is from Charles Willis Thompson, *Presidents I've Known and Two Near-Misses* (Indianapolis, Ind: Bobbs-Merrill, 1929), 118–9.

55. The quotation is from Oulahan, unpublished memoirs, "Harding," 6, Box 2, Oulahan Papers.

56. Davis, *Released for Publication*, 123–4.

57. T. W. Williams, "Temptations of a Young Journalist," *Cosmopolitan* 40 (April 1906): 680–1, discusses the consequences to a correspondent's career of angering Roosevelt or Loeb.

58. See Oulahan, unpublished memoirs, "TR Disciplines Newspapers," 3–5, Box 2; "Roosevelt's Back-fires," 6–7, Box 2, and in correspondence, 23 April 1926, Box 3; All in Oulahan Papers.

59. Archie Butt wrote in late 1908 that although few newspapers criticized Roosevelt, the President "cannot brook criticism." In Abbott, ed., *Letters of Archie Butt*, 1:233.

60. Oulahan, unpublished memoirs, "Roosevelt's Back-fires," 1–5, unpublished memoirs, Box 2, Oulahan Papers.

61. Archie Butt noted that Roosevelt kept the press "fed with news every hour of the day." In Abbott, ed., *Taft and Roosevelt: The Intimate Letters of Archie Butt,* 2:26–7. See also Gould, *The Presidency of Theodore Roosevelt,* 153–4.

62. Melville Stone, *Fifty Years a Journalist,* 313–4, said Roosevelt furnished the Associated Press with copies of some statements as much as six weeks in advance.

63. Louis Koenig, *The Invisible Presidency* (New York: Farrar and Rinehart, 1960), 172–7, describes Loeb as "in all but name the President's press secretary."

64. The quotation is from Roosevelt, *An Autobiography,* 369.

65. Folkerts and Teeter, *Voices of a Nation,* 246–53.

66. The leading women's magazines also had their own brand of muckraking. See Kathleen L. Endres, "Women and the 'Larger Household': The 'Big Six' and Muckraking," *American Journalism* 14 (Nos. 3–4, Summer-Fall 1997): 262–282.

67. Folkerts and Teeter, *Voices of a Nation,* 306–14.

68. Hofstadter, *The Age of Reform* (New York: Vintage Books, 1955), 204–14, discusses the privileged backgrounds of many of the magazine reformers.

69. The article appeared as William Allen White, "Platt," *McClure's* 18 (December 1901): 145–53. See Roosevelt to William Allen White, 31 December 1901, in Morison, *The Letters of Theodore Roosevelt,* 3:2246.

70. White, *The Autobiography of William Allen White* (New York: Macmillan, 1946), 346–7.

71. The article appeared in *McClure's* 28 (February 1907): 386–94. See Roosevelt to White, 28 November 1906, in Morison, *The Letters of Theodore Roosevelt,* 5:4152.

72. Roosevelt to Samuel Sydney McClure, 4 October 1902, in Morison, *The Letters of Theodore Roosevelt,* 5:3696.

73. Roosevelt to Lincoln Steffens, 12 March 1907, in Morison, *The Letters of Theodore Roosevelt,* 5:4269. Roosevelt to Steffens, 5 June 1908, 6:4740. The article was "Roosevelt-Taft-La Follette on What the Matter is in America and What to Do About It," *Everybody's* 18 (June 1908): 723–36.

74. See, as examples, Roosevelt to Ray Stannard Baker, 13 September 1905, in Morison, *The Letters of Theodore Roosevelt,* 5:3675, and Roosevelt to Baker, 28 November 1905, 5:3750.

75. The "muckrake" incident, which caused a breach between Roosevelt and the magazine writers, is described in Juergens, *News from the White House,* 72–9. Roosevelt also was critical of Phillips's searing political novel, *The Plum Tree,* which was serialized in the *Saturday Evening Post.* See Roosevelt to George Horace Lorimer, editor in chief of the *Post,* 12 May 1906, in Morison, *The Letters of Theodore Roosevelt,* 5:3912.

76. Roosevelt to Ray Stannard Baker, 9 April 1906, cited in Baker, *American Chronicle* (New York: Charles Scribner's Sons, 1945), 203. Roosevelt nevertheless kept up his letters trying to influence Baker's articles. See Roosevelt to Baker, 3 June 1908, in Morison, *The Letters of Theodore Roosevelt,*

6:4737. Lincoln Steffens was also displeased by Roosevelt's remarks. See Steffens, *The Autobiography of Lincoln Steffens,* 1:581.

77. Mark Sullivan, *Our Times: The Turn of the Century,* 1:80–1.

78. Dunn, *From Harrison to Harding,* 1:348.

79. Caroli, *First Ladies,* 119–22.

80. Gifford Pinchot, *Breaking New Ground* (New York: Harcourt Brace, 1947), 144–5.

81. Richard Norton Smith, "America's House," in Frank Freidel and William Pencak, eds., *The White House: The First Two Hundred Years* (Boston: Northeastern University Press, 1994), 32–3, 37–8. Gould, *The Presidency of Theodore Roosevelt,* 102. "Press Room at the White House," *Journalist* 32 (22 November 1902): 54.

82. See release 84, press release file, Theodore Roosevelt Papers, Library of Congress.

83. Gould, *The Presidency of Theodore Roosevelt,* 63. *Editor and Publisher* 2 (12 July 1902): 7, listed Washington correspondents at Oyster Bay from the *New York Times;* the *New York Sun;* Associated Press, Scripps-McRae, and the *Washington Evening Star.*

84. Somewhat defensively, the correspondents complained that local merchants were overcharging them. See, as examples, "Oyster Bay's Boom," *Washington Post,* 13 July 1902, and "Strenuous Time the Newspaper Men Are Having at Oyster Bay, the New Capital," *Los Angeles Record,* 8 July 1903.

85. Walter E. Clark to Erastus Brainerd, 1 July 1901, Box 2, Brainerd Papers.

86. Roosevelt to Paul Dana, 30 July 1902, in Morison, *The Letters of Theodore Roosevelt,* 3:2404. Oulahan, unpublished memoirs, "Roosevelt's Backfires," 6–7, Box 2, and correspondence dated 23 April 1926, Box 3, Oulahan Papers.

87. Lewis L. Gould, "Theodore Roosevelt, Woodrow Wilson and the Emergence of the Modern Presidency," *Presidential Studies Quarterly* 19 (Winter 1989): 43.

88. Juergens, *News from the White House,* 36–40. See also Stacey Rozek, "The First Daughter of the Land: Alice Roosevelt as Presidential Celebrity, 1902–1906," *Presidential Studies Quarterly* 19 (Winter 1989): 51–70.

89. Anthony, *First Ladies,* 312.

90. See Roosevelt to Theodore Roosevelt Jr., 2 October 1905, in Morison, *The Letters of Theodore Roosevelt,* 5:3694.

91. "Want More Privacy: Secretary Loeb Announces New Rule in White House," *Editor and Publisher* 6 (27 April 1907): 1.

92. Anthony, *First Ladies,* 295–313.

93. *Editor and Publisher* 44 (22 April 1905): 4, editorially sympathized with Roosevelt when he refused to allow reporters in his hunting camp.

94. *Editor and Publisher* subsequently published annual stories about the correspondents' summer colony at Oyster Bay. See, for example, "Fun at Oyster

Bay," *Editor and Publisher* 4 (27 August 1904), "Shades of Sagamore," *Editor and Publisher* 5 (8 August 1905), and "Oyster Bay: The Newspaper Corps is Entrenched at the Famous Long Island Town," *Editor and Publisher* 6 (15 June 1907).

95. I. H. Hoover, *Forty-Two Years in the White House* (Boston: Houghton Mifflin, 1934), 27.

96. For a detailed description of the controversy, see Tebbel and Watts, *The Press and the Presidency,* 341–8.

97. See, for example, "Teddy Calls on Nation to Sue New York World's Editor: Pulitzer is Now the Object of the President's Bitterest Wrath," *Seattle Star,* 16 December 1908.

98. The quotation is from an editorial, "Our Best Advertiser," in *Editor and Publisher* 8 (15 August 1908): 4. The journal also placed a picture of "Theodore Roosevelt: Journalist" on the front cover of its December 1908 Christmas issue.

99. Mark Sullivan, *Our Times: The Turn of the Century,* 1:71–2.

Chapter 3.
The White House and the First "Press Bureaus"

1. See Bernhard E. Fernow, *Report Upon the Forestry Investigation of the United States Department Agriculture, 1877–1898,* U.S. House of Representatives, 53rd Cong., 3rd sess., H.Doc. 181, 25.

2. *List of Publications of the Agriculture Department, 1862–1902* (Washington, D.C.: Government Printing Office, 1904), 2.

3. White, *The Republican Era,* 45–90.

4. See *Report of the Secretary of Agriculture* (Washington, D.C.: Government Printing Office, 1890).

5. See the 1889 *Report of the Secretary of Agriculture,* 2, 11–12, as well as White, *The Republican Era,* 234–44.

6. Both major biographers of Pinchot, M. Nelson McGeary, *Gifford Pinchot: Forester-Politician* (Princeton, N.J.: Princeton University Press, 1960), and Harold T. Pinkett, *Gifford Pinchot: Private and Public Forester* (Urbana, Ill.: University of Illinois Press, 1970), comment on his relentless pursuit of publicity, as does Pinchot himself in his autobiography, *Breaking New Ground* (New York: Harcourt, Brace, 1947).

7. See scrapbooks of clippings in the Gifford Pinchot Papers, Library of Congress, for articles on the Biltmore project and also about Pinchot's reform activities in New York City.

8. Pinchot, *Breaking New Ground,* 132.

9. For a case study of Pinchot's efforts to change public sentiment in the Northwest in 1897, see Stephen Ponder, "Conservation, Economics and Community Newspapering: The Seattle Press and the Forest Reserves Controversy of 1897," *American Journalism* 3 (January 1986): 50–60.

10. Pinchot, *Breaking New Ground,* 143.

11. Pinchot to R. C. Melward, 20 May 1903, Office of Reserves Correspondence, Record Group 95, National Archives.

12. Forest Service Order 80, 19 August 1905, Records of the Chief, Record Group 95, National Archives.

13. Minutes of the Service Committee, 24 November 1909, Record Group 95, National Archives.

14. Agency travel in 1907 and 1908 is documented in *A Statement of Members of the Forest Service at Meetings and Conventions During the Year 1907,* 60th Cong., 1st sess., S. Doc. 485. For the 1908 report, see the 25 February 1909 *Congressional Record,* U.S. Senate, 60th Cong., 2d sess., 43, pt. 6, 3092–4104.

15. U.S. Department of Agriculture, *Report of the Secretary, 1907,* 60th Cong., 1st sess., H. Doc. 6, 347.

16. U.S. Agriculture Department, *Report of the Secretary* (Washington. D.C.: Government Printing Office, 1902, 1908.)

17. In one indirect contact, Pinchot helped to supply Secretary of Agriculture James Wilson with briefing material for one of McKinley's western trips. See Pinchot to Wilson, 30 April 1901, William McKinley Papers, Library of Congress.

18. Peri E. Arnold, *Making the Managerial Presidency* (Princeton, N.J.: Princeton University Press, 1986), 4–21.

19. Roosevelt's outlines his expansive theory of executive authority in *An Autobiography,* 371. See also Gould, *The Presidency of Theodore Roosevelt,* 197–9.

20. An extensive literature exists on Theodore Roosevelt and the conservation movement. For an overview of Roosevelt's conservation policies as president, see Gould, *The Presidency of Theodore Roosevelt,* 199–207.

21. For Roosevelt's account of their collaboration, see *An Autobiography,* Chapter 11, "Natural Resources," which Pinchot helped to write.

22. For the list of statements, see Index Sheets, Box 575, Gifford Pinchot Papers, Library of Congress. Roosevelt to Pinchot, 16 September 1907, Roosevelt Papers. A draft speech to the 1906 Irrigation Congress, including Roosevelt's written changes, appears in correspondence with Pinchot for 24 August 1906, also Roosevelt Papers.

23. See Pinchot to Roosevelt, 30 March 1903, and Roosevelt to Pinchot, 11 May 1903; both in Roosevelt Papers.

24. See, for example, Theodore Roosevelt, "Forestry and Foresters," *Current Literature* 35 (September 1903): 337–8.

25. For example, see press release, 8 January 1905, Roosevelt Papers.

26. Roosevelt to Pinchot, 11 September 1903, Roosevelt Papers.

27. Pinchot, *Breaking New Ground,* 243–50. See also Pinchot to Roosevelt, 5 October 1903, and Roosevelt to W.A. Richards, 2 October 1903, both in Roosevelt Papers.

28. *Portland Oregonian,* 15 January 1904.

29. Pinchot, *Breaking New Ground,* 254.

30. See stories in the *New York Times, Chicago Tribune,* and *Seattle Post-Intelligencer,* among others, for 1 January 1905.

31. The quotation is from Pinchot, *Breaking New Ground,* 254.

32. On the goals of the various conservation commissions, see Charles R. Van Hise, *The Conservation of Natural Resources in the United States* (New York: Macmillan, 1913), 5–13.

33. Pinchot to Roosevelt, 20 May 1907, Roosevelt Papers.

34. Pinchot, *Breaking New Ground,* 329–30.

35. See, for example, Roosevelt's enthusiastic letter to his friend, Henry Cabot Lodge, 29 September 1907, Roosevelt Papers. The quotation is from Roosevelt, *An Autobiography,* 464.

36. See clippings, 2 October 1907 to 6 October 1907, in unorganized scrapbooks, Pinchot Papers. An informal review easily located front-page stories in the *New York Times,* the *Chicago Tribune,* and the *Seattle Post-Intelligencer,* among others.

37. On Pinchot's role in the conference, see McGeary, *Gifford Pinchot: Forester-Politician,* 96–9. A list of attenders is available in *Proceedings of a Conference of Governors, May 13–15, 1908* (Washington, D.C.: Government Printing Office, 1908). The quotation is from the *New York American,* 14 May 1908.

38. The quotations are from the *Chicago Record-Herald,* 1 May 1908, and the *Grand Rapids (Michigan) Press,* on 9 May 1908. Both are in scrapbooks, Pinchot Papers.

39. See the *Proceedings,* xi, for the press arrangements.

40. Pinchot, *Breaking New Ground,* 353.

41. Roosevelt, *An Autobiography,* 415.

42. Joseph Bucklin Bishop describes his duties in *Theodore Roosevelt and His Times,* 1: 449–55. See also "The Canal Secretary," *Editor and Publisher* 5 (5 September 1905): 1.

43. Carl E. Hatch, *The Big Stick and the Congressional Gavel* (New York: Pageant Press, 1967), 1–13, describes the 1907–1909 Congress as one of the most obstructive, particularly on natural resource issues.

44. Various correspondence documents this affair. See Roosevelt to Heyburn, 2 March 1904 and 13 June 1905. Pinchot to Roosevelt, 30 August 1904, and Roosevelt to Pinchot, 6 July 1905, all in the Roosevelt Papers. Pinchot, *Breaking New Ground,* 301. Pinchot reprinted the letters in *Forest Bulletin* 61 (Washington, D.C., Government Printing Office, 1905). For examples of the news stories, see "Heyburn in Black Book," *Spokane Spokesman-Review* and *Portland Oregonian,* both 1 October 1905.

45. Unidentified clipping, 17 January 1906, in scrapbooks, Pinchot Papers.

46. 11 May 1908, *Congressional Record,* U.S. Senate, 60th Cong., 1st sess., 42, pt. 7, 6072.

47. 3 February 1910, *Congressional Record,* U.S. House of Representatives, 61st Cong., 2d sess., 44, pt. 2, 1445.

48. The *Washington Post* comment appeared on 1 April 1908. The quotation from the *Washington Herald* appeared on 6 April 1908.

49. Walter E. Clark to Erastus Brainerd, 31 July 1907, Box 2, Brainerd Papers, University of Washington.

50. On Gilson Gardner, see correspondence from Pinchot to Herbert A. Smith, 9 April 1904, Box 92, Pinchot Papers.

51. U.S. House Rules Committee, *Departmental Press Agents: Hearing on House Resolution 545,* 62nd Cong., 2nd sess., 21 May 1912, 10. See also F. B. Marbut, *News from the Capitol* (Carbondale, Ill.,: Southern Illinois University Press, 1971), 194–5, and "After Press Agents: Congressman Nelson asks for Investigation of Publicity Bureaus," *Editor and Publisher* 11 (25 May 1912): 1.

52. Archie Butt to Mrs. Lewis F. B. Butt, 28 March 1909, in Abbott, *Letters of Archie Butt,* 1:28–32.

53. See Roosevelt to Hitchcock, 27 October 1906, in Morison, *The Letters of Theodore Roosevelt,* 5:4124.

54. See Roosevelt to Bishop, 29 August 1907, in Morison, *The Letters of Theodore Roosevelt,* 5:4422.

Chapter 4.
Taft: Avoiding the Press

1. On the contrasting philosophies of presidential leadership, see Donald E. Anderson, *William Howard Taft: A Conservative's Conception of the Presidency* (Ithaca, N.Y.: Cornell University Press, 1973), 289–306, and Paolo E. Coletta, *The Presidency of William Howard Taft* (Lawrence, Kans.: University Press of Kansas, 1973).

2. *New York Times,* 5 March 1913, cited in Henry F. Pringle, *The Life and Times of William Howard Taft,* 2 vols. (New York: Farrar and Rinehart, 1939), 1:855.

3. Cornwell, *Presidential Leadership of Public Opinion,* 13–5.

4. The quotation is from George Kibbe Turner, "How Taft Views His Own Administration," *McClure's* 35 (June 1910): 221. Hilderbrand, *Power and the People,* 76–7.

5. Ballinger used the term in a letter to William Hutchinson Cowles, 9 December 1909, Roll 3, Richard Achilles Ballinger Papers in microfilm, University of Washington.

6. For documentation of Oulahan's role, see correspondence between Oulahan and Taft in the fall of 1908 in the William Howard Taft Papers, Library of Congress. Davis, *Released for Publication,* 94–6.

7. Davis, *Released for Publication,* 127, 156–7, 162–6.

8. "Conservatism: The New Watchword at Washington Concerning White House News," *Editor and Publisher* 8 (27 March 1909): 1.

9. The quotation is from Edward G. Lowry, "The White House Now," *Harper's Weekly* 53 (15 May 1909): 7.

10. Archibald Butt to Mrs. Lewis F. B. Butt, 22 March 1909, in Abbott, *Letters of Archie Butt,* 1:26–7. Taft's vigorous response indicated that he would insist on conducting the presidency in his own way, and that he would not resume the press briefings popularized by Roosevelt.

11. The quotation is from "Taft—So Far," *American* 68 (July 1909): 308.

12. "Press censorship: Established De Facto at Washington by the Taft Cabinet," *Editor and Publisher* 8 (10 April 1909): 1.

13. Walter E. Clark to Erastus Brainerd, 3 July 1909, Box 2, Erastus Brainerd Papers, University of Washington.

14. Stone, *Fifty Years a Journalist,* 313–4. The quotation is from Archibald Butt to Mrs. Lewis F. B. Butt, 23 November 1909, in Abbott, *Letters of Archie Butt,* 1:218–19.

15. Archibald Butt to Mrs. Lewis F. B. Butt, 28 March 1909, in Abbott, *Letters of Archie Butt,* 1:28–32.

16. The quotation is from Taft to William Allen White, 20 March 1909, reprinted in White, *The Autobiography of William Allen White,* 451.

17. The quotation is from Archibald Butt to J. R. M. Taylor, 5 April 1910, in Abbott, *Letters of Archie Butt,* 1:319–20.

18. The quotation is from Dunn, *From Harrison to Harding* 2:109–12.

19. See Butt to Mrs. Lewis F. B. Butt, 4 July 1909, in Abbott, *Letters of Archie Butt,* 1:134–5.

20. Pollard, *The Presidents and the Press,* 61.

21. The quotation is from Butt to Mrs. Lewis F. B. Butt, 25 April 1910, in Abbott, *Letters of Archie Butt,* 1:336.

22. The quotation is from White, *Masks in a Pageant,* 328.

23. The quotation is from Lowry, *Washington Close-Ups,* 267.

24. The quotations are from Thompson, *Presidents I've Known and Two Near Misses,* 226–30.

25. Butt to Mrs. Lewis F. B. Butt, 4 July 1909, in Abbott, *Letters of Archie Butt,* 1:134–5.

26. The quotation is from Taft to William Dudley Foulke, 29 November 1909, William Howard Taft Papers, Library of Congress.

27. See Taft to Lucius B. Swift, 2 March 1910, Taft Papers.

28. The quotation is from Taft to Nancy Noelker, 11 September 1909, Taft Papers.

29. For Taft's role in the tariff bill and the negative response to news reports of the president's remarks, see Coletta, *The Presidency of William Howard Taft,* 45–75. For the correspondents' view of the Winona incident, see Davis, *Released for Publication,* 176–8.

30. The quotation is from Frances E. Leupp, "President Taft's Own View: An Authorized Interview," *Outlook* 99 (12 December 1911): 812.

31. Archibald Butt recounts the anecdote in a letter to Mrs. Lewis F. B. Butt, 21 March 1909, in Abbott, *Letters of Archie Butt,* 1:18.

32. Butt to Mrs. Lewis F. B. Butt, 1 June 1909, in Abbott, *Letters of Archie Butt,* 1:106.
33. The quotation is from Taft to William Kent, 19 September 1909, Taft Papers.
34. The quotation is from Taft to Mabel Boardman, 11 October 1909, Taft Papers.
35. Taft to Fred W. Carpenter, 24 October 1909, Taft Papers. The incident is also described in Archibald Butt to Mrs. Lewis F. B. Butt, 23 November 1909, in Abbott, *Letters of Archie Butt,* 1:218–9.
36. The quotation is from Taft to Mrs. William Howard Taft, 24 October 1909, Taft Papers.
37. Anthony, *First Ladies,* 320–9.
38. The incident is described by Archie Butt in a letter to Mrs. Lewis F. B. Butt, 29 August 1911, in Abbott, *Letters of Archie Butt,* 2:749.
39. Butt to Mrs. Lewis F. B. Butt, 31 July 1911, in Abbott, *Letters of Archie Butt,* 2:724.
40. Butt to Mrs. Lewis F. B. Butt, 12 December 1909, in Abbott, *Letters of Archie Butt,* 1:231–2.
41. The quotation is from Butt to Mrs. Lewis F. B. Butt, 20 July 1911, in Abbott, *Letters of Archie Butt,* 2:700–1.
42. See Anderson, *William Howard Taft,* 202–5.
43. The quotation is from Taft to R. L. O'Brian, 31 January 1910, Taft Papers.
44. The quotation is from Taft to J. H. Cosgrave, 23 February 1910, Taft Papers.
45. Juergens, *News from the White House,* 92–4.
46. The quotation is from Dunn, *From Harrison to Harding,* 2:101–3.
47. Michael Medved, *The Shadow Presidents: The Secret History of the Chief Executives and Their Top Aides* (New York: Times Books, 1979), 123–32.
48. "Newspaper Cabinet: Leading Washington Correspondents to Confer with President Once a Week," *Editor and Publisher* 10 (24 December 1910): 6.
49. J. Frederick Essary, "The Presidency and the Press," *Scribner's* 27 (May 1935): 305–7.
50. Dunn, *From Harrison to Harding,* 2:235–6.
51. See Oulahan, unpublished memoirs, "Taft's press conferences," 1–2, Richard V. Oulahan Papers, Herbert Hoover Presidential Library.
52. See Hilderbrand, *Power and the People,* 79–81.
53. See Brown to Erastus Brainerd, 29 September 1910, Box 1, Brainerd Papers.
54. Juergens, *News from the White House,* 104–5. See also Hilderbrand, *Power and the People,* 78–7.
55. Davis, *Released for Publication,* p. 184–185.
56. See, for example, the interviews with Turner, "How Taft Views His Own Administration," and with Leupp, "President Taft's Own View: An Authorized Interview."
57. "Washington: Gus J. Karger at the Helm of Taft Administration Publicity," *Editor and Publisher* 10 (15 April 1911): 1. See also David Lawrence, "Shop

Talk at Thirty," *Editor and Publisher* 77 (27 May 1944): 64, and Essary, *Covering Washington,* 88, 98.

58. Leupp, "The President and Mr. Wilson," 394–5.

59. "Taft Talks to Journalists," *Editor and Publisher* 11 (23 September 1911): 2. "Possum for Mr. Taft," *Editor and Publisher* 11 (28 October 1911): 1.

60. Taft to J. C. Hemphill, 16 November 1911, Box 18, Hemphill Family Papers, Special Collections Library, Duke University.

61. Taft to J. C. Hemphill, 16 November 1911, Box 18, 8, Hemphill Family Papers, Special Collections Library, Duke University.

Chapter 5.
The Consequences of "Nonpublicity"

1. U.S. House Committee on the Census, 24 January 1910, 61st Cong., 2d sess., H. Rep. 296 (serial 5594).

2. U.S. House Rules Committee, *Departmental Press Agents: Hearing on House Resolution 545,* 62nd Cong., 2nd sess., 21 May 1912, 10. See also Marbut, *News from the Capitol,* 194–5, and "After Press Agents: Congressman Nelson asks for Investigation of Publicity Bureaus," *Editor and Publisher* 11 (25 May 1912): 1.

3. Roosevelt's vigorous pursuit of leakers and Taft's lack of concern are compared in Archibald Butt to Mrs. Lewis F. B. Butt, 28 March 1909, in Abbott, *Letters of Archie Butt,* 1:28–32.

4. For an analysis of Roosevelt's conservation program, see Samuel P. Hays, *Conservation and the Gospel of Efficiency: The Progressive Movement, 1890–1920* (Cambridge, Mass.: Harvard University Press, 1959).

5. For a comprehensive discussion of this conflict, see James Penick Jr., *Progressive Politics and Conservation: The Ballinger-Pinchot Affair* (Chicago: University of Chicago Press, 1968)

6. However, Ballinger found it necessary to renew the contract a few months later. See Ballinger to E. L. Reber, 12 April 1909, and Don W. Carr to E. L. Reber, 1 November 1909, both in Box 14, Richard Achilles Ballinger Papers, University of Washington. An extensive bibliography of articles criticizing Ballinger, which he submitted to a Senate investigating committee, can be found in correspondence dated 3 February 1910, Box 13.

7. See correspondence between Ballinger and E. F. Baldwin, on 7 May 1909 and 10 May 1909, Roll 2, Ballinger Papers in microfilm. Ballinger did not fire Newell, but he reportedly considered replacing him with R. H. Thomson, the city engineer of Seattle, where Ballinger had been mayor. See "Ballinger is Here for Thomson," *Seattle Times,* 14 July 1909. For examples of newspaper and magazine coverage, see the scrapbooks for July and August 1909, Roll 12, the Ballinger papers in microfilm.

8. See Lawler to Ballinger, 21 July 1909, and Ballinger's dismissive reply, 30 July 1909. Both are in Box 8, Ballinger Papers.

9. Clark to Ballinger, 1 August 1909, Box 4, Ballinger Papers. Clark sent a similar letter to Erastus Brainerd, editor of the *Seattle Post-Intelligencer,* and a Ballinger sympathizer. See Clark to Brainerd, 1 August 1909, Box 3, Ballinger Papers.

10. In scrapbooks in the Ballinger Papers, see stories on 9 August 1909 and 10 August 1910 from numerous daily newspapers, including the *Washington Times, Baltimore World,* and the *Christian Science Monitor.* See U.S. Senate, 61st Cong., 3rd sess., S. Doc. 719 (Serial 5892), *Investigation of the Department of Interior and of the Bureau of Forestry,* 1:77.

11. For the speeches, see Arthur Hooker, ed., *Proceedings of the 17th National Irrigation Congress* (Spokane, Wash.: Shaw and Borden, 1910). For the extensive news coverage of the conference, see the *Washington Times,* 10 August 1909, among others, in clippings, Ballinger Papers.

12. See Penick, *Progressive Politics and Conservation,* 107–10; Oscar Lawler to Ballinger, 11 August 1909 and 13 August 1909, Roll 5, Ballinger Papers in microfilm, and the story itself, reprinted in the *Seattle Star,* 10 August 1909. For evidence of Pinchot's ties with Scripps, see E. W. Scripps to Pinchot, 10 June 1908 and 3 July 1908, as well as Scripps to E. W. Porterfield, 7 September 1909, in Boxes 11 and 12, E.W. Scripps Papers, Ohio University. See also Pinchot's boastful letter to his mother about the meeting, which described Scripps pointedly as the "second largest owner of newspapers in the United States." Pinchot to Mary E. Pinchot, 6 September 1909, Box 10, Gifford Pinchot Papers, Library of Congress. Pinchot, *Breaking New Ground,* 422–3.

13. On the coal claims issue, see Penick, *Progressive Politics and Conservation,* 77–106, and Coletta, *The Presidency of William Howard Taft,* 77–100.

14. For a useful chronology of events, see *Investigation,* 1:47–49.

15. See Pinchot to Garfield, 15 August 1909, Ballinger Files, Gifford Pinchot Papers, Library of Congress.

16. The quotation is from Pinchot to Taft, 10 August 1909, copy in Roll 8, Ballinger Papers in microfilm.

17. Penick, *Progressive Politics and Conservation,* 112–4.

18. See clippings in the *Washington Post, Chicago Tribune,* and other major newspapers, beginning 13 August 1909. Some of the banner headlines: "Ballinger's Foes Disclose Plans," *Chicago Tribune,* 14 August 1909; "Startling Developments May Be Expected at Any Time," *Washington Post,* 15 August 1909; "Pinchot to Fight it Out With Ballinger," *New York World,* 17 August 1909. All are from Roll 12, Ballinger Papers in microfilm.

19. For accounts of the leaking of documents to the *Post,* see Fred Dennett to Taft, 4 September 1909, reprinted in *Investigation,* 2:109–10, and H. H. Schwartz to Ballinger, 1 September 1909, *Investigation,* 2:264–7. For Taft's reply to the *Post,* see Taft to Ira E. Bennett, 27 August 1909, William Howard Taft Papers, Library of Congress.

20. Taft to Ballinger, 22 August 1909, Taft Papers. The quotation is from "Glavis, in Report, Accuses Chief," *Washington Post,* 25 August 1909. See

also the *Washington Star, New York Times,* and the *Washington Times* of the same date.

21. The quotation appeared in the *New York Times* and the *Chicago Record-Herald,* among others, 4 September 1909.

22. "Ballinger Heeds Taft's Subpoena," *Chicago Tribune,* 6 September 1909.

23. For the letter of vindication, see Taft to Ballinger 13 September 1909, Ballinger Papers. A handwritten postscript suggests that releasing it to the press was something of an afterthought.

24. See, for example, "Taft, in Most Sweeping Decision, Upholds Ballinger," *Washington Herald,* 16 September 1909.

25. For a discussion of the tariff debate and the Winona speech, see Coletta, *The Presidency of William Howard Taft,* 45–75.

26. The agency's role in suggesting and shaping the Glavis article is documented in letters from Overton Price to Pinchot, 14 September and 16 September 1909, in Ballinger File, Pinchot Papers. Norman Hapgood, *The Changing Years* (New York: Farrar and Rinehart, 1930), 183.

27. Penick, *Progressive Politics and Conservation,* 129–30, summarizes the major magazine articles. See also clippings, Ballinger Papers.

28. In a remarkable letter to Pinchot on 5 January 1910, Price and Shaw described the publicity campaign in detail and took full responsibility for it. The letter is reprinted in *Investigation,* 4:1275–1279. For the published reference to Price, see "Pinchot to Fight it out with Ballinger," *New York World,* 17 August 1909.

29. See correspondence from Lawler to Ballinger, 13 August, 14 August, 19 August, and 21 August 1909, Roll 5, Ballinger Papers in microfilm.

30. Ballinger to Taft, 15 August 1909, Taft Papers, and Ballinger to Taft, 4 September 1909, Roll 8, Ballinger Papers in microfilm.

31. Walter E. Clark to Ballinger, 11 September 1909, Roll 3, Ballinger Papers in microfilm.

32. Taft to Pinchot, 24 November 1909, copy in Ballinger Papers.

33. See "Taft May Let Them Fight It Out," 12 August 1909, Ballinger scrapbooks. See also Taft to E. F. Baldwin, 13 August 1909, Taft Papers.

34. Taft to Ira E. Bennett, 27 August 1909. See also Taft to Nicholas Longworth, 30 August 1909. Both are in the Taft Papers.

35. The quotation is from Taft to James Wilson, the Secretary of Agriculture, 31 August 1909, Taft Papers.

36. Taft to Ballinger, 13 September 1909. See also Taft to Ballinger, 30 September 1909, Box 13, Ballinger Papers.

37. Taft to Pinchot, 13 September 1909, Taft Papers.

38. The quotations are from Taft to Lawrence Abbott, 31 August 1909. Taft made similar remarks in a letter to Charles Nagel, his secretary of commerce and labor, 1 September 1909. All are in the Taft Papers.

39. Taft to George Wickersham, 7 October 1909, Taft Papers.

40. Taft to Horace D. Taft, 18 October 1909, Taft Papers.

41. Taft to Helen Herron Taft, 15 October 1909, Taft Papers.

42. See, for example, Ballinger's acknowledgement of support to Erastus Brainerd, on 25 August 1909, 17 November 1909, and 28 December 1909, among other references. Roll 2, Ballinger Papers in microfilm. Supportive articles from the Seattle newspapers can be found in the scrapbooks, Roll 12. On Clark's party activities, see correspondence in the Brainerd Papers.

43. See correspondence between Clark and Ballinger, 1 August 1909 and 7 August 1909, Box 4, Ballinger Papers.

44. Ballinger to E. F. Baldwin, 25 August 1909, Roll 2, Ballinger Papers in microfilm.

45. Ballinger to Erastus Brainerd, 25 August 1909, Roll 2, Ballinger Papers in microfilm.

46. Ballinger to Erastus Brainerd, 17 November 1909, Roll 2, Ballinger Papers in microfilm.

47. Ballinger to William Hutchinson Cowles, 9 December 1909, Roll 3, Ballinger Papers in microfilm.

48. See stories in the *Washington Post, Washington Times,* and the *Washington Star,* among others, on 28 and 29 August 1909.

49. *Chicago Record-Herald,* 30 August 1909.

50. "Warfare of Policies," *Washington Star,* 19 August 1909.

51. "Ballinger Will Get Full Inquiry," *Portland Oregonian,* 21 December 1909.

52. Ballinger to Taft, 6 December 1909, Taft to Ballinger, 6 December 1909, Taft Papers.

53. Taft to Horace D. Taft, 5 December 1909, Taft Papers.

54. Ballinger to Erastus Brainerd, 28 December 1909, Box 1, Brainerd Papers.

55. Pinchot to Dolliver, 5 January 1910, reprinted in *Investigation,* 4: 1281–5. See scrapbook, Roll 12, Ballinger Papers.

56. Hapgood, *The Changing Years,* 184–6.

57. *Investigation,* 4:1281–5.

58. Penick, *Progressive Politics and Conservation,* 151–2. See also the account of the hearings in McGeary, *Gifford Pinchot: Forester-Politician,* 165–73.

59. The quotation is from Taft to Horace D. Taft, 1 February 1910, Taft Papers.

60. McGeary, *Gifford Pinchot: Forester-Politician:* 171–2. Penick, *Progressive Politics and Conservation:* 152–5. For an editorial reply, see "Vertrees and Newspapers," *Philadelphia Record,* 29 May 1910.

61. Ormsby McHarg to Ballinger, Roll 6, Ballinger Papers in microfilm.

62. The quotation is from Brown to Erastus Brainerd, 31 March 1910, Box 1, Brainerd Papers.

63. See "The Ballinger Inquiry: The President, Congress and Country are Very Tired of It," *San Francisco Chronicle,* 2 May 1910. Ballinger ended up asking sympathetic editors in the Pacific Northwest to reprint clippings he sent them from the *Washington Post.* See Ballinger's correspondence with Edgar Piper, editor of the *Portland Oregonian,* on 3 May and 10 May 1910, Box 10, Ballinger Papers.

64. McGeary, *Gifford Pinchot: Forester-Politician,* 185–6.

65. The quotation is from Ashmun Brown to Erastus Brainerd, 11 March 1910, Box 1, Brainerd Papers.

66. See Penick, *Progressive Politics and Conservation,* 178–9.

67. For Taft's actions from 1910 to 1912, see, generally, Hilderbrand, *Power and the People,* 78–81.

Chapter 6.
Wilson: Centralizing Executive Information

1. See particularly Hilderbrand, *Power and the People,* 93–164, and Juergens, *News from the White House,* 126–77.

2. Tulis, *The Rhetorical Presidency,* 118–29, 182, 186. Niels Aage Thorsen, *The Political Thought of Woodrow Wilson, 1875–1910* (Princeton, N.J.: Princeton University Press, 1988), 107–10.

3. See, particularly, excerpts from Wilson's unpublished 1910 essay, "The Modern Democratic State," quoted in Thorsen, *The Political Thought of Woodrow Wilson,* 109–11. More generally, see Woodrow Wilson, *Constitutional Government in the United States* (New York: Columbia University Press, 1908).

4. The quotation is from Richard V. Oulahan, unpublished memoirs, "Presidents and Publicity," Chapter 4, Oulahan Papers, Herbert Hoover Presidential Library.

5. David Lawrence, *The True Story of Woodrow Wilson* (Murray, Hill, N.Y.: George H. Doran, 1924), 55–6.

6. See Remarks at press conference, 7 April 1913, in Arthur S. Link, ed., *The Papers of Woodrow Wilson,* 69 vols. (Princeton, N.J.: Princeton University Press, 1978): 27:263–4. Juergens, *News from the White House:* 154–5.

7. The quotation is from Ray Stannard Baker, *American Chronicle* (New York: Charles Scribner's Sons, 1945), 386–7.

8. Elmer C. Cornwell Jr., "The Press Conferences of Woodrow Wilson," *Journalism Quarterly* 39 (Summer 1962): 292–300, found that the conferences, even if off the record, were frequently followed by stories in the *New York Times.* See generally Hilderbrand, *Power and the People:* 94–104; Juergens, *News from the White House,* 140–54.

9. George E. Mowry, "Election of 1912," in Arthur M. Schlesinger Jr., ed., *History of American Presidential Elections, 1798–1968* (New York: Chelsea House, 1971), 3:2135–242.

10. For a discussion of Wilson's rocky experience with the press prior to the presidency, see Juergens, *News from the White House,* 126–40. Ray Stannard Baker, ed., *Woodrow Wilson: Life and Letters,* 7 vols. (London: William Heinemann, 1932), 4:229.

11. George Creel, "Woodrow Wilson—The Man Behind the President," *Saturday Evening Post* 203 (28 March 1931): 37.

12. The quotations are from Lowry, *Washington Close-Ups*, 19.

13. President Wilson to Newspapermen, 22 March 1913, copy in Box 47, Joseph P. Tumulty Papers, Library of Congress. Ritchie, *Press Gallery*, 205.

14. The quotation is from Remarks at press conference, 26 May 1913, in Link, *Papers of Woodrow Wilson*, 27:473, where the statement is also reprinted.

15. Remarks at press conference, 30 October 1913, in Link, *Papers of Woodrow Wilson*, 28:471–2.

16. See Oulahan, unpublished memoirs, "Wilson's Press Conferences," Chapters 21–3, Box 2, Oulahan papers.

17. Contrast, for instance, Thompson's comments to Reuben Adiel Bull, 3 March 1913, in Link, *Papers of Woodrow Wilson*, 27:164–6, with his postwar comment that "it was impossible to rely on anything he said." See Thompson, *Presidents I've Known and Two Near-Misses*, 297.

18. The quotation is from Hugh Baillie, *High Tension: The Recollections of Hugh Baillie* (New York: Harper and Brothers, 1959), 46–7.

19. Remarks at press conference, 3 January 1914, in Link, *Papers of Woodrow Wilson*, 29:98.

20. See entry in House's Diary, 14 February 1913, in Link, *Papers of Woodrow Wilson*, 27:112–3.

21. Baillie, *High Tension*, 47.

22. Lawrence, *The True Story of Woodrow Wilson*, 340–9.

23. The quotation is from Remarks at press conference, 9 October 1913, in Link, *Papers of Woodrow Wilson*, 28:379–80.

24. See Remarks at press conference, in Link, *Papers of Woodrow Wilson*, 29:174.

25. Remarks at press conference, 9 October 1913, in Link, *Papers of Woodrow Wilson*, 28:134, 310–1.

26. Caroli, *First Ladies*, 134–45. Anthony, *First Ladies*, 353–60.

27. Eleanor Wilson McAdoo, *The Woodrow Wilsons* (New York: Macmillan, 1937), 167.

28. For Wilson's outburst, see Remarks of press conference, in Link, *Papers of Woodrow Wilson*, 29:353–6.

29. See Cornwell, "Presidential News: The Expanding Public Image," 275–83, and Orman, "Covering the American President: Valenced Reporting in the Periodical Press," 381–90.

30. Ritchie, *Press Gallery*, 205. Hilderbrand, *Power and the People*, 97. Juergens, *News from the White House*, 151.

31. Richard V. Oulahan, unpublished memoirs, "Taft's Press Conferences," Chapter 14: 2–3, Oulahan Papers, Herbert Hoover Presidential Library.

32. Remarks at press conference, 2 February 1914, in Link, *Papers of Woodrow Wilson*, 29:212.

33. John Morton Blum, *Joe Tumulty and the Wilson Era* (Boston: Houghton Mifflin, 1951), 61–7.

34. The quotations are from Tumulty, "In the White House Looking Glass," Chapter 17, Box 120, Joseph P. Tumulty Papers, Library of Congress.

35. Anthony, *First Ladies,* 353–60.

36. Lawrence, *The True Story of Woodrow Wilson,* 333–4.

37. See correspondence in Baker, *Woodrow Wilson: Life and Letters,* 4:234.

38. J. A. R. Pimlott, *Public Relations and American Democracy* (Princeton, N.J.: Princeton University Press, 1951), 69–72.

39. Gifford Pinchot, "A Plan for Publicity," undated (1917?) memorandum to Theodore Roosevelt, Publicity File, Box 710, Gifford Pinchot Papers, Library of Congress.

40. Ritchie, *Press Gallery:* 205–6.

41. See "Washington Topics," *Editor and Publisher* 13 (16 August 1913): 166.

42. See, generally, Jeffrey E. Cohen, *The Politics of the U.S. Cabinet: Representation in the Executive Branch, 1789–1984* (Pittsburgh.: University of Pittsburgh Press, 1984); Richard F. Fenno Jr., *The President's Cabinet* (Cambridge, Mass.: Harvard University Press, 1959), and R. Gordon Hoxie, "The Cabinet in the American Presidency, 1789–1984," *Presidential Studies Quarterly* 14 (No. 2, Spring 1984): 209–30.

43. Kendrick A. Clements, *The Presidency of Woodrow Wilson* (Lawrence, Kans.: University Press of Kansas, 1992), 8. See also Sidney M. Milkis and Michael Nelson, *The American Presidency: Origins and Development, 1776–1990* (Washington, D.C.: Congressional Quarterly, 1990), 221–2.

44. August Heckscher, *Woodrow Wilson* (New York: Charles Scribner's Sons, 1991), 272.

45. Sullivan, *Our Times: Over Here, 1914–1918,* 5:148–57.

46. The number of Cabinet agencies also had increased, to ten by 1913, according to Paul P. Van Riper, "The American Administrative State: Wilson and the Founders," in Ralph Clark Chandler, ed., *A Centennial History of the American Administrative State* (New York: Free Press, 1987), 16.

47. See entry of 10 March 1913, in E. David Cronon, ed. *The Cabinet Diaries of Josephus Daniels, 1913–1921* (Lincoln, Nebr.: University of Nebraska Press, 1963), 6.

48. Clements, *The Presidency of Woodrow Wilson,* 32–3. In addition to his Post Office experience, Suter was a 25-year Washington reporter and former president of the National Press Club. See "Washington Topics," *Editor and Publisher* 13 (30 August 1913): 210.

49. For examples of Lane's frequent written exchanges with newspapermen, see Anne Wintermute Lane and Louise Herrick Wall, eds., *The Letters of Franklin K. Lane: Personal and Political* (Boston: Houghton Mifflin, 1922).

50. Wilson sidestepped the question. See Remarks of press conference, 11 April 1913, in Link, *Papers of Woodrow Wilson,* 27:284–9.

51. Remarks of press conference, 18 April 1913, in Link, *Papers of Woodrow Wilson,* 27:324. See Hilderbrand, *Power and the People,* 109–11.

52. See 17 May 1913 entry, in Cronon, *Cabinet Diaries of Josephus Daniels,* 67–8.

53. Remarks of press conference, 17 July 1913, in Link, *Papers of Woodrow Wilson,* 28:37–8.

54. Remarks of press conference, 6 October 1913, in Link, *Papers of Woodrow Wilson,* 50:255–63.

55. Secretary of the Navy Daniels, an admirer of Wilson, took extensive notes during substantive Cabinet discussions. See, for example, his diary entries following meetings in March and April 1913, reprinted in Link, *Papers of Woodrow Wilson,* 27:261–2, 267–69, 290–2, 328–33.

56. Remarks of press conference, 9 October 1913, in Link, *Papers of Woodrow Wilson,* 28:379–80.

57. The quotation is from David F. Houston, *Eight Years with Wilson's Cabinet, 1913–1920,* 2 vols. (Garden City, N.Y.: Doubleday, Page, 1926), 1:87–8. See also Baker, *Woodrow Wilson: Life and Letters,* 4:297–8.

58. Arthur S. Link, *The New Freedom* (Princeton, N.J.: Princeton University Press, 1960), 74–6. See also Heckscher, *Woodrow Wilson,* 282–3.

59. See Remarks of press conferences, 10 November, 17 November, and 20 November 1913, in Link, *Papers of Woodrow Wilson,* 28:516, 559, 568.

60. Remarks of press conference, 29 January 1914, in Hilderbrand, ed., *Papers of Woodrow Wilson,* 50:355–6.

61. Hilderbrand, *Power and the People,* 82–3.

62. See correspondence from Bryan to Wilson, 8 February, 12 February, and 18 February 1915, as well as an exchange of notes between Wilson and Tumulty on 19 February, and 20 February 1915. All are in Link, *Papers of Woodrow Wilson,* 32:245, 258, 265, 541. Hilderbrand, *Power and the People,* 109–11.

63. See Wilson to Eliot, 1 June 1914, quoted in Baker, *Woodrow Wilson: Life and Letters,* 4:234–5.

64. The quotation is from Link, *Papers of Woodrow Wilson,* 34:139.

65. Hilderbrand, *Power and the People,* 106–7.

66. See Hilderbrand, *Power and the People,* 132–34. See also Wilson to Lansing, 19 December and 21 December 1916, in Link, *Papers of Woodrow Wilson,* 40:276–7 and 306–7, and Lansing's 4 March 1917 memorandum, reprinted at 41:321–4.

67. See Entry of 21 March 1917, Diary of Thomas W. Brahany, a White House aide, in Link, *Papers of Woodrow Wilson,* 41:445.

Chapter 7.
Presidential Propaganda in World War I

1. For an overview, see James D. Startt, "The Media and National Crises, 1917–1945," in William David Sloan and James D. Startt, eds., *The Media in America: A History,* 3rd ed. (Northport, Ala.: Vision Press, 1996), 386–97. The definitive account of the Committee on Public Information is Vaughn, *Holding Fast the Inner Lines.*

2. See Harry N. Scheiber, *The Wilson Administration and Civil Liberties, 1917–1921* (Ithaca, N.Y.: Cornell University Press, 1960), and Donald

Johnson, "Wilson, Burleson and Censorship in the First World War," *Journal of Southern History* 28 (February 1962): 46–58, as well as James R. Mock, *Censorship 1917* (Princeton, N.J.: Princeton University Press, 1941).

3. George Creel, *Rebel at Large: Recollections of Fifty Crowded Years* (New York: G. P. Putnam's Sons, 1947), 157. Creel's involvement in censorship is described in Vaughn, *Holding Fast the Inner Lines,* 214–32.

4. Gary Dean Best, *The Critical Press and the New Deal: The Press and Presidential Power, 1933–1938* (Westport, Conn.: Praeger, 1993), 6–8.

5. Neil A. Wynn, *From Progressivism to Prosperity: World War I and American Society* (New York: Holmes and Meier, 1986), xvi–xix.

6. David M. Kennedy, *Over Here: The First World War and American Society* (New York: Oxford University Press, 1980), 1–41, describes the splintering of American society prior to the war years.

7. See correspondence from House to Wilson, 31 December 1916; Wilson to Howard, 2 January 1917; Howard to Wilson, 5 January 1917, and Wilson to Howard, 5 January 1917, in Link, *Papers of Woodrow Wilson,* 40:374–5, 381–2, 412. See also Robert E. Burke, "The Scripps West Coast Newspapers and the Election of 1916," in *A Celebration of E. W. Scripps: His Life, Works and Heritage* (Athens, Ohio: Scripps School of Journalism, 1990).

8. Hilderbrand, *Power and the People,* 143–6.

9. The quotation is from Remarks at press conference, 15 January 1917, in Link, *Papers of Woodrow Wilson,* 40:471–2.

10. For John Howard Whitehouse's memorandum of the 14 April 1917 meeting, see Link, *Papers of Woodrow Wilson,* 42:68.

11. Josephus Daniels to Wilson, 11 April 1917, with enclosed memorandum from George Creel, in Link, *Papers of Woodrow Wilson,* 42:39–41.

12. "Creel to Direct Nation's Publicity," *New York Times,* 15 April 1917, 1.

13. Diary of Josephus Daniels, 6 April 1917, reprinted in Link, *Papers of Woodrow Wilson,* 41:556.

14. Wilson to Edwin Yates Webb, 22 May 1917, in Link, *Papers of Woodrow Wilson,* 42: 369–70.

15. For overviews of the congressional debate on the Espionage Act, see Harry R. Scheiber, *The Wilson Administration and Civil Liberties* (Ithaca, N.Y.: Cornell University Press, 1960), 11–19, and Seward W. Livermore, *Politics is Adjourned: Woodrow Wilson and the War Congress, 1916–1918* (Middletown, Conn.: Wesleyan University Press, 1966), 32–6.

16. See complaints to Wilson from, among others, Max Eastman, Amos Pinchot, and John Reed as well as the President's and Burleson's responses, dated 13 July 1917 to 25 July 1917, in Link, *Papers of Woodrow Wilson,* 43: 164–5; 175–6; 187–8; 192; and 276–8.

17. John Morton Blum, *Woodrow Wilson and the Politics of Morality* (Boston: Little, Brown, 1956), 144.

18. Startt, "The Media and National Crises," in Sloan and Startt, *The Media in America,* 392.

19. The quotation is from Harold Lasswell, *Propaganda Techniques in the World War* (New York: Alfred P. Knopf, 1927), 2.

20. The quotation is from George Creel, *How We Advertised America* (New York: Harper and Brothers, 1920), 4.

21. Sullivan, *Our Times: Over Here, 1914–1918,* 5:65–6.

22. Vaughn, *Holding Fast the Inner Lines,* 43.

23. Juergens, *News from the White House,* 165.

24. The quotation is from point 4, Creel memorandum, 11 April 1917, in Link, *Papers of Woodrow Wilson,* 42:38–9. The phrase "central information bureau" is from Creel, *How We Advertised America,* 72.

25. Creel memorandum, 11 April 1917, in Link, *Papers of Woodrow Wilson,* 42:39–41.

26. Creel memorandum, 11 April 1917, in Link, *Papers of Woodrow Wilson,* 42:39–41.

27. Hilderbrand, *Power and the People,* 152.

28. In his memoirs, Lansing denounced Creel's "socialistic tendencies" and also expressed his distrust of Tumulty, the President's secretary. See Lansing, *War Memoirs* (Indianapolis, Ind.: Bobbs-Merrill, 1935), 323–4.

29. See correspondence in November and December 1917 among Wilson, Long, and Creel, in Link, *Papers of Woodrow Wilson,* 45:86–90, 152–3, 329.

30. For examples of Wilson's written support for Creel and the CPI, see Wilson to Creel, 17 May 1917, in Link, *Papers of Woodrow Wilson,* 42:304–13. See also James R. Mock and Cedric Larson, *Words That Won the War: The Story of the Committee on Public Information, 1917–1919* (Princeton, N.J.: Princeton University Press, 1939), 92.

31. Vaughn, *Holding Fast the Inner Lines,* 194.

32. Wilson, *Constitutional Government in the United States,* 126–7. See also Juergens, *News from the White House,* 175–7.

33. Creel, *How We Advertised America,* 208.

34. Wilson to Creel, 18 April 1917, from *Report of the Director of the Official U.S. Bulletin to the Chairman of the Committee on Public Information,* cited in Vaughn, *Holding Fast the Inner Lines,* 197–8.

35. Although Thomas Jefferson's *National Intelligencer* and other sponsored newspapers in the nineteenth century were de facto voices of their administrations, they were privately owned and published. See Ames, *A History of the National Intelligencer,* and Smith, *The Press, Politics and Patronage.*

36. For an overview of the *Official Bulletin* and its role, see Vaughn, *Holding Fast the Inner Lines,* 197–200.

37. Hilderbrand, *Power and the People,* 153–4.

38. Walton Bean, in "George Creel and His Critics: A Study of the Attacks on the CPI, 1917–1919" (Ph.D. dissertation, University of California, Berkeley, 1941), agreed that issues raised in the attacks on Creel were substantive ones but that his critics were motivated by partisanship, politics and personal disagreements. The quotation is from Bean, 13–4, and the *New*

York World, 13 May 1918. See also Hilderbrand, *Power and the President,* 148–56.

39. The quotation is from correspondence between Tumulty and Wilson, 11 July 1917, in Link, *Papers of Woodrow Wilson,* 43:145–6.

40. Wilson to Creel, 14 January 1918, in Link, *Papers of Woodrow Wilson,* 45:580–1.

41. The Food Administration has received limited scholarly attention. For the most comprehensive account, see George H. Nash, *The Life of Herbert Hoover: Master of Emergencies, 1917–1918* (New York: W. W. Norton, 1996). Prior to Nash, the most recent book-length study was that of Maxcy Robson Dickson, *The Food Front in World War I* (Washington, D.C.: American Council on Public Affairs, 1944). The official history, published by the Hoover Institution, is that of William Clinton Mullendore, *History of the United States Food Administration, 1917–1919* (Stanford, Calif.: Stanford University Press, 1941.) For a useful but brief overview, see Craig Lloyd, *Aggressive Introvert: A Study of Herbert Hoover and Public Relations Management, 1912–1932* (Columbus: Ohio State University Press, 1972), 45–52.

42. Robert Higgs, *Crisis and Leviathan: Critical Episodes in American Government* (New York: Oxford University Press, 1987), 137–8.

43. This summarizes the assessment given to the Cabinet by David Houston, Wilson's secretary of agriculture, in April 1917. See Houston, *Eight Years with Wilson's Cabinet,* 1:256–66, entry for 9 April 1917, and Cronon, *The Cabinet Diaries of Josephus Daniels,* entries of 8 and 9 May 1917, 148–9. See also Mullendore, *History of the United States Food Administration,* 47–50, and Herbert Hoover, *An American Epic,* 4 vols. (Chicago: Henry Regnery, 1960), 2:1–28.

44. The quotation is from Hoover to Emile Franqui, 14 November 1914, reprinted in George I. Gay, ed. *Public Relations of the Commission for Relief in Belgium,* 2 vols. (Stanford, Calif.: Stanford University Press, 1929), 1:13–4.

45. For a comprehensive discussion of Hoover's early humanitarian campaigns and his enthusiasm for publicity, see George H. Nash, *The Life of Herbert Hoover: The Humanitarian, 1914–1917* (New York: W. W. Norton, 1988). For Hoover's own account of the Belgian relief campaign, see *The Memoirs of Herbert Hoover: Years of Adventure, 1874–1920,* 3 vols. (New York: Macmillan, 1951), 1:152–216.

46. For Hoover's denial, see the *New York Times,* 9 May 1917. For Wilson's 19 May 1917 statement on the proposed legislation, see Link, *Papers of Woodrow Wilson,* 42:342–6.

47. "Senate May Delay Food Legislation: Stubborn Debate Predicted Over Extent of Powers Which President Shall Have," *New York Times,* 21 May 1917, 1.

48. For an overview of the congressional stalemate on food controls, see Livermore, *Politics is Adjourned,* 49–62.

49. The quotation is from Will Irwin, "First Aid to America: How Civilians Must Get Together and Get Behind Strong Leaders," *Saturday Evening Post* 189 (24 March 1917): 6.

50. "Suffrage Party Stands by Wilson," *New York Times*, 25 March 1917, 2. See correspondence between Carrie Chapman Catt, of the National American Woman's Suffrage Association, and Wilson, 17 May and 8 June 1917, in Link, *Papers of Woodrow Wilson*, 42:237, 241.

51. For the Cabinet discussion, see entry of 21 April 1917, in Cronon, *The Cabinet Diaries of Josephus Daniels*, 138.

52. "Women Food Savers Want Hoover as Head; National League Expects a Million Housewives to Help Conserve Supplies," *New York Times*, 3 May 1917, 6. "Womens' Groups Express Support," *New York Times*, 22 May 1917, 12. Ida Husted Harper, *The History of Woman Suffrage*, 6 vols. (New York: J. J. Little and Ives, 1922), 5:535–6.

53. "President Tells of Food News," *New York Times*, 20 May 1917, 1. Witold S. Sworakowski, "Herbert Hoover: Launching the food Administration, 1917," in Lawrence E. Gelfand, ed., *Herbert Hoover: The Great War and its Aftermath, 1914–1923* (Iowa City, Ia: University of Iowa Press, 1979), 40–60. For the text of Wilson's statement, see Link, *Papers of Woodrow Wilson*, 42:342–6.

54. The quotation is from the *New York Times*, 20 May 1917.

55. See "Woman's Part in the War: Ida Tarbell Says it is Conservation of Food and Doing Men's Work," *New York Times*, 26 May 1917, 8, and Tarbell, "Women Must Order Bread With Care," *New York Times*, 24 June 1917, 2.

56. The quotation is from Wilson to Hoover, 12 June 1917, in Francis William O'Brien, *The Hoover-Wilson Wartime Correspondence* (Ames: Iowa State University Press, 1974), 28–9. For the outline of the campaign, see correspondence between Wilson and Hoover, 12 June 1917, in Link, *Papers of Woodrow Wilson*, 42:480–6. See also "Wilson Orders Hoover to Start," *New York Times*, 17 June 1917, 1; and subsequent stories on 18, 19, and 20 June 1917.

57. Hoover's statement was reprinted in "Summons Women to save the Food," *New York Times*, 18 June 1917, 1.

58. See, as examples, "That Big Question of Food" and "'Food Saving' to be Text for Patriotic Sermons Today," *Portland Oregonian*, 1 July 1917, 4. See also "City Pastors Plead for Saving of Food," *New York Times*, 2 July 1917, 2.

59. "Mrs. Wilson's Food Pledge," *New York Times*, 9 July 1912, 2. Dickson, *The Food Front in World War I*, 17–8. Baker, *Woodrow Wilson: Life and Letters*, 7:149.

60. Caroli, *First Ladies*, 177. Anthony, *First Ladies*, 360–2.

61. See, for example, Harris Dickson, "Save and Serve With Hoover," *Collier's Weekly* 59 (11 August 1917): 5–7, 32; Herbert Hoover, "What I Would Like Women to Do," *Ladies Home Journal* 34 (August 1917): 25, and James H. Collins, "The Food Pledge," *McClure's*, November 1917: 70.

62. Vernon L. Kellogg, one of many Stanford University faculty members or students who joined the Food Administration, wrote to Hoover on 17

October 1917 that the pledge campaign needed stronger organizational support. See Box 9, Pre-Commerce Papers, Correspondence, Herbert Hoover Presidential Library.

63. The organization of the food conservation pledge campaign is described in Edgar Eugene Robinson and Paul Carroll Edwards, eds. *The Memoirs of Ray Lyman Wilbur* (Stanford: Stanford University Press, 1960), 258–61. Mullendore, *History of the United States Food Administration,* 86–7.

64. Sullivan, *Our Times: Over Here, 1914–1918,* 5:418–22.

65. Hoover's appeal to home economists received an enthusiastic response. See issues of the *Journal of Home Economics* 10 (1918), for accounts of their participation in the food campaigns.

66. The quotation is from Hoover to Wilson, 21 August 1917, in O'Brien, *The Hoover-Wilson Wartime Correspondence,* 66–7.

67. The quotation is from Mullendore, *History of the United States Food Administration,* 83.

68. Lloyd, *Aggressive Introvert,* 47.

69. Dickson, *The Food Front in World War I,* 26–33.

70. Hoover to Wilson, 17 January 1918, in Link, *Papers of Woodrow Wilson,* 46:19–21. The release was published in the *Official Bulletin,* 28 January 1918, 3.

71. Dickson, *The Food Front in World War I,* 28–29, 62. The quotation is from Herbert Kaufman, "Stop Eating Soldiers," a Food Administration release printed in *Cosmopolitan,* February 1918, 1.

72. Carol Reuss, "The *Ladies Home Journal* and Hoover's Food Program," *Journalism Quarterly* 49 (Winter 1972): 740–2.

73. Caroli, *First Ladies,* 177.

74. Mullendore, *History of the United States Food Administration,* 77.

75. The incident is described in Robinson and Edwards, *Memoirs of Ray Lyman Wilbur,* 261.

76. Albert N. Merritt, *Wartime Control of Distribution of Foods* (New York: Macmillan, 1920), vi. Mock and Larson, *Words That Won the War,* 92. Bean, "George Creel and His Critics," 82. Vaughn, *Holding Fast the Inner Lines,* 199.

77. For examples, see Hoover to Wilson, 12 June 1917, and a proposed presidential statement for the *Official Bulletin* in October 1917, both in Link, *Papers of Woodrow Wilson,* 42:480–6, and 44:443–4. While Wilson appreciated being kept informed, he did not enjoy Hoover's company and grew tired of the deluge of paperwork. See House Diary for 10 February 1918, reprinted in Link, *Papers of Woodrow Wilson,* 46:316.

78. Dickson, *The Food Front in World War I,* 13, 120–28. The $19 million estimate is from Mullendore, *A History of the Food Administration,* 89–90. See also David Burner, *Herbert Hoover: A Public Life* (New York: Alfred P. Knopf, 1979), 100–101.

79. Vaughn, *Holding Fast the Inner Lines,* 23–38.

80. The quotation is from *Report of the U.S. Food Administration for the Year 1918* (Washington. D.C.: Government Printing Office, 1919), 7.
81. The quotation is from Allen, undated, Food Administration Correspondence, Box 6, Allen Papers, Herbert Hoover Presidential Library.
82. The quotation is from Will Irwin, *Propaganda and the News* (New York: Whittlesey House, 1936), 186.
83. The phrase is from Stephen Fox, *The Mirror Makers* (New York: Vintage, 1984), 79–117. However, Daniel Pope, "The Advertising Industry and World War I," *Public Historian* 2 (Spring 1980):4–25, argues that the advertising volunteers were motivated less by idealism than a wish to take advantage of patriotic fervor to enhance the security and prestige of the industry itself.
84. Minna Lewinson and Henry Beetle Hough, *A History of the Services Rendered to the Public by the American Press During the Year 1917* (New York: Columbia University Press, 1918), 15.
85. See "Representative American Publishers Urge Paid-Advertising Policy for Nation," and "Newspapers of Country Are Flooded With Publicity Copy from Washington," *Editor and Publisher* 50 (16 March 1918), 5 and 7. Vaughn, *Holding Fast the Inner Lines,* 143–8.
86. Erika G. King, "Exposing the 'Age of Lies': The Propaganda Menace as Portrayed by American Magazines in the Aftermath of World War I," *Journal of American Culture* 21 (Spring 1989): 35–40.
87. For Creel's version of these events, see *Rebel at Large,* 222–5.
88. The remnants of the CPI were abolished in June 1919 by Congress, where Creel's critics refused to pay for printing the organization's final report. A frustrated Creel turned the report into his own book, *How We Advertised America,* ix.
89. See correspondence to Wilson and Grayson in Boxes 44 and 48, Joseph P. Tumulty Papers, Library of Congress.
90. See generally, Hilderbrand, *Power and the People,* 167–97, and Juergens, News from the White House, 205–65.
91. Ritchie, *Press Gallery,* 206–8.
92. Robert F. Himmelberg, "Hoover's Public Image, 1919–1920: The Emergence of a Public Figure and a Sign of the Times," in Gelfand, *Herbert Hoover: The Great War and its Aftermath,* 209–32. On Hoover's popularity after the war, see Burner, *Herbert Hoover: A Public Life* 153–4, and Gary Dean Best, *The Politics of American Individualism: Herbert Hoover in Transition, 1918–1921* (Westport, Conn.: Greenwood Press, 1975), 56.

Chapter 8.
Harding and Coolidge: Emergence of the Media Presidency

1. John D. Hicks, *Republican Ascendancy, 1921–1933* (New York: Harper, 1960), 24–5.

2. The term is from Fletcher Knebel, "The Placid Twenties," in Cabell Phillips, ed., *Dateline: Washington* (Garden City, N.Y.: Doubleday, 1949), 61–74.

3. Cornwell, *Presidential Leadership of Public Opinion,* 59–99.

4. William E. Leuchtenberg, *In the Shadow of FDR: From Harry Truman to Ronald Reagan,* rev. ed. (Ithaca, N.Y.: Cornell University Press, 1989), viii–xi. One factor limiting archival research into the executive-press relationship in the Harding and Coolidge administrations has been the truncated presidential manuscript collections. Large portions of Harding's presidential papers were burned, heavily edited, or discarded after his death. For accounts of the remarkable story of the Harding papers, see Carl Sferrazza Anthony, *Florence Harding: The First Lady, the Jazz Age, and the Death of America's Scandalous President* (New York: William Morrow, 1992), 485–98 and 528–30, Robert H. Ferrell, *The Strange Deaths of President Harding* (Columbia, Mo.: University of Missouri Press, 1996, 151–9, and Richard C. Frederick, ed., *Warren G. Harding: A Bibliography* (Westport, Conn.: Greenwood Press, 1992). As for Coolidge, the former President kept little more than the incoming mail. Surviving Coolidge Papers held by the Library of Congress were examined in microfilm.

5. In a 1995 survey of 58 presidential scholars, Harding ranked 38th of 38 Presidents; Coolidge, 26th, and Hoover, 24th. See Donald McCoy, "*Chicago Sun-Times* Poll," *Presidential Studies Quarterly* 26 (Winter 1996): 281–3. For overviews of the Harding administration, see Robert K. Murray, *The Harding Era* (Minneapolis: University of Minnesota, 1969), and Eugene P. Trani and David Wilson, *The Presidency of Warren G. Harding* (Lawrence, Kans.: Regents Press of Kansas, 1977). For a rare defense, see Ferrell, *The Strange Deaths of President Harding.*

6. Charles Willis Thompson, "Coolidge Has Learned the Art of Publicity," *New York Times,* 7 August 1927, 8:11. See also Tebbel and Watts, *The Press and the Presidency,* 391–414.

7. Pollard, *The Presidents and the Press,* 697–736.

8. On Hoover's publicity work as secretary of commerce, see James McCamy, *Government Publicity: Its Practice in Federal Administration* (Chicago: University of Chicago Press, 1939), 12, n. 19. Lloyd, *Aggressive Introvert,* 123–51.

9. The quotations are from J. Frederick Essary, *Covering Washington: Government Reflected to the Public in the Press* (Boston: Houghton Mifflin, 1927), 18. See also Essary, "Uncle Sam's Ballyhoo Men," *American Mercury* 23 (August 1931): 419–28.

10. Kernell, *Going Public: New Strategies of Presidential Leadership,* 55–64.

11. Ritchie, *Press Gallery,* 209–10.

12. Ritchie, *Press Gallery,* 208.

13. David Lawrence, "Reporting the Political News at Washington," *American Political Science Review* 22 (November 1928): 893–902.

14. Frank R. Kent, *The Great Game of Politics* (Garden City, N.Y.: Doubleday, Page., 1923), 210–3.

15. Wayne R. Whitaker, "Warren G. Harding and the Press" (Ph.D. dissertation, Ohio University, 1972), 68–78. Murray, *The Harding Era,* 50–2. Medved, *The Shadow Presidents,* 169–70. Laurin L. Henry, *Presidential Transitions* (Washington, D.C.: Brookings, 1960), 201, n. 19.

16. Anthony, *First Ladies,* 381.

17. Robert T. Barry, "Marion 'Front Porch' Organization Survives Capitol's Whimsies," *Editor and Publisher* 53 (26 March 1921): 10, 22. Robert T. Barry, "Assemble Order of the Elephant in Washington Saturday Night," *Editor and Publisher* 53 (2 April 1921): 9. "Harding Elephants' Host," *New York Times,* 8 April 1921, 3. Whitaker, "Warren G. Harding and the Press," 36–78. See also Pollard, *The Presidents and the Press,* 691–700, and Cornwell, *Presidential Leadership of Public Opinion,* 63–5.

18. The quotation is from "Harding in Capitol, Calls Upon Wilson," *New York Times,* 4 March 1921, 1.

19. "Harding Will Call Special Session for April 4 or 11," *New York Times,* 8 March 1921, 1.

20. Karger to Harding, 21 January 1921, cited in Whitaker, "Warren G. Harding and the Press," 127–9, and Appendix A.

21. The quotation is from Lowry, *Washington Close-Ups,* 18–20. See also Robert T. Barry, "President Strives for Working Agreement with Press," *Editor and Publisher* 53 (12 March 1921): 7.

22. The quotation is from Richard V. Oulahan, unpublished memoirs, "Harding," Chapter 15, Box 2, Oulahan Papers, Herbert Hoover Presidential Library.

23. J. Frederick Essary, "President, Congress and the Press Correspondents," *American Political Science Review* 22 (November 1928): 902–9.

24. F. B. Marbut, *News from the Capitol* (Carbondale, Ill.: Southern Illinois University Press, 1971), 172. "Praises 'We Boys' Ouster," *Editor and Publisher* 53 (23 April 1921): 40. "Propagandists Barred from White House Press Conference," *Editor and Publisher* 56 (27 October 1923): 12. Thomas L. Stokes, *Chip Off My Shoulder* (Princeton, N.J.: Princeton University Press, 1940), 70–1. Whitaker, "Warren G. Harding and the Press," 137.

25. Pollard, *The Presidents and the Press,* 704–5. Cornwell, 66–7. Stokes, *Chip Off My Shoulder,* 107–8.

26. The quotation is from Edward G. Lowry, "Mr. Harding Digging In," *New Republic* 26 (18 May 1921): 341–2.

27. See Archie Butt to Mrs. Lewis F. B. Butt, 4 July 1909, in Abbott, *Letters of Archie Butt,* 1:134–5.

28. See Wilson to Rudolph Forster, 9 August 1917, in O'Brien, *The Hoover-Wilson Wartime Correspondence,* 56–8.

29. Anthony, *Florence Harding,* 205–6.

30. The quotation is from Lowry, "Mr. Harding Digging In," 342.

31. Cornwell, *Presidential Leadership of Public Opinion,* 68.

32. Anthony, *Florence Harding, 278–80.*

33. Caroli, *First Ladies,* 158, 161–4.

34. Anthony, *First Ladies,* 390–3.

35. Sam W. Bell, "Editor Harding Fails to Win a Place on Washington Golf Team," *Editor and Publisher* 55 (3 June 1922): 16.

36. "Harding Says Hobby is to Revive Hope," *New York Times,* 8 March 1921, 4.

37. "Harding Declares Return to Normalcy Big Result of Year," *New York Times,* 5 March 1922, 1.

38. See, for example, "Harding and Davis Laud Editor's Work," *New York Times,* 27 April 1921, 10, a story for the presidential statement sent to the annual directors' luncheon of the Associated Press. "Harding Lauds Reporters," *New York Times,* 26 April 1922, 3, reflects a similar statement sent to a dinner of the American Newspapers Publishers Association.

39. "No Banker Swayed Him, Says Harding," *New York Times,* 29 April 1923, 1.

40. Hicks, *Republican Ascendancy,* 74–5.

41. Anthony, *Florence Harding,* xiii-ix.

42. For an overview of the Harding scandals, see Trani and Wilson, *The Presidency of Warren G. Harding,* 179–185.

43. Burl Noggle, *Teapot Dome: Oil and Politics in the 1920s* (New York: Norton, 1962), 1–25.

44. Noggle, *Teapot Dome,* 25–31.

45. Noggle, *Teapot Dome,* 32–58.

46. The quotation is from Olive Ewing Clapper, *Washington Tapestry* (New York: Whittlesey House, 1946), 67.

47. The quotation is from "Press Agent Urged as Harding Adjunct," *New York Times,* 3 April 1923, 1.

48. The quotation is from Oulahan, unpublished memoirs, "Harding," Chapter 15, unpublished memoirs, Box 2, Oulahan Papers, Herbert Hoover Presidential Library.

49. See "Harding Puts End to Publicity Plan," *New York Times,* 5 April 1923, 2. "No Publicity Agent," *New York Times,* 11 April 1923, 16.

50. Nan Britton, *The President's Daughter* (New York: Elizabeth Ann Guild, 1927). See also Anthony, *Florence Harding,* 530–2. Trani and Wilson, *The Presidency of Warren G. Harding,* 178.

51. Anthony, *Florence Harding,* 141, 208–10. See also Anthony, "Scandal in the Oval Office, *Washington Post National Weekly Edition,* 25 June 1998, 6–7.

52. Anthony, *Florence Harding,* 337.

53. Neal Gabler, *Winchell: Gossip, Power, and the Culture of Celebrity* (New York: Alfred A. Knopf, 1994), xii, 78.

54. Hicks, *Republican Ascendancy,* 73–4.

55. The quotation is from William Allen White, *A Puritan in Babylon: The Story of Calvin Coolidge* (New York: Macmillan, 1938), 230.

56. The quotation is from "The President," *Editor and Publisher* 56 (4 August 1921): 26.

57. The quotation is from Sam Bell, "Ours Was the Honor of the President's Requiem," *Editor and Publisher* 56 (11 August 1923): 5–6.

58. See Commerce File, Reel 7, Coolidge Papers in microfilm.

59. Robert T. Barry, "President Strives for Working Relationship with Press," *Editor and Publisher* 53 (12 March 1921): 7.

60. "Correspondents Hear Coolidge in First Speech as President," *New York Times,* 5 August 1923, 1, and "Coolidge Meets 150 Correspondents," *New York Times,* 15 August 1923, 3.

61. Calvin Coolidge, *The Autobiography of Calvin Coolidge* (New York: Cosmopolitan, 1929), 183–4.

62. The quotations are from Frederic William Wile to Calvin Coolidge, 17 August 1923, File 36, Reel 39, Coolidge Papers in microfilm.

63. "Coolidge Declines to Revive Aninias Club; Will Ignore All Purporting to Quote Him," *New York Times,* 22 September 1923, 1.

64. Coolidge, *The Autobiography of Calvin Coolidge,* 215–6.

65. See "Memorandum of Questions Which May Be Put to the President at This Afternoon's Press Conference," 12 June 1925 and 16 June 1925, in File 36, Reel 39, Coolidge Papers in microfilm. The same file contains written questions submitted by correspondents in 1928–9.

66. For partial transcripts of Coolidge's press conferences, see Howard H. Quint and Robert H. Ferrell, eds., *The Talkative President: The Off-the-Record Press Conferences of Calvin Coolidge* (Amherst, Mass.: University of Massachusetts Press, 1964).

67. Robert Barry, "'Silent Cal' Causes Dearth of News," *Editor and Publisher* 56 (6 October 1923): 12.

68. Philip Schuyler, "What Press Conferences Mean to Washington Correspondents," *Editor and Publisher* 56 (10 May 1924): 3.

69. J. Bart Campbell, "White House Rules Out Stenographers," *Editor and Publisher* 58 (27 June 1925): 14. David Lawrence, "President Coolidge's Step Backward in Official Press Relationship," *Editor and Publisher* 58 (4 July 1925): 3, 12.

70. Alfred H. Kirchhofer, "Coolidge and 'Spokesman' Satisfied with Summer White House News," *Editor and Publisher* 59 (31 July 1926): 6. Thompson, *Presidents I've Known and Two Near Misses,* 380–2.

71. Bart Campbell, "Barton Interview Not News Matter, Coolidge Tells Correspondents," *Editor and Publisher* 59 (2 October 1926): 3, 10.

72. The quotation is Raymond Clapper, "White House Spokesman Mystery Stirs Senate Curiosity at Last," *Editor and Publisher* 59 (15 January 1927): 15.

73. Willis Sharp, "President and Press," *Atlantic Monthly* 140 (August 1927): 239–45

74. For examples of the association and Gridiron meetings that Coolidge attended, see "Daugherty Puts Honor Above Office," *New York Times,* 9 March 1924, 1. J. Bart Campbell, "Coolidge Beams on White House Men at Annual Press Banquet," *Editor and Publisher* 57 (28 March 1925): 29. "Gridiron's History Reviewed by Depew," *New York Times,* 24 April 1925, 10. "Coolidge is Guest of News Writers," *Editor and Publisher* 58 (12 March 1926): 40.

75. "Coolidge Declares Non-Interference His Foreign Policy," *New York Times,* 9 April 1926, 1.

76. "Coolidge's Party for Editors Filmed," *Editor and Publisher* 57 (3 January 1925): 34. White, *A Puritan in Babylon,* vi–xiii.

77. The quotation is from David Lawrence, "The President and the Press," *Saturday Evening Post* 200 (27 August 1927): 27, 117–8.

78. "Coolidge Narrowly Escapes Bad Fall," *New York Times,* 10 July 1925, 1. Despite the headline, the bulk of the story was a detailed description of Coolidge's hospitality on the presidential yacht.

79. "Coolidge Urges Obedience to Law," *New York Times,* 29 August 1923, 19, to the Southern Newspaper Publishers Association. "Coolidge for a New Arms Conference," *New York Times,* 23 April 1924, 1, to the Associated Press annual luncheon. "Coolidge Declares Press Must Foster America's Idealism," *New York Times,* 18 January 1925, 1, to the American Society of Newspaper Editors. "News Service Binds People of Americas, Coolidge Tells Press Congress," *Editor and Publisher* 58 (10 April 1925): 23, 66, to United Press.

80. Baillie, *High Tension,* 69.

81. "'Values of Advertising Underestimated'—Coolidge," *Editor and Publisher* 59 (30 October 1926): 3. Fox, *The Mirror Makers,* 97.

82. For another example, see "Senators Beat Red Sox, 6–2, Before President and Mrs. Coolidge," *New York Times,* 13 April 1927, 21. For a description of Coolidge's extensive publicity activity during his summer vacation in South Dakota in 1927, see Claude M. Fuess, *Calvin Coolidge: The Man From Vermont* (Boston: Little, Brown, 1940), 390–1.

83. Caroli, *First Ladies,* 166–71.

84. Anthony, *First Ladies,* 397–432.

85. "Coolidge for a New Arms Conference," *New York Times,* 23 April 1924, 1.

86. Louise M. Benjamin, "Broadcast Campaign Precedents from the 1924 Presidential Election," *Journal of Broadcasting and Electronic Media* 31 (Fall 1987): 449–60.

87. "Coolidge Cuts Off Inaugural Pomp," *New York Times,* 11 February 1925, 1.

88. Cornwell, *Presidential Leadership of Public Opinion,* 89–94.

89. The quotations are from Lindsay Rogers, *The American Senate* (New York: Alfred A. Knopf, 1926), 215–41.

90. Knebel, "The Placid Twenties," 64.

91. The quotation is from Stokes, *Chip Off My Shoulder*, 138–9.

92. Delbert Clark, *Washington Dateline* (New York: Frederick A. Stokes, 1941), 62–6; Leo Rosten, *The Washington Correspondents* (New York: Harcourt, Brace, 1937): 28–9.

93. Kent, "Mr. Coolidge," 385–90.

Chapter 9.
Herbert Hoover and Cabinet Publicity in the 1920s

1. Harding's instructions on Cabinet publicity are outlined in "Harding's Cabinet Meets First Time in 2-Hour Session," *New York Times*, 9 March 1921, 1.

2. See memorandum from Karger to Harding, 15 January 1921, reprinted in Whitaker, "Warren G. Harding and the Press," 127–9 and Appendix A.

3. Trani and Wilson, *The Presidency of Warren G. Harding*, 38–45. Murray, *The Harding Era*, 93–144. See also Henry, *Presidential Transitions*, 148–206, and Fenno, *The President's Cabinet*, 30–1.

4. See, for example, "Harding Conciliator on Bureau Recasting," *New York Times*, 8 May 1922, 30. Henry, *Presidential Transitions*, 205–6.

5. The quotation is from Richard V. Oulahan, unpublished memoirs, "Presidents and Publicity," Chapter 4, 4–5, Box 1, Oulahan Papers, Herbert Hoover Presidential Library. See also Oulahan, "Hoover, the Handy, Plays Many Parts," *New York Times Magazine*, 22 November 1925, 3.

6. Trani and Wilson, *The Presidency of Warren G. Harding*, 35–45. See also Noggle, *Teapot Dome: Oil and Politics in the 1920s*.

7. "Harding Aides at Work," *New York Times*, 3 April 1921, 8:3, described how the various Cabinet members were carrying out the President's wishes.

8. T. Swann Harding, "Genesis of One 'Government Propaganda Mill,'" *Public Opinion Quarterly* 10 (Summer 1947): 227–35.

9. Paul J. Croghan to Christian A. Herter, 3 August 1921, Commerce Department: Foreign and Domestic Commerce File, Box 135, Commerce Papers, Herbert Hoover Presidential Library.

10. Stokes, *Chip Off My Shoulder*, 79.

11. The quotation is from Richard Barry, "Mr. Hughes Humanized: A Study of the Secretary of State," *Outlook* 128 (6 July 1921): 412–3.

12. See Lansing, *War Memoirs*, 323–4.

13. For overviews of Hughes's service as secretary of state, see Mario J. Pusey, *Charles Evans Hughes*, 2 vols. (New York: Macmillan, 1951), and Charles Cheney Hyde, "Charles Evans Hughes," in Samuel F. Bemis, ed., *The American Secretaries of State*, 20 vols. (New York: Alfred P. Knopf, 1929), 10:232–401.

14. "Hughes Restricts News Publications: New Secretary of State Would Limit Correspondents to Official Statements," *New York Times*, 8 March 1921, 3.

15. Marbut, *News from the Capital*, 200–1.

16. Lowry, "Mr. Harding Digging In," 341–2.

17. "Shears for Hughes for 'Gordian Knots,'" *New York Times*, 12 March 1922, 9.

18. "Hughes Has Man's Job," *New York Times*, 27 March 1922, 8:3.

19. The primary single-volume biographies of Hoover are Burner, *Herbert Hoover: A Public Life*, and Joan Hoff Wilson, *Herbert Hoover: Forgotten Progressive* (Boston: Little, Brown, 1975).

20. The quotation is from John Lee Mahim to Herbert Hoover, 5 July 1922, Publicity File, Box 487, Commerce Papers, Herbert Hoover Presidential Library.

21. Burner, *Herbert Hoover: A Public Life*, 114–58. See also Best, *The Politics of American Individualism*, 34–56.

22. Abbot, *Watching the World Go By*, 272. Steel, *Walter Lippmann and the American Century*, 167–8.

23. J. R. Williams, "Hoover, Harding and the Harding Image," *Northwest Ohio Quarterly* 45 (Winter/Spring 1972–73):4–20, and Henry, *Presidential Transitions*, 161–2, 182–90.

24. Peri E. Arnold, "The 'Great Engineer' as Administrator: Herbert Hoover and Modern Bureaucracy," *Review of Politics* 42 (July 1980): 331–3.

25. Hoover, *Memoirs*, 2:42.

26. Peri E. Arnold, "Ambivalent Leviathan: Herbert Hoover and the Positive State," in David J. Greenstone, ed., *Public Values and Private Power in American Politics* (Chicago: University of Chicago Press, 1982), 114. Wilson, *Herbert Hoover: Forgotten Progressive*, 80–3.

27. "Hoover Advocates Less Regulation," *New York Times*, 12 May 1925, 10.

28. See, for example, "Hoover Predicts Coming Years Will be Best Since the War," *New York Times*, 1 January 1925, 1.

29. Hoover to David Lawrence, 29 December 1927, Box 364, Commerce Papers, Herbert Hoover Presidential Library. See also Hoover, *Memoirs*, 2: 61–3. Peri H. Arnold, "Herbert Hoover and the Department of Commerce: A Study of Ideology and Policy" (Ph.D. dissertation, University of Chicago, 1972), 89, argues that Hoover's approach was a radical one, in effect the curtailment of free market competition among businesses by government sharing of competitive information.

30. For an overview of the Hoover publicity machine in the 1920s, see Lloyd, *Aggressive Introvert*, 59–72.

31. See, for example, "President to Call Conference Soon on Unemployment," *New York Times*, 29 August 1921, 1, based on a statement by Hoover.

32. Robert K. Murray, "Herbert Hoover and the Harding Cabinet," in Ellis W. Hawley, ed., *Herbert Hoover as Secretary of Commerce: Studies in New Era Thought and Practice* (Iowa City, Ia.: University of Iowa Press, 1981), 21–3. Wilson, *Herbert Hoover, Forgotten Progressive*, 80–6.

33. Paul F. Croghan to Frederick Feiker, 28 May 1921, Commerce Department—Foreign and Domestic Commerce, Croghan, P. J., 1921–22 File, Commerce Papers, Herbert Hoover Presidential Library.

34. The quotation is from Paul J. Croghan to Christian A. Herter, 29 April 1921, Commerce Department—Foreign and Domestic Commerce, Croghan, P. J., 1921–22 File, Commerce Papers, Box 135, Herbert Hoover Presidential Library.

35. Julius Klein to Herbert Hoover, 1 August 1924, Commerce Department Achievements File, Box 121, Commerce Papers, Herbert Hoover Presidential Library.

36. *Tenth Annual Report of the Secretary of Commerce: 1922* (Washington, D. C.: Government Printing Office, 1922), 4–5.

37. Memorandum by O. P. Hopkins, assistant director of the Bureau of Foreign and Domestic Commerce, 15 December 1921, Commerce Department-Foreign and Domestic Commerce, Croghan, P. J., 1921–22 File, Box 135, Commerce Papers, Herbert Hoover Presidential Library. Lloyd, *Aggressive Introvert*, 71–2.

38. See Julius Klein to Hoover, 3 January 1922, and Paul J. Croghan to Julius Klein, 10 March 1922, both in Press Release Service File, Box 484, Commerce Papers, Herbert Hoover Presidential Library.

39. *Ninth Annual Report of the Secretary of Commerce* (Washington.: Government Printing Office, 1921), 46.

40. Donald Wilhelm to Hoover, 4 February 1922, Commerce Department—Standards, Donald Wilhelm, 1919–22 File, Box 148, Commerce Papers, Herbert Hoover Presidential Library. Lloyd, *Aggressive Introvert,* 64–6.

41 The quotation is from Donald Wilhelm to S. W. Stratton, 29 March 1922, Commerce Department—Standards, Donald Wilhelm, 1919–22 File, Box 148, Commerce Papers, Herbert Hoover Presidential Library.

42. Donald Wilhelm to Hoover, 30 October 1922, and memorandum of 1 November 1922, both in Commerce Department—Standards, Donald Wilhelm, 1922–1923 File, Box 148, Commerce Papers, Herbert Hoover Presidential Library.

43. See, generally, William R. Tanner, "Secretary Hoover's War on Waste," 1–235; David E. Lee, "Herbert Hoover and the Development of Commercial Aviation, 1921–26," 36–65; and Carl E. Krog, "Organizing the Production of Leisure," 66–94, all in Carl E. Krog and William R. Tanner, eds., *Herbert Hoover and the Republican Era: A Reconsideration* (Lanham, Md: University Press of America, 1984). Essary, "Uncle Sam's Ballyhoo Men," 425.

44. Arnold, "The 'Great Engineer,'" 345–6.

45. See, for example, United Press dispatch, 24 September 1924, Commerce Department Miscellaneous File, 1923–24, Box 120, Commerce Papers, Herbert Hoover Presidential Library. Bruce Catton, "Handouts," 164–5, in Phillips, *Dateline: Washington.* Marbut, *News from the Capitol,* 198.

46. David Lawrence to Harold Phelps Stokes, 18 December 1925, David Lawrence File, Box 364, Commerce Papers, Herbert Hoover Presidential Library.

47. The quotation is from Herbert Corey, "The Presidents and the Press," *Saturday Evening Post* 204 (9 January 1932): 25, 96–104.

48. The quotation is from Paul Y. Anderson, "Hoover and the Press," *Nation* 133 (14 October 1931): 382–4.

49. Memorandum of 18 April 1921, Commerce Department—Foreign and Domestic Commerce, Croghan, P. J., 1921–22 File, Box 135, Commerce Papers, Herbert Hoover Presidential Library.

50. Memorandum of 4 January 1923, Commerce Department—Foreign and Domestic Commerce, Croghan, P. J., 1923–25 File, Box 144, Commerce Papers, Herbert Hoover Presidential Library.

51. Arnold, "The 'Great Engineer,'" 345.

52. "Hoover Guest of Editors," *New York Times,* 13 April 1921, 2. "Business Editors Will Help Hoover Solve Nation's Trade Problems," *Editor and Publisher* 46 (16 April 1921): 11.

53. "Herbert Hoover Principal Speaker at First Convention Session," *Editor and Publisher* 57 (9 May 1925): 73. "Advertising Reduces Both Costs and Prices—Secretary Hoover to AACW," *Editor and Publisher* 57 (16 May 1925):5.

54. Alfred Pearce Dennis, "Humanizing the Department of Commerce," *Saturday Evening Post* 197 (6 June 1925), 8–9, 181–2, 184, and 186.

55. A. H. Ulm, "Hoover Emerges as a One-Man Cabinet," *New York Times Magazine,* 19 September 1926, 1.

56. The quotation is from Louis Rothschild to Wayne R. Whitaker, 5 March 1972, cited in Whitaker, "Warren G. Harding and the Press," 131. Clinton Gilbert, *The Mirrors of Washington* (New York: G. P. Putnam's Sons, 1921), 120–1.

57. For Hoover's frequent publicity suggestions to Coolidge and the negative responses, see Commerce File, Reel 6, Calvin Coolidge Papers in microfilm, Library of Congress.

58. Hoover's most recent biographer, George H. Nash, describes relations between Hoover and Coolidge as correct but tense. See Nash, "The 'Great Enigma' and the 'Great Engineer': The Political Relationship of Calvin Coolidge and Herbert Hoover," in John Earl Haynes, ed. *Calvin Coolidge and the Coolidge Era* (Washington, D. C.: Library of Congress, 1998), 132–48.

59. See, for example, "Hoover Asks Nation for $2 Million More in Appeal by Radio," *New York Times,* 29 May 1927, 1.

60. Louis W. Liebovich, *Bylines in Despair: Herbert Hoover, the Great Depression, and the U.S. News Media* (Westport, Conn: Praeger, 1994), 46–9, describes the press coverage of Hoover's flood relief efforts.

61. The phrases are from White, *A Puritan in Babylon,* 353. For examples of the stories, see Richard V. Oulahan, "Capitol Mystified on Hoover's Status with the President," *New York Times,* 16 April 1927, 1. "Resentment Widens on Hoover Remarks," *New York Times,* 19 April 1927, 8. "White House Praises Hoover's Ability," *New York Times,* 20 April 1927, 9.

62. See memorandum, Croghan to Christian A. Herter, 18 April 1921, Commerce Department—Foreign and Domestic Commerce, Croghan, P. J.,

1921–22 File, Box 135, Commerce Papers, Herbert Hoover Presidential Library.

63. Liebovich, *Bylines in Despair,* 36–7.

64. The quotation is from McCamy, *Government Publicity: Its Practice in Federal Administration,* 12, n. 19.

65. The phrase is from Harper Leech and John C. Carroll, *What's the News?* (Chicago: Pascal Covici, 1926), 160.

66. The quotation is from Essary, "Uncle Sam's Ballyhoo Men," 419–28.

67. The memorandum is in Commerce Department—Foreign and Domestic Commerce, Croghan, P. J., 1926–27 File, Box 135, Commerce Papers, Herbert Hoover Presidential Library. See also Lloyd, *Aggressive Introvert,* 76–9.

68. See, for example, "Hoover Predicts Coming Years Will Be Best Since the War," *New York Times,* 1 January 1925, 1, a story based on the Commerce Department's annual economic survey.

Chapter 10.
Hoover: The Press and Presidential Failure

1. For a historiographic overview, see Ellis W. Hawley, "Herbert Hoover and Modern American History: Sixty Years and After," 1–38, in Mark Dodge, ed., *Herbert Hoover and the Historians* (West Branch, Ia.: Herbert Hoover Presidential Library Association, 1989).

2. Martin L. Fausold, *The Presidency of Herbert C. Hoover* (Lawrence, Kans.; University Press of Kansas, 1985), 203–5.

3. Joan Hoff Wilson, "Herbert Hoover: The Popular Image of an Unpopular President," in Lee Nash, ed., *Understanding Herbert Hoover: Ten Perspectives* (Stanford, Calif.: Hoover Institution Press, 1987), 1–26. See also Wilson, *Herbert Hoover: Forgotten Progressive.*

4. Burner, *Herbert Hoover: A Public Life,* 253–6.

5. Lloyd, *Aggressive Introvert,* 154–75.

6. For the most comprehensive examination of Hoover's relations with the press in the White House, see Liebovich, *Bylines in Despair.*

7. John Kenneth Galbraith, *The Great Crash of 1929* (New York: Avon, 1979), 120–6, 149. A revised view of Hoover's long public career has emerged since opening of the Herbert Hoover Presidential Library archives in 1966. See, for example, Richard Norton Smith, *An Uncommon Man: The Triumph of Herbert Hoover* (New York: Simon and Schuster, 1984).

8. The quotation is from Anderson, "Hoover and the Press," 382–4.

9. Malcolm M. Willey and Stuart A. Rice, eds., *Communications Agencies and Social Life* (New York: McGraw-Hill, 1933), 167–70.

10. Kernell, *Going Public,* 58–60.

11. William Press Beazell, "The Party Flag Comes Down," *Atlantic Monthly* 147 (March 1931): 366–72. See also Beazell, "Tomorrow's Newspaper," *Atlantic Monthly* 146 (July 1930): 24–30.

12. Schudson, *The Power of News,* 62–3.

13. Walter Lippmann, "Two Revolutions in the American Press," *Yale Review* 20 (March 1931): 433–41. On the development of objectivity as a professional norm, see Schudson, *Discovering the News.*

14. Raymond G. Carroll, "Reform v. the Washington Correspondent," *Editor and Publisher* 61 (21 July 1928):7, 44.

15. William G. Shepherd, "The White House Says," *Collier's* 83 (February 1929):19, 47–9.

16. Emery and Emery, *The Press and America,* 319–21.

17. "Praises 'We Boys' Ouster," *Editor and Publisher* 53 (23 April 1921): 40.

18. "Coolidge Protest as Writers Dash Out," *Editor and Publisher* 57 (21 March 1925): 8.

19. "White House Corps Elects," *Editor and Publisher* 61 (6 April 1928): 8.

20. George H. Manning, "White House Writers Hold Annual Frolic," *Editor and Publisher* 62 (15 March 1930): 26.

21. "White House Group Host to Hoover," *Editor and Publisher* 64 (12 March 1932): 14.

22. See, as examples, William G. Shepherd, "Our Ears in Washington," *Everybody's* 43 (October 1920): 68–73. "How the White House Became a Glass House," *Literary Digest* 88 (20 February 1926): 38, 40, 45. J. Frederick Essary, "Presidents, Congress and the Press Correspondents," *American Political Science Review* 22 (November 1928): 902–9.

23. See, for example, L. Ames Brown, "President Wilson and Publicity," *Harper's Weekly* 58 (1 November 1913): 19–21.

24. T. W. Williams, "Temptations of a Young Journalist," *Cosmopolitan* 40 (April 1906): 680–1.

25. Kernell, *Going Public,* 60, 63–4.

26. Baillie, *High Tension,* 69.

27. The quotations are from Kent, "Mr. Coolidge," 385–90.

28. See, for example, Schuyler, "What Press Conferences With Coolidge Mean to Washington Correspondents," 3.

29. J. Bart Campbell, "White House Rules Out Stenographers," *Editor and Publisher* 58 (27 June 1925): 14.

30. See David Lawrence, "President Coolidge's Step Backward in Office Press Relationship," *Editor and Publisher* 58 (4 July 1925): 3. A. H. Kirchhofer, "Correspondent Wrathful at His Fellows Covering the White Court," *Editor and Publisher* 58 (8 August 1925): 6.

31. The quotation is from Oswald Garrison Villard, "The Press and the President: Should the President be Quoted Directly and Indirectly," *Century* 111 (December 1925): 195–200. See also Bulkley Southworth Griffin, "The Public Man and the Newspapers," *Nation* 120 (17 June 1925): 689–90.

32. Charles Merz, "Silent Mr. Coolidge," *New Republic* 47 (2 June 1926): 51–4.

33. See, for example, "Government by Publicity," *New Republic* 48 (22 September 1926): 110–1.

34. Clapper, "White House Spokesman Mystery Stirs Senate Curiosity at Last," 15.

35. David Lawrence, "The President and the Press," *Saturday Evening Post* 200 (27 August 1927): 27, 117–8. Willis Sharp, "President and Press," *Atlantic Monthly* 140 (August 1927): 239–45. Charles W. Thompson, "Coolidge Has Learned the Art of Publicity," *New York Times,* 7 August 1927, 8, 11.

36. See, for example, the editorial, "Inviting Misunderstanding," *New York Times,* 8 September 1926, 24.

37. "News Writers Expect Hoover to Continue 'Spokesman' Plan," *Editor and Publisher* 61 (10 November 1928): 18. George H. Manning, "Liberalizing of President's Contacts with Press Hoped for from Hoover," *Editor and Publisher* 61 (12 January 1929): 5–6.

38. "Confer with Hoover on News Methods," *Editor and Publisher* 61 (2 March 1929): 12. George H. Manning, "Hoover Liberalizes Press Conferences," *Editor and Publisher* 61 (9 March 1929): 7. Liebovich, *Bylines in Despair,* 90–1.

39. George H. Manning, "Hoover's Press System Best Instituted by Any President, Capital Writers Say," *Editor and Publisher* 61 (16 March 1929): 5.

40. Medved, *The Shadow Presidents,* 188–91.

41. "AP Vote on Radio News Reports Expected," *Editor and Publisher* 61 (20 April 1929); 7–8, 50 "President Hoover Calls on Nation's Press to Aid Cause of Law Enforcement," *Editor and Publisher* 61 (27 April 1929): 9–10. Liebovich, *Bylines in Despair,* 91–3.

42. Ray T. Tucker, "Mr. Hoover Lays a Ghost," *North American Review* 227 (June 1929): 661–9. For Tucker's pre-election view, see "Is Hoover Human?" *North American Review* 226 (November 1928): 513–9.

43. The quotations are from Paul Y. Anderson, "The President Goes Into Action," *Nation* 128 (3 April 1929): 394–5.

44. *Editor and Publisher* even praised the quality of information in routine handouts. See "Hoover Aiding Writers," *Editor and Publisher* 61 (11 May 1929): 18.

45. George H. Manning, "White House Corps in New Quarters," *Editor and Publisher* 62 (5 October 1929): 8. "Reporters Hoover's Guests after Fire," *Editor and Publisher* 63 (28 December 1929): 10.

46. Fauneil J. Rinn, "President Hoover's Bad Press," *San Jose Studies* 1 (February 1975): 32–44. Stanley and Niemi, *Vital Statistics on American Politics,* 50.

47. Rinn, "President Hoover's Bad Press," 34, argues that the correspondents' expectations were unrealistic, based on a wishful interpretation of Hoover's limited intentions.

48. George H. Manning, "President Cancels a Press Conference," *Editor and Publisher* 62 (7 September 1929): 12.

49. Harold Brayman, "Hooverizing the Press," *Outlook and Independent* 156 (24 September 1930): 123–5, 155, outlines the complaints of the correspondents. Liebovich, *Bylines in Despair,* 112–4.

50. "Hoover Action Bars Publicity 'Experts,'" *Editor and Publisher* 62 (17 August 1929): 6.

51. Liebovich, *Bylines in Despair,* 93.

52. Anthony, *First Ladies,* 441–6. Caroli, *First Ladies,* 183.

53. George H. Manning, "White House is Best Source for Rapidan Camp 100 Miles Away," *Editor and Publisher* 62 (13 July 1929): 15. Anderson, "Hoover and the Press," 383.

54. "Press Boxing: By the Gentleman at the Keyhole," *Collier's* 88 (26 September 1931): 61.

55. For a collection of the various complaints by the correspondents, see George H. Manning, "President Hoover and White House Corps at Odds over News 'Leaks,'" *Editor and Publisher* 64 (11 July 1931): 15, and "Strained Air Pervades White House Circles as White House 'Leak' is Sought," *Editor and Publisher* 64 (18 July 1931): 10. Manning, "Hoovers Seek Source of 'Talkie' Story," *Editor and Publisher* 64 (14 November 1931): 8. Liebovich, *Bylines in Despair,* 146–7.

56. For a prescient observation, see J. Fred Essary, "Hoover, Sensitive to Criticism, Will Tighten Relations with Press," *Editor and Publisher* 61 (16 February 1929): 8. See also I. H. Hoover, *Forty-Two Years in the White House,* 188.

57. The quotation is from Olive Ewing Clapper, *Washington Tapestry,* 16.

58. Robert S. Allen and Drew Pearson, *Washington Merry-Go-Round* (New York: Horace Liveright, 1931). "Political Notes: Merry-Go-Round," *Time* 18 (4 September 1931): 18. George H. Manning, "Monitor's Financial Chief Dismissed," *Editor and Publisher* 64 (September 1931): 12.

59. TRB, "Washington Notes," *New Republic* 61 (22 January 1930): 248–9.

60. Will Kollock, "The Story of a Friendship: Mark Sullivan and Herbert Hoover," *Pacific Historian* 18 (Spring 1974), 31–48. I. H. Hoover, *Forty-Two Years at the White House,* 209.

61. Allen and Pearson, *Washington Merry-Go-Round,* 321–7.

62. Richard V. Oulahan, "Capitol Corps Praised for Diligence," *Editor and Publisher* 63 (25 April 1931): 32. See also Ritchie, *Press Gallery,* 213–6.

63. TRB, "Washington Notes," *New Republic* 61 (22 January 1930): 248–9.

64. "Michelson Helping to Fill 'News Gaps,'" *Editor and Publisher* 62 (13 July 1929): 14.

65. Frank R. Kent, "Charley Michelson," *Scribner's* 88 (September 1930): 290–6.

66. Lloyd, *Aggressive Introvert,* 172. George H. Manning, "Wickersham Report Easily Handled," *Editor and Publisher* 63 (24 January 1931): 6.

67. "Press Services Pick Big Stories of 1931," *Editor and Publisher* 64 (30 January 1932): 3.

68. For the first two installments, see George H. Manning, "Subtle Censorship on Government News is Arising Steadily in Washington," *Editor and Publisher* 64 (5 September 1931): 5–6, and Manning, "Washington Corps Plans Committee to Check Official News Stifling," *Editor and Publishing* 64 (12 September 1931): 12. See also an editorial, "No Political Censorship," *Editor and Publisher* 64 (26 September 1931): 48, and Manning, "White House News Ban on Bank Parley Upset by Correspondents," *Editor and Publisher* 64 (10 October 1931): 4–5.

69. George H. Manning, "Joslin Suggests News 'Consultations,'" *Editor and Publisher* 64 (19 September 1931): 7.

70. Elliott Thurston, "Hoover Can Not Be Elected," *Scribner's* 91 (January 1932): 13–16.

71. Ray T. Tucker, *The Mirrors of 1932* (New York: Brewer, Warren and Putnam, 1931), 23.

72. Liebovich, *Bylines in Despair,* 101–47.

73. Herbert Corey, "The Presidents and the Press," *Saturday Evening Post* 204 (9 January 1932): 25, 96–104. On Lorimer's role, see Tebbel and Watts, *The Press and the Presidency,* 415–7.

74. Louis Liebovich, "Press Reaction to the Bonus March of 1932," *Journalism Monographs* 122 (August 1990).

75. Walter Millis, "The President," *Atlantic Monthly* 149 (March 1921): 265–78.

Chapter 11.
Conclusion: The Media Presidency

1. Winfield, *FDR and the News Media,* 28–9.

2. Richard W. Steele, *Propaganda in an Open Society: The Roosevelt Administration and the Media, 1933–41* (Westport, Conn.: Greenwood Press, 1985), 1–51.

SELECTIVE BIBLIOGRAPHY

Manuscript Collections

Ben Allen. Papers. Herbert Hoover Presidential Library, West Branch, Iowa.

Richard Achilles Ballinger. Papers. University of Washington, Seattle.

Erastus Brainerd. Papers. University of Washington. Seattle.

Walter E. Clark. Papers. University of Washington, Seattle.

Calvin Coolidge. Papers. Library of Congress, Washington, D.C.

George B. Cortelyou. Papers. Library of Congress, Washington, D.C.

Hemphill Family. Papers. Duke University, Durham, N.C.

Herbert Hoover. Papers. Herbert Hoover Presidential Library, West Branch, Iowa.

Robert M. LaFollette. Papers. Library of Congress, Washington, D.C.

William G. McKinley. Papers. Library of Congress, Washington, D.C.

Richard V. Oulahan. Papers. Herbert Hoover Presidential Library, West Branch, Iowa.

Theodore Roosevelt. Papers Library of Congress, Washington, D.C.

E.W. Scripps. Papers. Ohio University, Athens.

William Howard Taft. Papers. Library of Congress, Washington, D.C.

Joseph P. Tumulty. Papers. Library of Congress, Washington, D.C.

Woodrow Wilson. Papers. Library of Congress, Washington, D.C.

Government Documents

List of Publications of the Agriculture Department, 1862–1902. Washington, D.C.: Government Printing Office, 1904).

Proceedings of a Conference of Governors, May 13–15, 1908. Washington, D.C.: Government Printing Office, 1908.

U.S. Department of Commerce, *Annual Reports.*

U.S. Congress. Senate. *Congressional Record.* 60th Cong., 2nd sess., 43, pt. 6.

U.S. Congress. House. *Report Upon the Forestry Investigation of the United States Department of Agriculture, 1877–1898.* 53rd Cong., 3rd sess., H. Doc. 181.

U.S. Congress. Senate. *A Statement of Members of the Forest Service at Meetings and Conventions During the Year 1907.* 60th Cong., 1st sess., S. Doc. 485.

U.S. Congress. House Committee on Rules. *Departmental Press Agents: Hearing on House Resolution 545,* 62nd Cong., 2nd sess., 21 May 1912.

U.S. Congress. Senate. Select Committee to Investigate the Executive Agencies of Government, *Preliminary Report.* 75th Cong., 1st sess., 1937.

U.S. Congress. Senate. *Investigation of the Department of Interior and of the Bureau of Forestry,* 61st Cong., 3rd sess., S. Doc. 719 (Serial 5892), 1910.

U.S. Department of Agriculture. *Annual Report of the Secretary.* Washington, D.C.: Government Printing Office.

U.S. Food Administration. *Report for the Year 1918.* Washington; D.C.: Government Printing Office, 1919).

U.S. Forest Service. Records. Group 95, National Archives. Washington, D.C.

Books

Abbott, Lawrence F., ed. *Taft and Roosevelt: The Intimate Letters of Archie Butt,* 2 vols. New York: Doubleday, Doran, 1930.

Abbott, Willis. *Watching the World Go By.* Boston: Little, Brown, 1924.

Allen, Robert S., and Pearson, Drew. *Washington Merry-Go-Round.* New York: Horace Liveright, 1931.

Anderson, Donald E. *William Howard Taft: A Conservative's Conception of the Presidency.* Ithaca, N.Y.: Cornell University Press, 1973.

Anthony, Carl Sferrazza. *Florence Harding: The First Lady, the Jazz Age, and the Death of America's Most Scandalous President.* New York: William Morrow, 1998.

Anthony, Carl Sferrazza. *First Ladies: The Saga of the President's Wives and their Power, 1789–1961.* New York: William Morrow, 1992.

Arnold, Peri E. *Making the Managerial Presidency.* Princeton, N.J.: Princeton University Press, 1986.

Baillie, Hugh. *High Tension: The Recollections of Hugh Baillie.* New York: Harper and Brothers, 1959.

Baldasty, Gerald J. *The Commercialization of News in the Nineteenth Century.* Madison: University of Wisconsin Press, 1992.

Baker, Ray Stannard. *American Chronicle.* New York: Charles Scribner's Sons, 1945.

Baker, Ray Stannard. *Woodrow Wilson: Life and Letters,* 7 vols. London: William Heinemann, 1932.

Barry, David S. *Forty Years in Washington.* Boston: Little, Brown, 1924.

Bean, Walton. "George Creel and His Critics: A Study of the Attacks on the CPI, 1917–1919." Unpublished diss., University of California, Berkeley, 1941.

Bellamy, Edward. *Looking Backward from the Year 2000.* New York: New American Library, 1960 [1888].

Bemis, Samuel F., ed. *The American Secretaries of State.* 20 vols. New York: Alfred P. Knopf, 1929.

Best, Gary Dean. *The Critical Press and the New Deal: The Press and Presidential Power, 1933–1938.* Westport, Conn.: Praeger, 1993.

Best, Gary Dean. *The Politics of American Individualism: Herbert Hoover in Transition, 1918–1921* Westport, Conn.: Greenwood Press, 1975.

Binkley, Wilfred E. *President and Congress,* 3d rev. ed. New York: Vintage Books, 1962.

Bishop, Joseph Bucklin. *Theodore Roosevelt and His Times,* 2 vols. New York: Charles Scribner's Sons, 1920.

Blum, John Morton. *Woodrow Wilson and the Politics of Morality.* Boston: Little, Brown, 1956.

Blum, John Morton. *Joe Tumulty and the Wilson Era.* Boston: Houghton Mifflin, 1951.

Brownlow, Louis, *A Passion for Politics,* 2 vols. Chicago: University of Chicago Press, 1955.

Burner, David. *Herbert Hoover: A Public Life.* New York: Alfred P. Knopf, 1979.

Caroli, Betty Boyd. *First Ladies,* exp. ed. New York: Oxford University Press, 1995.

Cater, Douglass. *The Fourth Branch of Government.* New York: Vintage Books, 1959.

Clapper, Olive Ewing. *Washington Tapestry.* New York: Whittlesey House, 1946.

Clark, Delbert. *Washington Dateline.* New York: Frederick A. Stokes, 1941.

Clements, Kendrick A. *The Presidency of Woodrow Wilson.* Lawrence, Kans.: University Press of Kansas, 1992.

Cohen, Jeffrey E. *The Politics of the U.S. Cabinet: Representation in the Executive Branch, 1789–1984.* Pittsburgh, Penn.: University of Pittsburgh Press, 1984.

Coletta, Paolo E. *The Presidency of William Howard Taft.* Lawrence, Kans.: University Press of Kansas, 1973.

Cook, Timothy E. *Governing with the News: The News Media as a Political Institution.* Chicago: University of Chicago Press, 1998.

Coolidge, Calvin. *The Autobiography of Calvin Coolidge.* New York: Cosmopolitan, 1929.

Cornwell, Elmer C., Jr. *Presidential Leadership of Public Opinion.* Westport, Conn.: Greenwood Press, 1979 [1965].

Cronon, E. David, ed. *The Cabinet Diaries of Josephus Daniels, 1913–1921.* Lincoln, Neb.: University of Nebraska Press, 1963.

Creel, George. *Rebel at Large: Recollections of Fifty Crowded Years.* New York: G. P. Putnam's Sons, 1947.

Creel, George. *How We Advertised America.* New York: Harper and Brothers, 1920.

Davis, Oscar King. *Released for Publication: Some Inside Political History of Theodore Roosevelt and His Times.* Boston: Houghton Mifflin, 1925.

Dickson, Maxcy Robson. *The Food Front in World War I.* Washington, D.C.: American Council on Public Affairs, 1944.

Dodge, Mark, ed. *Herbert Hoover and the Historians.* West Branch, Ia: Herbert Hoover Presidential Library Association, 1989.

Dunn, Arthur Wallace. *From Harrison to Harding,* 2 vols. New York: G. P. Putnam's Sons, 1922.

Dunn, Arthur Wallace. *Gridiron Nights.* New York: Frederick A. Stokes, 1915.

Edwards, George III. *The Public Presidency: The Pursuit of Popular Support.* New York: St. Martin's Press, 1983.

Emery, Michael, and Edwin Emery. *The Press and America,* 8th ed. Boston: Allyn and Bacon, 1996.

Entman, Robert. *Democracy Without Citizens.* New York: Oxford, 1989.

Essary, J. Frederick. *Covering Washington: Government Reflected to the Public in the Press.* Boston: Houghton Mifflin, 1927.

Fallows, James. *Breaking the News.* New York: Pantheon, 1996.

Fausold, Martin. *The Presidency of Herbert C. Hoover.* Lawrence, Kans.: University Press of Kansas, 1985.

Fenno, Richard F. Jr. *The President's Cabinet.* Cambridge, Mass: Harvard University Press, 1959.

Ferrell, Robert H. *The Strange Deaths of President Harding.* Columbia, Mo.: University of Missouri Press, 1996.

Feuss, Claude. *Calvin Coolidge: The Man from Vermont.* Boston: Little, Brown, 1940.

Folkerts, Jean, and Dwight L. Teeter. *Voices of a Nation,* 3rd ed. New York: Macmillan, 1998.

Fox, Stephen. *The Mirror Makers.* New York: Vintage, 1984.

Frederick, Richard C., ed. *Warren G. Harding: A Bibliography.* Westport, Conn.: Greenwood Press, 1992.

Freidel, Frank, and William Pencak, eds. *The White House: The First Two Hundred Years.* Boston: Northeastern University Press, 1994.

Galbraith, James Kenneth. *The Great Crash of 1929.* New York: Avon, 1979.

Gatewood, William B. Jr. *Theodore Roosevelt and the Art of Controversy.* Baton Rouge, La.: Louisiana State University Press, 1970.

Gay, George I., ed. *Public Relations of the Commission for Relief in Belgium,* 2 vols. Stanford, Calif.: Stanford University Press, 1929.

Gelfand, Lawrence E., ed. *Herbert Hoover: The Great War and its Aftermath, 1914–1923.* Iowa City, Ia.: University of Iowa Press, 1979.

Gilbert, Clinton. *The Mirrors of Washington.* New York: G. P. Putnam's Sons, 1921.

Gould, Lewis L. *The Presidency of Theodore Roosevelt.* Lawrence, Kans.: University Press of Kansas, 1991.

Gould, Lewis L. *The Presidency of William McKinley.* Lawrence, Kans.: Regents Press of Kansas, 1980.

Gramling, Oliver K. *AP: The Story of News.* New York: Farrar and Rinehart, 1940.

Greenstone, David J., ed. *Public Values and Private Power in American Politics.* Chicago: University of Chicago Press, 1982.

Grossman, Michael Baruch, and Martha Joynt Kumar. *Portraying the President: The White House and the News Media.* Baltimore, Md.: Johns Hopkins University Press, 1981.

Hapgood, Norman. *The Changing Years.* New York: Farrar and Rinehart, 1930.

Harper, Ida Husted. *The History of Woman Suffrage,* 6 vols. New York: J. J. Little and Ives, 1922.

Hatch, Carl. *The Big Stick and the Congressional Gavel.* New York: Pageant Press, 1967.

Hawley, Ellis W., ed. *Herbert Hoover as Secretary of Commerce: Studies in New Era Thought and Practice.* Iowa City, Ia.: University of Iowa Press, 1981.

Hays, Samuel P. *Conservation and the Gospel of Efficiency: The Progressive Movement, 1890–1920.* Cambridge, Mass.: Harvard University Press, 1959.

Henry, Laurin. *Presidential Transitions.* Washington, D.C.: Brookings, 1960.

Hess, Stephen. *The Government-Press Connection.* Washington, D.C.: Brookings, 1984.

Hicks, John D. *Republican Ascendancy, 1921–1933.* New York: Harper, 1960.

Higgs, Robert. *Crisis and Leviathan: Critical Episodes in American Government.* New York: Oxford University Press, 1987.

Hilderbrand, Robert C. *Power and the People: Executive Management of Public Opinion in Foreign Affairs, 1897–1921.* Chapel Hill: University of North Carolina Press, 1981.

Hofstadter, Richard. *The Age of Reform: From Bryan to FDR.* New York: Vintage, 1955.

Hooker, Arthur, ed. *Proceedings of the 17th National Irrigation Congress.* Spokane, Wash.: Shaw and Borden, 1910.

Hoover, Herbert. *An American Epic,* 4 vols. Chicago: Henry Regnery, 1960.

Hoover, Herbert. *Memoirs,* 3 vols. New York: Macmillan, 1951.

Hoover, I. H. *Forty-Two Years in the White House.* Boston: Houghton Mifflin, 1934.

Houston, David F. *Eight Years with Wilson's Cabinet, 1913–1920,* 2 vols. Garden City, N.Y.: Doubleday, Page, 1926.

Humphrey, Carol Sue. *The Press of the Young Republic, 1783–1833.* Westport, Conn.: Greenwood Press, 1996.

Irwin, Will. *The American Newspaper.* Ames, Ia: Iowa State University Press, 1966 [1911].

Irwin, Will. *Propaganda and the News.* New York: Whittlesey House, 1936.

Jones, Charles O. *The Presidency in a Separated System.* Washington, D.C.: Brookings, 1994.

Juergens, George. *Joseph Pulitzer and the New York World.* Princeton, N.J.: Princeton University Press, 1996.

Juergens, George. *News from the White House: The Presidential-Press Relationship in the Progressive Era.* Chicago: University of Chicago Press, 1981.

Kennedy, David M. *Over Here: The First World War and American Society.* New York: Oxford University Press, 1980.

Kent, Frank R. *The Great Game of Politics.* Garden City, N.Y.: Doubleday, Page, 1923.

Kernell, Samuel. *Going Public: New Strategies of Presidential Leadership,* 2nd ed. Washington, D.C.: Congressional Quarterly Press, 1993.

Koenig, Louis. *The Invisible Presidency.* New York: Farrar and Rinehart, 1960.

Krog, Carl E., and William R. Tanner, eds. *Herbert Hoover and the Republican Era: A Reconsideration.* Lanham, Md.: University Press of America, 1984.

Kurtz, Howard. *Spin Cycle: Inside the Clinton Propaganda Machine.* New York: Free Press, 1998.

Lane, Anne Wintermute and Louise Herrick Wall, eds. *The Letters of Franklin K. Lane: Personal and Political.* Boston: Houghton Mifflin, 1922.

Lasswell, Harold. *Propaganda Techniques in the World War.* New York: Alfred P. Knopf, 1927.

Lawrence, David. *The True Story of Woodrow Wilson.* Murray Hill, N.Y.: George H. Doran, 1924.

Leech, Harper, and John C. Carroll. *What's the News?* Chicago: Pascal Covici, 1926.

Leech, Margaret. *In the Days of McKinley.* New York: Harper and Brothers, 1959.

Leuchtenberg, William E. *In the Shadow of FDR: From Harry Truman to Ronald Reagan,* rev. ed. Ithaca, N.Y.: Cornell University Press, 1989.

Lewinson, Minna, and Henry Beetle Hough. *A History of the Services Rendered to the Public by the American Press during the Year 1917.* New York: Columbia University Press, 1918.

Liebovich, Louis. *Bylines in Despair: Herbert Hoover, the Great Depression and the U.S. News Media.* Westport, Conn.: Praeger, 1994.

Link, Arthur S., ed. *The Papers of Woodrow Wilson,* 69 vols. Princeton, N.J.: Princeton University Press, 1978.

Link, Arthur S. *The New Freedom.* Princeton, N.J.: Princeton University Press, 1956.

Livermore, Seward W. *Politics is Adjourned: Woodrow Wilson and the War Congress, 1916–1918.* Middletown, Conn.: Wesleyan University Press, 1966.

Lowry, Edward G. *Washington Close-Ups: Intimate Views of Some Public Figures.* Boston: Houghton Mifflin, 1921.

Lloyd, Craig. *Aggressive Introvert: A Study of Herbert Hoover and Public Relations Management, 1912–1932* Columbus, Ohio: Ohio State University Press, 1972.

Maltese, John Anthony. *Spin Control: The White House Office of Communications and the Management of Presidential News,* 2nd ed. Chapel Hill: University of North Carolina Press, 1994.

Marbut, F. B. *News from the Capitol.* Carbondale, Ill: Southern Illinois University Press, 1971.

Marcosson, Isaac F. *Adventures in Interviewing.* New York: John Lane, 1919.

McAdoo, Eleanor Wilson. *The Woodrow Wilsons.* New York: Macmillan, 1937.

McCamy, James. *Government Publicity: Its Practice in Federal Administration.* Chicago: University of Chicago Press, 1939.

McCulluogh, David. *Mornings on Horseback.* New York: Simon and Schuster, 1981.

McGeary, M. Nelson. *Gifford Pinchot: Forester-Politician.* Princeton, N.J.: Princeton University Press, 1960.

McGerr, Michael. *The Decline of Popular Politics.* New York: Oxford University Press, 1986.

Medved, Michael. *The Shadow Presidents: The Secret History of the Chief Executives and their Top Aides.* New York: Times Books, 1979.

Merritt, Albert N. *Wartime Control of Distribution of Foods.* New York: Macmillan, 1920.

Milkis, Sidney M. and Michael Nelson. *The American Presidency: Origins and Development, 1776–1990*. Washington, D.C.: Congressional Quarterly, 1990.

Mock, James R. *Censorship 1917*. Princeton, N.J.: Princeton University Press, 1941.

Mock, James R., and Cedric Larson. *Words that Won the War: The Story of the Committee on Public Information, 1917–1919*. Princeton, N.J.: Princeton University Press, 1939.

Morgan, H. Wayne. *William McKinley and His America*. Syracuse, N.Y.: Syracuse University Press, 1963.

Morison, Elting S., ed. *The Letters of Theodore Roosevelt*, 10 vols. Cambridge, Mass: Harvard University Press, 1951.

Morris, Edmund. *The Rise of Theodore Roosevelt*. New York: Coward, McCann and Geoghegan, 1979.

Mott, Frank Luther. *American Journalism: A History of Newspapers in the United States through 250 Years, 1690–1940*. New York: Macmillan, 1949.

Mullendore, William Clinton. *History of the United States Food Administration*. Stanford, Calif.: Stanford University Press, 1941.

Murray, Robert K. *The Harding Era*. Minneapolis: University of Minnesota Press, 1969.

Nash, George H. *The Life of Herbert Hoover: Master of Emergencies, 1917–1918*. New York: W. W. Norton, 1996.

Nash, George H. *The Life of Herbert Hoover: The Humanitarian, 1914–1917*. New York: W. W. Norton, 1988.

Nash, Lee, ed. *Understanding Herbert Hoover: Ten Perspectives*. Stanford, Calif.: Hoover Institution Press, 1987.

Nelson, W. Dale. *Who Speaks for the President? The White House Press Secretary from Cleveland to Clinton*. Syracuse, N.Y.: Syracuse University Press, 1998.

Neustadt, Richard. *Presidential Power*. New York: John Wiley and Sons, 1980.

Noggle, Burl. *Teapot Dome: Oil and Politics in the 1920s*. New York: Norton, 1962.

O'Brien, Francis William, ed. *The Hoover-Wilson Wartime Correspondence*. Ames, Ia.: Iowa State University Press, 1974.

Parker, George F. *Recollections of Grover Cleveland*. New York: Century, 1911.

Patterson, Thomas E. *Out of Order*. New York: Vintage, 1994.

Penick, James L. *Progressive Politics and Conservation: The Ballinger-Pinchot Affair*. Chicago: University of Chicago Press, 1968.

Phillips, Cabell, ed. *Dateline: Washington*. Garden City, N.Y.: Doubleday, 1949.

Pimlott, J. A. R. *Public Relations and American Democracy*. Princeton, N.J.: Princeton University Press, 1951.

Pinchot, Gifford. *Breaking New Ground*. New York: Harcourt, Brace, 1947.

Pinkett, Harold T. *Gifford Pinchot: Public and Private Forester*. Urbana, Ill: University of Illinois Press, 1970.

Pollard, James E. *The Presidents and the Press*. New York: Macmillan, 1947.

Pringle, Henry F. *The Life and Times of William Howard Taft*, 2 vols. New York: Farrar and Rinehart, 1939.

Pringle, Henry F. *Theodore Roosevelt: A Biography*. New York: Harcourt, Brace, 1931.

Pusey, Mario J. *Charles Evans Hughes,* 2 vols. New York: Macmillan, 1951.

Quint, Howard H., and Robert H. Ferrell, eds. *The Talkative President: The Off-the-Record Press Conferences of Calvin Coolidge.* Amherst: University of Massachusetts Press, 1964.

Riis, Jacob. *How the Other Half Lives.* New York: Charles Scribner's Sons, 1907 [1890].

Ritchie, Donald A. *Press Gallery: Congress and the Washington Correspondents.* Cambridge, Mass: Harvard University Press, 1991.

Robinson, Edgar Eugene, and Carroll Edwards, eds. *The Memoirs of Ray Lyman Wilbur.* Stanford, Calif.: Stanford University Press, 1960.

Rodgers, Lindsay. *The American Senate.* New York: Alfred P. Knopf, 1926.

Roosevelt, Nicholas. *The Man as I Knew Him.* New York: Dodd, Mead, 1967.

Roosevelt, Theodore. *An Autobiography.* New York: Macmillan, 1914.

Ross, Edward Alysworth. *Sin and Society.* Boston: Houghton Mifflin, 1907.

Rossiter, Clinton, ed. *The Federalist Papers.* New York: Mentor, 1961.

Rosten, Leo. *The Washington Correspondents.* New York: Harcourt, Brace, 1937.

Sabato, Larry J. *Feeding Frenzy: How Attack Journalism Has Transformed Politics.* New York: Free Press, 1991.

Scheiber, Harry N. *The Wilson Administration and Civil Liberties, 1917–1921.* Ithaca, N.Y.: Cornell University Press, 1960.

Schiller, Dan. *Objectivity and the News.* Philadelphia: University of Pennsylvania Press, 1981.

Schlesinger, Arthur W. Jr. *The Imperial Presidency.* Boston: Houghton Mifflin Co., 1973.

Schlesinger, Arthur W. Jr., ed. *History of American Presidential Elections, 1798–1968.* New York: Chelsea, 1971.

Schudson, Michael. *The Power of News.* Cambridge, Mass: Harvard University Press, 1995.

Schudson, Michael. *Discovering the News.* New York: Basic Books, 1978.

Sigal, Leon V. *Reporters and Officials: The Organization and Politics of Newsmaking.* Lexington, Mass: D. C. Heath, 1973.

Sloan, William David, and James D. Startt, eds. *The Media in America: A History,* 3rd ed. Northport, Ala.: Vision Press, 1996.

Smith, Culver H. *The Press, Politics and Patronage: The American Government's Use of Newspapers.* Athens, Ga.: University of Georgia Press, 1977.

Smith, J. Allen. *The Spirit of American Government.* Cambridge, Mass.: Harvard University Press, 1965 [1909].

Smith, Richard Norton. *An Uncommon Man: The Triumph of Herbert Hoover.* New York: Simon and Schuster, 1984.

Stanley, Harold W., and Richard G. Niemi. *Vital Statistics on American Politics.* Washington, D.C.: CQ Press, 1988.

Stealey, O. O. *Twenty Years in the Press Gallery.* Privately published by O. O. Stealey, 1906.

Steel, Ronald. *Walter Lippmann and the American Century.* New York: Vintage, 1981.

Steele, Richard W. *Propaganda in an Open Society: The Roosevelt Administration and the Media, 1933–41* Westport, Conn.: Greenwood Press, 1985.

Steffens, Lincoln. *The Shame of the Cities,* Louis Joughin, ed. New York: Hill and Wang, 1966 [1911].

Steffens, Lincoln. *The Autobiography of Lincoln Steffens,* 2 vols. New York: Harcourt, Brace, 1931.

Stoddard, Henry L. *As I Knew Them: Presidents and Politics from Grant to Coolidge.* New York: Harper and Brothers, 1927.

Stokes, Thomas L. *Chip Off My Shoulder.* Princeton, N.J.: Princeton University Press, 1940.

Stone, Melville E. *Fifty Years a Journalist.* Garden City, N.Y.: Doubleday, Page, 1921.

Sullivan, Mark. *Our Times,* 7 vols. New York: Charles Scribner's Sons, 1926.

Summers, Mark Wahlgren. *The Press Gang: Newspapers and Politics, 1865–1878.* Chapel Hill: University of North Carolina Press, 1994.

Tebbel, John, and Sarah Miles Watts. *The Press and the Presidency.* New York: Oxford University Press, 1985.

Thompson, Charles Willis. *Presidents I've Known and Two Near-Misses.* Indianapolis, Ind.: Bobbs-Merrill, 1929.

Thorsen, Niels Aage. *The Political Thought of Woodrow Wilson, 1875–1910.* Princeton, N.J.: Princeton University Press, 1988.

Trani, Eugene P., and Wilson, David L. *The Presidency of Warren G. Harding.* Lawrence, Kans.: Regents Press of Kansas, 1977.

Tucker, Ray T. *The Mirrors of 1932.* New York: Brewer, Warren and Putman, 1931.

Tulis, Jeffrey K. "The Two Constitutional Presidencies." In Michael Nelson, ed., *The Presidency and the Political System,* 3rd ed. Washington, D.C.: Congressional Quarterly, 1990.

Tulis, Jeffrey K. *The Rhetorical Presidency.* Princeton, N.J.: Princeton University Press, 1987.

Van Hise, Charles R. *The Conservation of Natural Resources in the United States.* New York: Macmillan, 1913.

Van Riper, Paul P. "The American Administrative State: Wilson and the Founders." In Ralph Clark Chandler, ed., *A Centennial History of the American Administrative State.* New York: Free Press, 1987.

Vaughn, Stephen. *Holding Fast the Inner Lines: Democracy, Nationalism and the Committee on Public Information.* Chapel Hill, N.C.: University of North Carolina Press, 1980.

Walsh, Kenneth. *Feeding the Beast: The White House versus the Press.* New York: Random House, 1996.

Welch, Richard E. Jr. *The Presidencies of Grover Cleveland.* Lawrence, Kans.: University Press of Kansas, 1988.

Whitaker, Wayne R. "Warren G. Harding and the Press," (unpublished Ph.D. diss., Ohio University, 1972).

Wiebe, Robert H. *The Search for Order.* New York: Hill and Wang, 1967.

White, Leonard D. *The Republican Era: 1869–1901.* New York: Macmillan, 1958.

White, William Allen. *The Autobiography of William Allen White*. New York: Macmillan, 1946.

White William Allen. A *Puritan in Babylon: The Story of Calvin Coolidge*. New York: Macmillan, 1938.

White, William Allen. *Masks in a Pageant*. New York: Macmillan, 1928.

Willey, Malcolm M. and Stuart A. Rice, eds. *Communications Agencies and Social Life*. New York: McGraw-Hill, 1933.

Wilson, Joan Hoff. *Herbert Hoover: Forgotten Progressive*. Boston: Little, Brown, 1975.

Wilson, Woodrow. *Constitutional Government in the United States*. New York: Columbia University Press, 1908.

Wilson, Woodrow. *Congressional Government*. Boston: Houghton Mifflin, 1886.

Winfield, Betty Houchen. *FDR and the News Media*. Urbana, Ill.: University of Illinois Press, 1990.

Wynn, Neil A. *From Progressivism to Prosperity: World War I and American Society*. New York: Holmes and Meier, 1986.

Articles

Adams, Henry C. "What is Publicity?" *North American Review* 175 (December 1902): 894.

Anderson, Paul Y. "Hoover and the Press." *Nation*, 14 October 1931, 382–4.

Anderson, Paul Y. "The President Goes into Action." *Nation*, 3 April 1929, 394–5.

Arnold, Peri E. "The 'Great Engineer' as Administrator: Herbert Hoover and Modern Bureaucracy." *Review of Politics* 42 (1980): 331–3.

Baldasty, Gerald J. "The Press and Politics in the Age of Jackson." *Journalism Monographs* 89 (1984)

Baldasty, Gerald J., and Jeffrey Rutenbeck. "Money, Politics and Newspapers: The Business Environment of Press Partisanship in the Late Nineteenth Century." *Journalism History* 13 (1989): 60–9.

Balutis, Alan. "The Presidency and the Press." *Presidential Studies Quarterly* 7 (1977): 244–51.

Barry, David S. "George Bruce Cortelyou." *World's Work* 5 (1903): 3337–40.

Barry, David S. "News-Getting at the Capitol." *Chautauquan* 26 (1897): 282.

Barry, Richard. "Mr. Hughes Humanized: A Study of the Secretary of State." *Outlook* 128 (6 July 1921): 412–3.

Beazil, William Press. "The Party Flag Comes Down." *Atlantic Monthly*, March 1931, 366–72.

Beazil, William Press. "Tomorrow's Newspaper." *Atlantic Monthly*, July 1930, 24–30.

Benjamin, Louise M. "Broadcast Campaign Precedents from the 1924 Presidential Election." *Journal of Broadcasting and Electronic Media* 31 (1987): 449–60.

Bishop, Joseph Bucklin. "Newspaper Espionage." *Forum* 1 (1886): 528–37.

Bloomfield, Douglas M. "Joe Tumulty and the Press." *Journalism Quarterly* 42 (1965): 413–21.

Blumenthal, Sidney. "The Syndicated Presidency." *New Yorker*, 5 April 1993, 42–7.

Brayman, Harold. "Hooverizing the Press." *Outlook and Independent,* 24 September 1930, 123–5.

Brown, L. Ames. "President Wilson and Publicity." *Harper's Weekly,* 1 November 1913, 19–21.

Bruere, Henry. "Government and Publicity." *Independent* 63 (12 December 1907): 1422–6.

Corey, Herbert. "The Presidents and the Press." *Saturday Evening Post,* 9 January 1932, 25.

Cornwell, Elmer C. Jr. "The Press Conferences of Woodrow Wilson." *Journalism Quarterly* 39 (Summer 1962): 292–300.

Cornwell, Elmer C. Jr. "Presidential News: The Expanding Public Image." *Journalism Quarterly* 36 (1959): 275–83.

Creel, George. "Woodrow Wilson—The Man Behind the President." *Saturday Evening Post,* 28 March 1931.

Dennis, Alfred Pearce. "Humanizing the Department of Commerce." *Saturday Evening Post,* 6 June 1925, 8.

Dickinson, J. J. "Theodore Roosevelt, Press Agent: And What His Newspaper 'Cuckoos' Have Done for Him." *Harper's Weekly,* 28 September 1907.

Domke, David, et al. "News Media, Candidates and Issues, and Public Opinion in the 1996 Presidential Campaign." *Journalism and Mass Communications Quarterly* 74 (1997): 718–37.

Dooley, Patricia I., and Paul Grosswiler. "'Turf Wars': Journalists, New Media and the Struggle for Control of Political News." *Press/Politics* 8 (No. 2, Summer 1997): 31–51.

Endres, Kathleen L. "Women and the 'Larger Household': The 'Big Six' and Muck-raking." *American Journalism* 14 (Nos. 3–4, Summer-Fall 1997): 262–82.

Essary, J. Frederick. "The Presidency and the Press." *Scribner's* 27 (1935): 305–7.

Essary, J. Frederick. "Uncle Sam's Ballyhoo Men." *American Mercury,* August 1931.

Essary, J. Frederick. "President, Congress and the Press Correspondents." *American Political Science Review* 22 (1928): 902–9.

Gardner, Gilson. "Inside the Quotes." *Editor and Publisher* 5 (1906), 1.

Gould, Lewis L. "Theodore Roosevelt, Woodrow Wilson and the Emergence of the Modern Presidency." *Presidential Studies Quarterly* 19 (1989): 41–50.

Griffin, Bulkley Southworth. "The Public Man and the Newspapers. *Nation,* June 1925, 689–90.

Gropkin, Adam. "Read All About It." *New Yorker,* 12 December 1994.

Halstead, Albert. "The President at Work—A Character Sketch." *Independent* 53 (1901): 2081.

Harding, T. Swann. "Genesis of One 'Government Propaganda Mill.'" *Public Opinion Quarterly* 10 (1947): 227–35.

Hoover, Herbert. "What I Would Like Women to Do." *Ladies Home Journal,* August 1917, 25.

Hoxie, R. Gordon. "The Cabinet in the American Presidency, 1789–1984." *Presidential Studies Quarterly* 14 (No. 2, Spring 1984): 209–30.

Irwin, Will. "First Aid to America: How Civilians Must Get Together Behind Strong Leaders." *Saturday Evening Post,* 24 March 1917, 6.

Johnson, Donald. "Wilson, Burleson and Censorship in the First World War." *Journal of Southern History* 28 (1962): 46–58.

Kaplan, Richard. "The Economics and Politics of Nineteenth-Century Newspapers: The Search for Markets in Detroit, 1865–1900." *American Journalism* 10 (Nos. 1–2, Winter-Spring 1993): 84–101.

Kent, Frank R. "Charley Michelson." *Scribner's,* September 1930, 290–6.

Kent, Frank R. "Mr. Coolidge." *American Mercury,* August 1924, 385–90.

King, Erika G. "Exposing the 'Age of Lies': The Propaganda Menace as Portrayed by Magazines in the Aftermath of World War I." *Journal of American Culture* 12 (1989): 35–40.

Kollock, Will. "The Story of a Friendship: Mark Sullivan and Herbert Hoover." *Pacific Historian* 18 (1974): 31–48.

Kumar, Martha Joynt. "The White House Beat at the Century Mark." *Press/Politics* 2 (No. 3, Summer 1997): 10–13.

Lawrence, David. "Reporting the Political News at Washington." *American Political Science Review* 22 (1928): 893–902.

Lawrence, David. "The President and the Press." *Saturday Evening Post,* 27 August 1927, 117–8.

Lemert, James B. "Adapting to Clinton and the New Media Reality." *Media Studies Journal* 8 (1994): 53–8.

Leupp, Frances E. "The President—and Mr. Wilson." *Independent,* 27 November 1913.

Leupp, Frances E. "President Taft's Own View: An Authorized Interview." *Outlook,* 12 December 1911.

Liebovich, Louis. "Press Reaction to the Bonus March of 1932." *Journalism Monographs* 122 (1990).

Lippmann, Walter. "Two Revolutions in the American Press." *Yale Review* 20 (1931): 433–41.

Lowry, Edward G. "Mr. Harding Digging In." *New Republic,* 18 May 1921, 341–2.

Lowry, Edward G. "The White House Now." *Harper's Weekly,* 15 May 1909.

Marbut, Frederick B. "Decline of the Official Press in Washington." *Journalism Quarterly* 33 (1956): 335–41.

McCoy, Donald. "*Chicago Sun-Times* Poll." *Presidential Studies Quarterly* 26 (Winter 1996): 281–3.

McLeod, Jack. "The Impact of Traditional and Nontraditional Media Forms in the 1992 Presidential Election." *Journalism and Mass Communications Quarterly* 73 (1996): 401–16.

Merz, Charles. "Silent Mr. Coolidge." *New Republic,* 2 June 1926, 51–4.

Millis, Walter. "The President." *Atlantic Monthly,* March 1931, 265–78.

Orman, John. "Covering the American Presidency: Valenced Reporting in the Periodical Press." *Presidential Studies Quarterly* 14 (1984): 381–90.

Oulahan, Richard V. "Roosevelt, the Politician." *Saturday Evening Post,* 21 September 1907.

Patterson, Thomas E. "Legitimate Beef: The Presidency and a Carnivorous Press." *Media Studies Journal* 8 (1994): 21–6.

Ponder, Stephen. "That Delightful Relationship: Presidents and White House Correspondents in the 1920s." *American Journalism* 14 (1997): 164–81.

Ponder, Stephen. "Popular Propaganda: The Food Administration in World War I." *Journalism and Mass Communications Quarterly* 72 (1995): 539–50.

Ponder, Stephen. "'Nonpublicity' and the Unmaking of a President: William Howard Taft and the Ballinger-Pinchot Controversy of 1909–1910." *Journalism History* 19 (1994): 111–20.

Ponder, Stephen. "Presidential Publicity and Executive Power: Woodrow Wilson and the Centralizing of Government Information." *American Journalism* 11 (1994): 257–69.

Ponder, Stephen. "The President Makes News: William G. McKinley and the First White House Press Corps, 1897–1901." *Presidential Studies Quarterly* 24 (1994): 823–36.

Ponder, Stephen. "E. W. Scripps and the Progressive Movement." In *A Celebration of the Legacies of E. W. Scripps.* Athens, Ohio: Ohio University, 1990.

Ponder, Stephen. "The Progressive Drive to Shape Public Opinion, 1898–1913." *Public Relations Review* 16 (1990): 94–104.

Ponder, Stephen. "Gifford Pinchot: Press Agent for Forestry." *Journal of Forest History* 31 (1987): 26–35.

Ponder, Stephen. "Conservation, Economics and Community Newspapering: The Seattle Press and the Forest Reserves Controversy of 1897." *American Journalism* 3 (1986): 50–60.

Ponder, Stephen. "Executive Publicity and Congressional Resistance, 1905–1913." *Congress and the Presidency* 13 (1986): 177–86.

Ponder, Stephen. "Federal News Management in the Progressive Era." *Journalism History* 13 (1986): 42–8.

Pope, Daniel. "The Advertising Industry and World War I." *Public Historian* 2 (1980): 4–25.

Price, W. W. "How the Work of Gathering White House News Has Changed." *Washington Evening Star,* 16 December 1902.

Price, W. W. "Secretaries to the Presidents." *Cosmopolitan,* March 1901, 491.

Reuss, Carol. "The *Ladies Home Journal* and Hoover's Food Program." *Journalism Quarterly* 49 (1972): 740–2.

Ridings, William J. Jr., and McIver, Stuart B. "1990s Presidential Poll." *Presidential Studies Quarterly* 25 (1995): 375–7.

Rinn, Fauneil J. "President Hoover's Bad Press." *San Jose Studies* 1 (1972): 32–44.

Ritchie, Donald A. "'The Loyalty of the Senate': Washington Correspondents in the Progressive Era." *Historian* 50 (1989): 574–91.

Roosevelt, Theodore. "Forestry and Foresters." *Current Literature,* September 1903, 337–8.

Rozek, Stacey. "The First Daughter of the Land: Alice Roosevelt as Presidential Celebrity, 1902–1906." *Presidential Studies Quarterly* 19 (1989): 51–70.

Rutenbeck, Jeffrey. "Newspaper Trends in the 1870s: Proliferation, Popularization, and Political Independence." *Journalism Quarterly* 72 (1995): 361–75.

Rutenbeck, Jeffrey. "The Stagnation and Decline of Partisan Journalism in Late Nineteenth-Century America." *American Journalism* 10 (1993): 38–60.

Schudson, Michael. "Toward a Troubleshooting Manual for Journalism History." *Journalism and Mass Communications Quarterly* 74 (1997): 463–76.

Schudson, Michael. "The Politics of Narrative Form." *Daedulus* 3 (1982): 101–2.

Sharp, Willis. "President and Press." *Atlantic Monthly*, August, 1927, 239–45.

Shepherd, William G. "The White House Says." *Collier's*, February 1929, 19.

Shepherd, William G. "Our Ears in Washington." *Everybody's*, October 1920, 68–73.

Sloan, William David. "The Early Party Press: The Newspaper in American Politics, 1789–1812." *Journalism History* 9 (1982): 18–24.

Smythe, Ted Curtis. "The Reporter, 1880–1900: Working Conditions and Their Influence on News." *Journalism History* 7 (1980): 1–10.

Steffens, Lincoln. "Roosevelt-Taft-La Follette on What the Matter is in America and What to Do about It." *Everybody's*, June 1908, 723–36.

Steffens, Lincoln. "The Business of a Newspaper." *Scribner's* 22 (1897): 446–7.

Streitmatter, Rodger. "Theodore Roosevelt: Public Relations Pioneer." *American Journalism* 1 (1990): 96–113.

Streitmatter, Rodger. "William W. Price: First White House Correspondent and Emblem of an Era." *Journalism History* 16 (1989): 32–41.

Stuckey, Mary. "The Rhetorical Presidency: A Nexus for Scholarship." *PRG Report* 20 (No. 2, Fall 1997): 6–8.

Tarbell, Ida. "President McKinley in War Times." *McClure's*, July 1898, 214.

Thurston, Elliott. "Hoover Can Not be Elected." *Scribner's*, January 1932, 13–16.

Tucker, Ray T. "Mr. Hoover Lays a Ghost." *North American Review*, June 1929, 661–9.

Tucker, Ray T. "Is Hoover Human?" *North American Review*, November 1928, 513–9.

Turner, George Kibbe. "How Taft Views His Own Administration." *McClure's*, June 1910, 221.

Vance, Arthur T. "The Value of Publicity in Reform." *Annals* 29 (January 1907): 87–92.

Villard, Oswald Garrison. "Should the President be Quoted Directly and Indirectly." *Century*, December 1925, 195–200.

Waber, Jennifer. "Secrecy and Control: Reporters Committee says Clinton Administration's dealings with the press have become more antagonistic." *Editor and Publisher*, 24 May 1997, 10–13, 33–4.

White, William Allen. "Roosevelt: A Force for Righteousness." *McClure's*, February 1907, 386–94.

White, William Allen. "Platt." *McClure's*, December 1901, 145–53.

Williams, J. R. "Hoover, Harding and the Harding Image." *Northwest Ohio Quarterly* 45 (1972): 4–20.

Williams, T. W. "Temptations of a Young Journalist." *Cosmopolitan*, April 1906), 680–1.

Trade Journals

Editor and Publisher
The Journalist
The Newspaper Maker

Newspapers

Chicago Record-Herald
Chicago Tribune
Christian Science Monitor
Philadelphia Record
Portland (Oregon) Daily News
Portland Oregonian
Los Angeles Record
New York American
New York Commercial Advertiser
New York Dispatch
New York Mail and Express
New York Sun
New York Times
New York Tribune
New York World
Ohio State Journal (Columbus)
San Diego Sun
San Francisco Chronicle
Seattle Post-Intelligencer
Seattle Star
Seattle Times
Spokane Spokesman-Review
Washington Evening Star
Washington Herald
Washington Post
Washington Times

INDEX